Y0-BRG-514

Gladys M. Stern
June 2001

Emphatics

THE VANDERBILT LIBRARY OF AMERICAN PHILOSOPHY offers interpretive perspectives on the historical roots of American philosophy and on present innovative developments in American thought, including studies of values, naturalism, social philosophy, cultural criticism, and applied ethics.

SERIES EDITOR

Herman J. Saatkamp, Jr.
Indiana University & Purdue University at Indianapolis

EDITORIAL ADVISORY BOARD

Kwame Anthony Appiah (Harvard University)
Larry A. Hickman (Southern Illinois University)
John Lachs (Vanderbilt University)
John J. McDermott (Texas A&M)
Joel Porte (Cornell University)
Hilary Putnam (Harvard University)
Ruth Anna Putnam (Wellesley College)
Andrew J. Reck (Tulane University)
Beth J. Singer (Brooklyn College)
John J. Stuhr (Pennsylvania State University)

Emphatics

Paul Weiss

VANDERBILT UNIVERSITY PRESS

NASHVILLE

© Vanderbilt University Press 2000
All rights reserved

First Edition 2000

04 03 02 01 00 5 4 3 2 1

Library of Congress Cataloging-in-Publication Data

Weiss, Paul, 1901–
Emphatics / Paul Weiss.— 1st ed.
p. cm. — (The Vanderbilt library of American philosophy)
Includes indexes.
ISBN 0-8265-1353-0 (alk. paper)
1. Ontology. I. Title. II. Series.
B945.W3963 E57 2000 191—dc21
00-008055

Published by Vanderbilt University Press
Printed in the United States of America

In Memory of I. C. Lieb

CONTENTS

PREFACE

Some sixty years ago, I was convinced that I would never be able to get to the root of what there was in the large and the little, the important and the unimportant, the fixed and the transient, surfaces and depths, unless I carried out a systematic, comprehensive, self-critical study about the existence and natures of primary realities, determined the kind of knowledge that was required, what their warrants were, and what, if anything, was being presupposed. I was convinced that I had to identify the major claims, both those explicitly and those implicitly made in daily living and in major enterprises, and that I also had to determine their scope, warrant, implications, and consequences, if I were to know them as well as they could be known. All pivotal claims, I held—and still do—were to be examined separately and in relation to one another and tested to see how they withstood doubts and criticisms.

Before I presented a manuscript to a publisher, I rewrote and rewrote, qualified, and often discarded much of what I had written. I made many changes in the galleys, and then in the page proofs, so many in fact that after these many years I have only now been able to pay off, out of royalties, the charges that I had accumulated. And then, again and again, I found it desirable to make corrections in the final, printed works.

When I began a new study, usually making an advance on or applying what I thought I had identified, I found it had been maintained earlier, or that I had dealt with it from new positions and in other contexts. Although some of the radical moves were made by me only recently, particularly in the discussions of Being and its relations to other realities, I do not think that there are any serious conflicts between the views that were held long ago and those advanced later. Often, though, new terms were required to mark off what was novel or had not been well understood by me or others. Again and again, I found that I had sometimes moved too quickly and had skipped too lightly over intermediate and crucial issues.

All that I now claim is that, what was later maintained, makes advances at particular points, and that it remedies what had been inadequately dealt with elsewhere. Since I do not have a good memory, and rarely look at what I had once published, I am not sure now what in them I would or should repudiate or qualify today. Apart from a somewhat careless continuation of a common philosophic practice of using "God" to refer to what is not the object of faith—Aristotle, Descartes. Leibniz, Spinoza, and Whitehead did that—but who, in some mysterious way, solves or eliminates major difficulties that the philosopher cannot, I would not be surprised to find that some of my earlier treatments of some issues, or that even entire works, were preferred to those written later.

The temper of a philosopher concerned with knowing the major kinds of reality and how they are related to one another is closer to that of an artist than it is to that of a scientist or a mathematician; the procedure is more like that of an explorer than it is of a logician or technician. Like an artist the philosopher tries to make each work complete and excellent. Like an explorer the philosopher is alert to the need to approach the same territory again and again from new angles, while remaining ready to enter new places at any time.

Being and Other Realities, the systematic study that preceded this, displaced but did not completely replace other works, particularly those that were primarily occupied with the study of special topics, such as art, politics, history, or sport. For the most part, it focused on issues that had been previously slighted or overlooked by me, and it approached them with an alertness to the ways in which what necessarily is affects what need not be. What is here maintained modifies some claims previously made, though it was not designed to do so. It also makes some signal advances beyond some of the positions that had been arrived at—a most desirable outcome.

Nothing much is gained by following a common practice that contents itself with rejecting what must be accepted in order that a negation have a terminus. Since every negation clings to what it would eliminate, the more successful skeptics are, the more evident it becomes that there is nothing that they could show that they had accomplished. For something to be destroyed, it must be real enough to require an acknowledgment.

A negation must be empowered if it is to be effective. "Not x" is not identifiable with "non-x." "Not" addresses, "non" invades. Perhaps aware of that fact, some have been content to speak vaguely of a language of humanity to replace the ones we otherwise use or speak of, as somehow being able to know the untarnished past by continuing further and further into the future, and both carry out and complete a deconstruction of what they or others had understood the past to have been. Others suppose that, if they are scrupulously careful in what they say, what they say will be right or true. Sometimes they are answered in similar ways. Nothing much, though, is gained when opponents match affirmations with affirmations or negations with negations.

The fact that major issues deserve to be dealt with resolutely is promoted if one faces oneself with difficult questions, directed at major claims. I have, therefore, continued the practice that I had initiated in *Being and Other Realities*. At the end of each chapter, I have raised questions and have tried to offer answers that help clarify and that sometimes take us beyond the point where the preceding discussion apparently ended.

It has sometimes been said that I have offered a number of systems; it is to be expected that there will be some who will take the present work to present another system, presumably to be followed by others. I do not agree. The different works that were published over the decades were the outcomes of a steady attempt to understand primary, pivotal realities by themselves, and as related to one another, with many of the same issues dealt with from different angles. Later works, for the most part, made additions to and subtletized what had been previously examined. There are, though, some discussions in the earlier studies that I now think should have been carried out under different headings, or were poor anticipations of what is now evident. However, the present work presupposes no acquaintance with any of the others.

I would today rewrite the entire chapter on God in *Modes of Being* and try to make evident that the discussion there is about Being, dealt with in better ways in later works. I now see that what was dealt with in *Being and Other Realities* as "the Habitat" is the Dunamis, somewhat misconstrued. It has also now become evident that Being is both presupposed by and participated in and that both adumbrations and discernments go over the same routes, but in a direction opposite to that over which emphatics are expressed. The present work, though, does not presuppose an acquaintance with any of these other studies.

I have been singularly fortunate in having a number of acute readers and careful thinkers give a good deal of time and thought to understanding, correcting, and questioning what I presented in earlier drafts. Their acute observations and corrections have led me to understand emphatics in a more comprehensive, systematic, and illuminating way than my initial conception allowed.

The help and advice I have received from William Desmond, Tom Krettek, S.J., John Lachs, Robert C. Neville, Andrew Reck, and Jonathan A. Weiss have helped me turn a not-well-focused work into one that, I think, will open up a neglected and promising field of inquiry. They stopped me again and again at crucial places, and they raised issues that could not be mastered until I rethought and rewrote the entire work a number of times, from beginning to end. They are not to be held accountable for this final version. They prompted me to rewrite it, but its faults are my own.

March 1999
Washington, D.C.

Emphatics

Chapter 1

Some Well-Known Emphatics

An emphatic is an intrusion that alters the import of that which it is intruded on. When we are ebullient, rebellious, resistant, restrained, at play, courteous or discourteous, or participate in formal gatherings or when we make use of capitals, commas, periods, and question marks, we provide many different kinds of emphatics, usually in considerable accord with the practices of others.

The failure to produce an emphatic may itself function as an emphatic. If one does not answer a greeting, one provides an emphatic that underscores the fact that an expected emphatic had not been produced. Evidently an expectation may mark a place where an emphatic can, but need not, be expressed. An expectation, though, is not an emphatic unless it in fact intrudes on something and thereupon affects its import.

Although we are confronted with emphatics many times during the day and although there are books on etiquette, protocol, and composition, as well as well-entrenched conventions about appropriate speech, dress, and behavior, there appears to be no systematic study that is devoted just to this topic, making evident not only when, why, and how the emphatics are used, but also trying to understand their sources, their sustainers, and their effects as well. Nor does there seem to be any systematic, detailed study of those emphatics that are intruded by realities that exist outside the daily world, beyond the point where a recognizable sympathy, love, hate, fear, or admiration begins and ends. A sustained inquiry into the subject is needed, if for no other reason than to discover their variety and to make us aware of emphatics that are not usually noticed, even though they make a difference to the import of that on which they impinge and may reveal something about their sources that might otherwise remain unnoticed.

A good introduction to the subject is provided by taking note of some of the more familiar, commonly used emphatics and by making evident the differences they make to that on which they impinge. That will make it possible to set in relief another set of emphatics, "ontological" ones, that begin and end beyond the positions where the others do. The present study is primarily occupied with understanding the nature and roles of ontological emphatics.

Nothing odd or unusual may result from the use of many of the more familiar emphatics. We are so accustomed to expressing some, that we rarely ask if they intruded on and affected what was routine and commonplace. Those that are frequently used, like a line distinguishing a sequence of numbers from their sum, or a nod of recognition, punctuation marks, common terms of address, or the salute of an officer, may be so readily and almost automatically expressed that their omission rather than their expression may have emphatic roles, registering an inappropriate laxness, rejection, contempt, ignorance, or childishness.

An emphatic does not cease to be one because it is commonly used or because it makes no appreciable difference to the import of that on which it intrudes. If it is not imposed where, when, or how it should be, it may provoke the use of another that rejects it as having been properly produced. Bad manners are emphatics that are sometimes met by silences intended to convey rejections, dismissals, or contempt—emphatics that give the bad manners a new import.

It is not to be expected that there ever will be an exact matching of the kind and degree of an emphatic's expression with the emphatic as received. What it intrudes on affects it, sometimes greatly, sometimes in hardly noticeable ways. A personal slur, on some occasions, may not be worth noticing; it may have been uttered by someone who was drunk or hurt, or it may be intended to and in fact provoke a violent reaction.

Nothing is so passive that it makes no difference to what intrudes on it. If it made no difference, it would, of course, not be able to provide a place where an emphatic could both intrude and be sustained. That does not mean that the emphatic need affect the way in which what it intrudes on will act. An emphatic adds a tonality that may have no effect on what its recipient may then do. It could be welcomed, disdained, or ignored, but that will not necessarily affect the change it introduces.

A "Q.E.D.," a "damn!," a smile, or a sneer alters the tonality of that on which it intrudes. It makes a difference even when it is ignored, disdained, or misconstrued. Bad manners are emphatics that are sometimes met by silences, conveying dismissals, rejections, or contempt. Those silences give the bad manners a new import, without necessarily extinguishing the difference they made.

It is not to be expected that there will be an exact matching of the kind and degree in the expression of an emphatic and the receiving of it. Expressed, it intrudes. Received, it is qualified by that which sustains it. Nor is anything so passive that it makes no difference to what intrudes on it; if it made none, of course, it would not be able to provide a place where an emphatic could both intrude and be sustained. This does not mean that an emphatic need affect the way in which what it intrudes upon will act.

There are a number of different kinds of emphatics that are in common use. A distinguishing of them from one another, and an understanding of what is common to all of them, provides a good introduction to, a guide for, and a contrast with "ontological" emphatics—the primary concern of this work.

1. Grammatical Emphatics

Commas, semi-colons, colons, periods, question and exclamation marks—even underlinings and italics—are emphatics. They reach backwards toward what precedes, sometimes toward the beginning of an expression, just as a capital letter at the beginning of a word, affects the rest of it. They are so often and so readily used that their emphatic roles are overlooked or minimized.

The string of *x*'s that an adolescent adds to a written letter says no more, and may convey less, than one or two exclamation marks would. Sometimes, though, it is necessary to insist on an emphatic again and again, particularly when something serious is amiss, and insufficient attention has been aroused. "Look out!" may need to be repeated before it is properly grounded. No matter how strongly an emphatic is insisted on, it needs support if it is to be more than something intended.

A cascade of "thank you's" for a small favor turns an underscoring of a kindness into an annoyance, while revealing its user's poor sense of values and appropriate behavior. It would, perhaps, not be amiss to take the repetition to be an unintended emphatic used to make one's intentions or feelings evident. Repeated curses, and to some extent, a multiplicity of holidays, tend to become tiresome and burdensome, losing some of their impact on what they otherwise might have affected more radically.

Often enough, an emphatic, that is expressed at the end of a sentence, may play a role throughout most of it, or even all of it. Capital letters, exclamation points, commas, colons, semi-colons, and periods qualify expressions of diverse lengths. Spanish is a language that makes sure one does not overlook the scope of a question or an exclamation, by setting the marks of these both before and after a complete expression. The practice reflects the fact that those linguistically expressed emphatics intrude on what they qualify, not by affecting it at just one position, but throughout. A pair of brackets, one set before and the other after an expression, serves a similar purpose.

When I was an undergraduate at City College in New York, students had to take a class in public speaking. I remember my surprise at learning that it was incorrect to say "Lawn-gylan" when one intended to refer to Long Island. Those with whom we daily spoke had no difficulty in understanding us, but we were being taught how to speak to others as well. Teachers in isolated regions spend some of their time helping children make similar adjustments in the ways the children had learned to speak at home or in the neighborhood. The speakers, unknowingly, produced emphatics that revealed their failure to function as fully assimilated members of a dominant, and supposedly a normative group.

Silence may have an emphatic role. It is not always identifiable with a soundless, unnoticed interval. As musicians, poets, and actors know, it should sometimes be lived through as an emphatic that both separates and joins what is before and after it, thereupon giving them a new import. It is quite different from an intermission; this is not part of a performance.

Like a semi-colon or a colon, a silence may affect what occurs before and after it. It is not possible to play a piece without making a sound, as John Cage tried to do, since silence in a musical performance is an emphatic that affects what precedes and what follows it. After a work has been performed, what follows immediately after. is not the kind of silence that was lived through in the performance. Instead, it is an emphatic that defines what preceded it to be a completed work.

2. Etiquette

A large number of familiar emphatics fit under the heading of etiquette, or rules for proper behavior. It encompasses many different kinds of expression, having reference to decency and conventions. Note is taken of expressions of interest, comity, and their omissions, as well as of exaggerations and of what is inappropriate. Alert to vulgarities, as well as aware of the speech, dress, and acts that make others feel uneasy or hurt, the works assume that individuals have rights and dignities, and the works try to show what and how acts are to be expressed and respected, on usual as well as on special occasions. Tending to favor the practices of the socially established, respectful of protocol, distrustful of novelties, they determine what emphatics it would be appropriate to express in various social situations.

Works on etiquette are inclined to ignore discussions of jokes, emergencies, or the need to adjust and subtletize. They make it hard to distinguish between accepted moves that have become routine for special, privileged groups and those that promote harmony, respect, and perhaps fellowship. The first are part of a code, designed to promote good social functioning. The second are designed to make social life pleasant and peaceful. The two overlap at many points. Both are to be expressed, easily and appropriately, as though it were normal, and presumably normative, behavior. "Eureka!" shouted the naked Archimedes, excited by his great discovery, running down the street. He would be roundly condemned by any work of etiquette that took note of him, and any such work would be backed by those who saw to it that one met some standards of dress before he left his home, no matter how excited he was or how important the message. They would not be wrong to do so, but that does not mean that Archimedes was not expressing an emphatic worthy of his great discovery. Excitement, no matter what the reason, would not, for them, provide a sufficient excuse.

Try as one might, it is sometimes not possible to avoid raising one's eyebrows, looking askance, withholding and withdrawing, and thereby meeting the social demand that one not notice some errors or affronts. Some jokes, loud laughter, crooked smiles, odd topics, indeed almost anything that would likely disrupt the pace or direction of people amicably together, apart from emergencies, would be taken by the arbiters of etiquette to be emphatics that make it too likely that something unpleasant or even disruptive will ensue.

Formal gatherings of governmental officials or business leaders, conduct in a court room, wedding ceremonies, and funerals have their own distinctive rules of etiquette, requiring that distinctive things be done and others things be avoided. Few need to be told about the inappropriateness of loud laughter at the bedside of one who is dying, wracked with pain.

Even grammatical and arithmetical emphatics may be expressed on inappropriate occasions. A semicolon may be put in the wrong place; a sum may have been incorrectly arrived at. To know what, when, and where particular emphatics should be expressed, it is necessary to understand the needs, rights, customs, and promise of that on which they intrude and to be aware of the likely effects. A study of the emphatics that are commonly used requires an understanding of the differences these make, not only to that on which the emphatics are intruded, but elsewhere as well. A broker's or a salesman's welcome may serve to alert fellow workers of the likelihood of a sale. The emphatic is introduced in such a way that the others become aware of the weakness in one who is taken to be the ostensible object of a personalized greeting.

Use is sometimes made of emphatics in order to hide what is meant. Sometimes praise is used to hide contempt, fear, or jealousy. Gestures, movements of the eyes and hands, silences and half-hidden frowns sometimes add new meanings to what had already been emphasized in other ways. There is no necessary limit to the imposition of emphatics on what has already been subject to one of them, though the result may reduce the import of each. The art of flattery is occupied with producing emphatics that enrich what presumably could have been, or had already been, enriched by a gesture, a posture, or an expression.

Sometimes emphatics are used at the wrong times or in the wrong ways. Applause before a play or a concert is completed is an undesirable emphatic, even when well intentioned, but applause may be appropriate and desired many times, over the course of a political address. Effuse thanks for small favors add emphatics that overwhelm and may hide what should have been allowed to provide a closure. Evidently it is not enough to know some of the major emphatics. One should also know when, where, and how they should be used and the differences they make when imposed on what had already been subject to other emphatics. A child and a dog may need to hear an emphatic expressed a number of times before it becomes aware of the difference that the emphatic is supposed to make on its behavior or attitude.

3. Status

Status, the standing one has relative to others, is expressed in many ways. Uniforms, medals, titles, possessions, invitations, rejections, handcuffs, gifts, grammar, accents, and attitudes are emphatics or loci for emphatics, and sometimes both. Officers in the military display their ribbons. Some of those who are honored in national and international biographical works buy plaques, clocks, medals, and other paraphernalia with indications that they are listed in those works, which they can then display to a presumably impressionable audience.

Germans have a long-established practice of making uniforms and title function as unmistakable emphatics, signalizing the distinctive roles of those who have been so honored. They are supposed to make evident the distinctive status of those who possess them, the kind of respect they deserve, and even the kind of respect that is due to their wives. It shocks the English to see a learned German colleague's calling card or letterhead, with its string of honors trailing after his or her name, all the while that the English person remains acutely aware of the accents of those he or she daily encounters, treating them as emphatics expressing the speaker's status in a stratified society.

Other cultures have other ways of emphasizing differences in social ranking. Lacking the long-established indications of standing that are characteristic of the Germans and the English, Americans readily provide indications of their importance by making conspicuous use of such titles as C.E.O. or manager. The size and number of expensive automobiles and homes that they own, the parties they give and to which they are invited, even the charities that they support, and their acquaintance with those who are mentioned often in the major media—all provide means used by many to distinguish supposed superiors from most of their fellows. I once was at the lowest level of an office hierarchy in which I had the grand title of "Assistant Manager"; despite my puny salary, I was emphatically set above the telephone operator and the cleaning woman. Thorstein Veblen was acutely aware of the emphatics that were used to express differences in rank in the United States. His *Theory of the Leisure Class* is a neglected classic.

Medals, titles, box seats, locations of homes and vacation spots, dining places, guards, varsity letters, trophies, and even the brand of shoes that are worn by outstanding athletes have emphatic roles. At commencement exercises, faculties proudly display evidences of the honors and degrees that they received from that and other institutions, the more vivid and exotic the better. Learning makes it claim to status as surely as earning does.

Although emphatics that indicate one's status may not be acknowledged by others, at least to the degree and in the manner they supposedly deserve, they are intended to express the distinctive standing one has in a society, state, institution, or some section of these. They are representative emphatics, emphatics that are produced by those who supposedly act on behalf of these controlling powers.

Bureaucrats have little power beyond that of mediating, accelerating, obstructing, and redirecting emphatics that have other sources. The stamps, certificates, channelings, delays, and short cuts that they provide are emphatics that supposedly originate elsewhere and which they then carry forward, often in a considerably modified and weakened form. These emphatics could be identified as providing stages through which other emphatics must pass in order to be appropriately expressed and to be provided with needed lodgings.

One of the marks of a bureaucracy is the obstructive role so many employees seem to assume. It is saddening to see citizens waiting hours upon hours to be noticed, waiting for their simple yet serious requests to be dealt with, presumably as a first step in the production of an emphatic that makes life more livable. Were one to collect all the different ways in which roles in life, or status, are expressed by making use of emphatics, one would form a class containing many different kinds.

It would be illuminating to have a social study devoted to an examination of the various ways in which status is emphasized, as well as of the consequences and the determinations of the manner and degree in which emphatics affect the lives of those who are subject to them. The users of the emphatics may or may not be alert to the differences the same emphatics make on themselves, and on others, both those who may and those who will not gain from taking note of those emphatics.

4. Natural Emphatics

These are exhibited by thunder, lightning, sunrise, sunset, the wind, snow, and rain, the changing seasons, earthquakes, storms, floods, deserts, mountains, cliffs, canyons, and valleys. When the U.S. Congress, in an attempt to underline a decision it wanted to have prevail, closed down the national parks and other places the public wanted to visit, it learned something about the emphatic roles those places had for many. Other emphatics, such as forest fires, drought, and hurricanes, may be feared. They may have the status of emphatics for anyone who takes a stand at what these intrude upon, but they are rarely viewed as emphatics that serve to make nature's diversity evident. Natural in origin, course, and outcome, they have emphatic roles only relative to what is taken to be usual, normal, or desirable.

For those to whom nature offers a challenge or an opportunity, some things stand out, and others serve as background. Sometimes people intrude their own emphatics into them, selecting some places, times, objects, and creatures as signaling the presence or the absence of something crucial or arresting. It is tempting for them to suppose that what they focus on is an emphatic that was produced by themselves and not by the objects in nature. Dewey yielded to that temptation and, as Santayana noted, dealt with nature as though it had a distinctive humanly relevant foreground and an irrelevant background. Nature is not subdivided in that way. It existed before there were any humans. When they deal with nature, they submit to the mediation of a vitalized rationality, enabling them to begin from what is in their persons or the humanized world and to arrive at what is in nature.

What in nature is humanly relevant is what humans have qualified by introducing emphatics that give those occurrences another role. Darwin's *Origin of Species* does not provide a satisfactory base for his *Descent of Man*. Only in the latter does he make such an incredible jump from the posture of an ape before the setting sun to the ape as supposedly engaged in a primitive form of prayer. From the position of the occupants of nature, the laws to which they are subject are emphatics. They do not know that, of course. The efficacy of an emphatic does not necessarily depend on anyone's being aware of it.

In the absence of an emphatic, natural occurrences might fit well together but might not be compelled to do so. Law-abiding, natural occurrences are subject to emphatics that limit and direct their courses and interplays. As long as we keep focused on what occurs in nature, we will neglect the laws and other emphatics that are relevant only to persons, to the members of the humanized world, or to the members of the cosmos.

The acknowledgment of governing laws, and the differences these make to what is subject to them, requires the use of emphatics in the guise of instantiations of those laws. The laws need not be only those that hold in nature. The fall of a body provides a locus for an evident emphatic expression of a law of gravitation. A red light at an intersection demands that movement stop. A failure to acknowledge emphatics makes a mystery of the instantiation of any kind of law. The emphatics may not be deliberately produced, but they always need something to sustain their expressions.

5. Religious Emphatics

Emphatics that supposedly originate with a divine being, paradoxically, are acknowledged by those who are religious, but are ignored by theologians. Since some of these are religious, what they claim fails to do justice to what they in fact believe. Again and again they speak of symbols. Neville has underscored the fact that such symbols are "broken" and could conceivably have many different kinds of termini.

Symbols are produced by humans and refer to what is distinct from them and their users. They might have no terminus in what is eternal, and surely they do not tell us anything about this. The pious attend to what they take to be emphatic expressions of the divine, believing that these will provide beginnings for moves that will take them to or toward this. Those emphatics, presumably expressed in holy books, hymns, a cross, a star, a covered head, a church, a synagogue, or a mosque, and the like, are both familiar and have a presumed transcendent source.

So-called religious symbols are made by humans. None could ever do more than direct one to what is not known to exist. The pious, when they express their religious faith, never use them. Instead they treat their prayers, meeting places, sacred objects, and sometimes their acknowledged leaders and guides, as already emphatically qualified by their God. Those who do not participate in a particular religion's activities, and those who do not accept that what it claims are the loci of divinely produced emphatics, can and sometimes do respect the practices of those who believe that they know some of those emphatics and can in fact make effective use of them to arrive at their divine source directly or with the help of intermediaries.

A theology that focuses on symbols, which people are supposed to use to refer to a God, or to an intermediary, turns things upside down. Instead of recognizing that the pious are occupied with doing what they take to be emphatics produced by the divine, it takes them to be using special, finite objects and acts, directed at a reality that is distanced from all. Many look upward as though the object of their symbols were somewhere else in space.

What is disdained by outsiders as an idol is what a worshiper takes to be a place where a divine emphatic is expressed and which can be used to begin a move toward its source. It is questionable whether there ever was a religious person who was idolatrous, paying homage to some inanimate object.

A sympathetic approach to every religion and its practices would take each to find specific objects and acts to be more warranted or evident loci of divinely produced emphatics than other objects and acts are. If, with Thomas Aquinas, one makes an Aristotelian distinction between a substance and accidents and holds that priests are enabled to transform the substance of bread and wine into the body and blood of Christ while leaving the accidents untouched, one would, with him, have to suppose that they undergo an ontological transformation in order to be able to do this. Nothing more, though, need be supposed than that the priests enable believers to find that Christ is emphatically present when those priests carry out various acts.

Protestants, Jews, Muslims, among others, deny the availability of a divine emphatic in the objects that Catholics identify. They take other objects and acts to be loci of divine emphatics, whose proper acceptance and use rituals and other practices make evident, available, and usable. Quakers refuse to accept any object, no matter what its

11

supposed sanction, to be a place where a divine emphatic might be expressed and used to begin a move back to its source. Verging on a mysticism, they await an occasion when they are able to make themselves be avenues through which a divine spirit will evidently express itself. In effect they suppose that this is always available but that its presence is usually overlooked because one allows irrelevancies to get in the way.

A theology that is satisfied with taking some sanctioned objects as symbols, pointing one toward a divine being or an intermediary, turns things upside down. Instead of recognizing that the pious are occupied with using what they take to be emphatics produced by the divine, it takes them to be directing finite objects and acts at a reality that exists apart from all of them and that conceivably might not be reached by and might not attend to any of them.

A sympathetic approach to religion takes each to provide one of a number of practices acknowledging different objects, usually in special circumstances, to be evident loci of supposed divinely produced emphatics. The idea is not endorsed by any one of them. Each is confident that it provides the best or the only way to make emphatics, which are due to a divine being, available to those who have a needed faith and who carry out some prescribed acts. Conceivably, though, were there a God, He would make Himself available everywhere in the guise of emphatics, leaving it to the different religions to find different ways and places where they could acknowledge and make use of some of them.

Those who find no emphatic that is unquestionably due to a God are in no position to deny that some may be acquainted with such emphatics, while those who are confident that they know and use emphatics that have been made available by God have no way to show that those who do not acknowledge any divinely produced emphatics would identify and use them if only they allowed someone, perhaps one who has devoted his or her life to religious practices, to show them ways to make those identifications and carry out the needed activities.

It is doubtful that there are any sure ways to convince either believers or nonbelievers that they are mistaken. Some have become religious after a period when they were irreligious; some give up one religion and adopt another; some stop being religious altogether.

There is no way to show that anyone of them is right or mistaken. Where some can find no divinely produced emphatics, the others are sure that they can identify a number and can use them to begin a move to their God and that everyone else, even those who use some other objects or acts as loci of divinely produced emphatics, is mistaken—or, at most, has not found the best ways to identify or use the emphatics that would enable them to move toward and perhaps reach Him. Sometimes others are persuaded and give up one religion for another or stop being skeptics or unbelievers. Sometimes, though, particularly when a fervent prayer is unanswered, some cease to carry out any religious practices and may even be strongly opposed to others doing so.

There is no sure way to convince either that he or she is mistaken. I have not found that those who are professedly religious to be more honorable than those who claim to be nonreligious. Nor have I found any warrant for supposing that those who profess an inability to identify or to use divinely produced emphatics are inferior in mind or character to those who are convinced that they can make the identifications and carry out moves that will take them from available emphatics to a divine source.

An emphatic could be more readily available in one place than in another, without precluding its presence everywhere. The acts and objects that some religion endorses as being where the divine is most readily available to its practitioners does not compromise the use of other objects and acts by other religions. Those who accept no religion could conceivably find emphatics whose source is transcendent and eternal and is both participated in and presupposed by every finite being. Usually they are not interested enough to make the effort.

A ritual may promote a desirable attitude that makes possible a more ready identification and use of an emphatic that supposedly originated with a God. It could also encourage a use of various means for preparing for and celebrating the fact. Once an emphatic has been identified as having God as its source, one is in a position to arrive at Him, only if this is acceptable to Him. It is possible, also, for one to acknowledge an emphatic as having a divine source, without this being used as a beginning for a movement to that source.

Some suppose that a receptivity is all that is required for a divinely produced emphatic to be identified. In this age, when a great deal of

13

time is spent on daily concerns, rituals are assigned a time and a place. Sometimes a limit is imposed on the time when a supposed divinely produced expression will become available. A few, Quakers particularly, suppose that a receptive attitude is all that is required. In some Quaker meetings, a clock is visible, allowing all to know the span within which the divine will usually express itself in and through someone. Other religions mark off well-defined times and places when and where the divine will be most available.

The acknowledgment of divinely produced emphatics takes one in a different direction from that which other emphatics do. Most of these others are due to singulars with limited powers and range. Some, though, are due to Being. This is not only eternal, presupposed, and participated in by everything; it also can be known. No faith, no participation in any ritual, no submission to or guidance by an authority is required. Anyone can come to know it by reflecting on such questions as the origin of contingencies, what exists necessarily and is other than every finite being, or what is perfect and participated in by everything.

A philosophic account, that is true to its calling, acknowledges nothing that cannot be known. If it finds itself trapped within the compass of a mind, as personalists and existentialists confessedly are, it will retrace its steps and try to find out why and how it failed to see that there would be no one to talk to or ever know that what it claimed was true. It refuses to accept anything on faith and recognizes no authority, political or intellectual, as rightfully putting any issue beyond the reach of examination, criticism, acceptance, qualification, or rejection.

6. Works of Art

Works of art—paintings, poems, stories, plays, sculptures, music, dance, architecture, film, among others—present emphatics whose intrusive presence is evident. Each says what can be partially translated as "Indeed!" "Yes!" "Lo!" It makes evident an insistence whose acknowledgment needs nothing more than a readiness to attend, a willingness to allow it to present itself, and the awakening of an awareness of the singular, rich depth that is being expressed in and through what it presents.

A work of art makes a difference to the way one sees, hears, or feels, to the degree that one allows it to alert one to what is beyond appearances and to sense what is singular and rich beyond the reach of prosaic description. The fact is overlooked when references are made to harmony, beauty, symmetry, and the like. It is caricatured in the claim that art pleases, awakens, or arrests those who allow it to present itself. The work makes evident what it is to be—a fire at sea, a woman with a child, a ruler, a man seeking revenge, a poet among school children, a murderer of a guest, the beginning of spring, even something for which one has no name, unless it be the "Dunamic-Rational," flux and necessity combined and envisaged as existing below the level where individuals are.

References to the "beauty" and "harmony" of a work of art betray a disinterest in the emphatic that it is the major purpose of the work to express. Use of such terms make evident an insensitivity to what is being shown or an inability to express what in fact is being made evident and appreciated.

Since emphatics expressed in works of art are not only commonplace, but make evident the depths of beings, they will be dealt with again, when we attend, not to the fact that the emphatics produced by works of art are common, but to the fact that their emphatics are like, while they contrast with, those that are due to training, disciplining, and education.

7. Conventions

The wearing of hats, vests, beards, corsets, veils, stockings, and ties express emphatics at various times. They are matched by other conventions that are expressed by those who seek to make their nonconformity evident by refusing to make use of those that are commonly used. When initially used or used by a few, they challenge the established ways. Common use may sometimes make them acceptable, with their neglect or miscues understood to express emphatic additions.

A convention can be understood to be an emphatic, giving a social import to what otherwise would be one occurrence among many. Since changes in a convention assume the status of emphatics that are intruded on what is already acceptable, some emphatics may not only be imposed on others that are already acceptable, but may qualify or cancel some. Traditionalized practices limit, channel, and modify uncontrolled and disturbing acts, imposing acceptable emphatic meanings and roles on what would otherwise be rejected as inappropriate and therefore improper.

Works on etiquette have a short life and are quickly replaced by others that are more attuned to the emphatic roles that are characteristic of the time, places, diverse roles, and shifts in the importance of various positions in society and state. In the absence of such works, recourse must be had to conventions that indicate the ways to act on special occasions.

Power must be exercised if beings are to be constrained. If conventions are to be able to introduce emphatics that will have a restraining role, they must exercise some power. This will sometimes be obtained from some of the beings that will be affected. Usually, they express the power of what constrains and controls. Just as one can use a whip, strike oneself, or make a chair on which one can sit, so can one provide controls and guides for what that one and/or others are to do.

8. Encyclopedias

Encyclopedias focus on various items that are ordered in accord with the place the first letter of a key word has in the alphabet. They have counterparts in geographies that focus on places oriented toward some fixed position and in histories where dates are used in order to determine the order in which items will be dealt with. Everyone of the selected items in an encyclopedia could, and ideally would, have a subsection indicating how a selected item is or should be emphatically used.

I open a handy encyclopedia at random and note that a reference is being made to Pindling, who was a prime minister of the Bahamas, followed by a reference to Pindus, a mountain range in Greece, and this by a reference to pine, a tree. The choices express emphatics that distinguish each of the three from the other two, and from rejected or skipped listings, some having the same names or whose spelling would place them between two of the selected items. The work's identification of an official, a mountain range, and a tree, and what it says about them, points up occasions when each is appropriately used as an emphatic.

Each entry in an encyclopedia could have a subsection in which distinctive emphatic uses of the entry would be focused on. The editors could decide to point up the kind of respect and privileges that the minister demanded, the effect that the mountain range had and has on its inhabitants and weather, and, conversely, and the difference that the tree makes to the environment as well as the difference the environment makes to the tree. Those emphatics would not exhaust the number and kinds of emphatics that each of the distinguished occurrences intrudes on others or that others intrude on each of them. In new editions, or in competing works, other items may be listed and, more likely than not, Mr. Pindling will no longer have a place, though he will surely be given one in a good history of the Bahamas.

Encyclopedias use the alphabet in one way, dictionaries in another. Some reference works, e.g., those dealing with health and medicine, use it in still other ways, with all making an overarching use of the entire alphabet as a convenient device and, incidentally, allowing for quick references by numbering their pages sequentially. Diagrams may dispense with the use of the alphabet or may use it in nonsequential ways. Specialized works focus on what are important emphatics in some area or discipline, using the alphabet as a convenient device and incidentally allowing for quick references by numbering their pages sequentially.

By its inclusions and exclusions, an encyclopedia points up what it takes to deserve the status of an emphatic. It could, and perhaps should, add a subsection to every listed item, pointing up the occasions when they could have other, distinctive uses. Every one of the kinds of emphatics that are discussed in this work could find a place in a wide-ranging study, showing when the items that had already been noted and perhaps discussed had additional emphatic roles.

Reference works are sometimes referred to as "tools." They would be more appropriately characterized as "guides." Tools await a controlled use if they are to have effective roles. What the alphabet and other established ways of ordering items provide, though, are tools, neatly arranged for ready use. Although clocks, pumps, telephones, and computers perform a number of tasks without supervision, so far as they are used, they depend on their users to activate or manipulate them and thereby make them become effective means for the achievement of some objective.

9. Psychiatry

Institutionalized religions have a practical aim. So does psychiatry. Both are occupied with knowing some major kinds and roles of emphatics that originate deep within their sources. The pious are primarily concerned with using emphatics that supposedly have been made available by God and could be used by those who approach in a proper spirit the objects in which they are expressed. "Idolatry" is a term of abuse directed at those who find divine emphatics available where others do not.

In contrast with the pious, psychiatrists focus on emphatics that individuals have themselves produced and that may have adversely affected the tenor of their lives. It tries to discover sources deep within a person and to make evident other emphatics that one had traumatically suffered. Where a religion focuses on emphatics that are traceable to a divine being, or some representative of this, psychiatry is concerned with understanding those emphatics that had intruded on, or had been expressed by those who function in unacceptable ways. Both are occupied with what had a presumed great effect on what sustains the emphatics, the one attending to individuals and their expressions in and through their persons, lived bodies, and organisms, the other attending mainly to what is personally undergone or is done in disturbing ways.

One may misunderstand the sources of emphatics that affect one's person, while knowing how to alter the effects those sources have and even how to alter the ways these will emphatically express themselves. Those who find fault with psychiatry because its theories and practices do not fit well with those that interest physicists, biologists, or experimental psychologists, misconstrue its interests and objectives. The determination of whether or not the source of some emphatic has been properly identified and whether or not the remedies proposed will preclude its use or alter or reduce its effectiveness may not, of course, be beyond the reach of a reasonable doubt.

Representatives of religious institutions sometimes take themselves to provide indispensable emphatics that have intermediate roles, translating some supposed divinely produced emphatics into others that are more accessible to most. They thereupon strengthen the claims that a participation in a religion's practices is needed. At the same time they ignore or even reject the claim that others, following other practices, could arrive at the divine. A midway position would allow for the understanding of different institutions as desirable, but dispensable, and therefore for emphatics that could but need not be used or allow for bypassing them in times of crises. Roman Catholicism grants legitimacy to baptisms performed by atheists in crises when no one else is available. Although Catholicism takes the successful meeting of sperm and egg in a womb to be a human being, it has not yet allowed for any way to baptize the fetus.

Each of us knows that he or she has a depth, diversely expressed in various ways and degrees. If an emphatic is initiated there, perhaps in one's character or in the singular being that owns and expresses itself through this, something like psychoanalysis, as now understood, may be required. Attempts to reach an unconscious, in any case, must move part of the way along which a patient's sympathies, loves, and fears were expressed, but in the opposite direction.

We are often aware that what we say and do is not exactly what we intend. Our awareness of the unifying control that we impose on what we express and on what impinges on us, as well as our insight into what other finite beings are and intend, sometimes alert us to the fact that other finite beings also are singulars who not only own what they express, but both subjugate and unify what impinges on them and may unknowingly introduce their own emphatics. Others sometimes make evident what they are in depth by their walk and by their clothes, sometimes even by their apparent casual moves and unnoticed quickenings and hesitations.

A discernment traverses a path from surface to depth in a single, intensive move. An adumbration moves only part of the distance. An ordered number of adumbrations could presumably end where a single act of discernment does, but only if those adumbrations are so ordered that where one ended others began to move beyond it. Love is carried out over a discerning route. As friendships mature, adumbrations progress toward the position that love may reach in a single move.

One may dream of having failed a test that one had already passed successfully or that one may soon confront, thus making it the locus of a dreamed failure. Such dreams were explored by Freud with great skill, originality, and perceptiveness. One need not, though, accept his view of the unconscious as a kind of reservoir into which the disagreeable is consigned and from which it might be expressed in a distorted form or on inappropriate occasions. Recesses of the mind, characters, and singulars are not receptacles in which the disagreeable is churned into a hardly identifiable mixture, able to express itself in emphatic ways.

10. Ontological Emphatics

The foregoing brief discussions of a number of different kinds of emphatics deal with only some of the familiar kinds. Some, it was noted, have sources that are more recessive than others have. Those that are usually acknowledged by religions, focused on by works of art, or referred to by Freudians are more or less familiar. The primary task of the present work is to deal with emphatics that make evident the nature and activity of pivotal realities and their distinctive natures and effects. To know such emphatics is to be in a position to answer questions about the nature of others, signs, truth, particulars, time, contingencies, evil and wrong, what prompts us to provide emphatics, and what we always emphatically presuppose.

In addition to dealing with issues that have been slighted by myself and others, the following examinations make evident two signal advances over what was maintained in *Being and Other Realities,* the work that preceded this. It abandons the supposition that there is a primal Habitat and affirms instead that the Dunamis is and does what the Habitat was mistakenly thought to do and, in addition, notes its involvement with the Rational and its irreducible vitalizing effectiveness. In addition it recognizes that every being has a three-fold relation to Being—it presupposes this, participates in it, and emphatically refers to it. As a result it is able to exist in contradistinction to Being and is also able to exist apart from and be related to other beings. Both the venture and its results preclude atomisms and monisms without denying that there are singulars and that all realities are together in a single totality. Realities affect one another, and all realities are related to others. Sooner or later atomists allow for a supervening being, mind, or laws, enabling the atoms to act in some accord. Sooner or later monists distinguish themselves from what they claim alone exists.

Distinct beings are interrelated. They may produce emphatics, and they may sustain some. Conceivably there might never have been any emphatic, but then there would never be anything other than Being. That, though, is impossible. When and as Being is, it is possible. When and as Being is possible, its possibility is sustained and referred to

Being. Were there no finite, transient beings, there would still be Being, its possibility, and the sustaining and referring of that possibility to Being. Being necessarily produces what emphatically refers Being's possibility to it. If so, we must, in addition to taking note of some of the emphatics in daily use, take account of others that have deeper groundings and that result from distinctive kinds of expressions.

Beyond the emphatics in common use are others that originate with and are sometimes received by beings at depths where they are received and used in distinctive ways. The rest of this work will attend mainly to those emphatics that make possible a better understanding of what is real.

Question: I read this survey as an introduction to a first attempt to deal with a complex, neglected, and arresting subject. Yet most of it is devoted to making evident the presence of emphatics that you do not intend to deal with in the rest of the work. An introduction is surely needed. Since you have elsewhere presented what purports to be a comprehensive, systematic account of what there is, one would reasonably expect you to deal with emphatics—indeed, with every subject—by examining them in the light of what you had finally understood to be the main realities and pivotal points of your view. Why did you not do that?

Answer: It was tempting to try, but it also entrained many risks, not the least of which was a neglect of what had not been of primary interest at that time. What I have maintained over the years is, I think, sound, by and large. I have, though, subtletized and developed some of my previously maintained views. In some cases, particularly with reference to Being, I have found it necessary to withdraw some claims and to advance some others.

Being, as I now understand it, is both participated in and presupposed by every other reality. A source of emphatics, it is also a terminus of many ventures that begin with their acknowledgment. It necessarily produces the ultimate conditions in order to have its possibility, a possibility in it and therefore of it, become a sustained possibility for it. It and finite beings are others of and for one another. Between the two are the ultimate conditions, necessarily produced by Being, and both owned and used by whatever finite beings that those ultimate conditions jointly confine.

Q: Why do you suppose that there is anything more to know than what the sciences certify, unless perhaps it is mathematics and logic, which provide the sciences with tools and checks?

A: "Science" is an honorific, cherished term today, as some sociologists, psychologists, and linguists make evident when they try to escape classifications that place them among the humanities. It is one thing, though, to acknowledge and honor a discipline for what it has achieved and what it seems likely to master, and another to suppose that it alone can tell us what can and what does occur. Not only do the sciences accept the outcome of mathematical endeavors and submit to logical tests, they cannot account for the emphatics that they express and those evident in that to which they attend. Those emphatics originate within beings from positions that can be reached only by carrying out intensive, convergent acts, outside the reach of experiment and observation.

Q: How could one know that there were such origins?

A: In a number of ways. We can and do become aware of others as intruding on us and/or other realities. We also become aware of the fact that what we intrude on and what intrudes on us is received in ways and with results that we had not expected.

Q: Could emphatics be imposed on objects to make these noticeable or respectable?

A: Yes. Different emphatics may be imposed on the same object and thereupon make evident that this has different roles and meanings when approached from different positions.

Q: When emphatics are expressed, do they continue to be connected with their sources?

A: Not always. They are, though, always oriented toward them, enabling one to use them to begin a move toward those sources.

Q: Could there be an emphatic that was sustained by nothing?

A: If it could find no lodgment, it would at best be a thrust.

Q: Although phenomenologists pay scrupulous attention to what they confront, they can know neither emphatics nor what biologists, linguists, and psychologists might accept as places where emphatics are expressed?

A: They could be said to focus on nothing but emphatics, while pre-cluding themselves from knowing anything about the sustainers or sources of any of them. The bracketing of what they want to examine subjects this to an emphatic of which no notice is taken, as though it did not affect that which was being examined.

Q: Is every denial, rejection, or repulsion an emphatic?

A: Yes.

Q: Is it dependent on the presence of something on which it can intrude?

A: Yes and no. It may be expressed but may find no lodgment. I think I hear a knock on the door and call out, "come in!" but then, after a silence, get up and discover that there is no one at the door. "Come in!" is an emphatic.

Q: Even the most radical of skeptics accepts something?

A: Yes. That skeptic supposes that his or her denials are sustained and that there are humans who are being addressed.

Q: Why are you not content to note that each reality is insistent and then take supposed emphatics to do no more than provide evi-dences or qualifications of unusual insistencies?

A: Emphatics make evident that some, perhaps all, realities have an abil-ity to express themselves. The realities may express themselves in ways and at times that are unexpected and may make an otherwise inexplicable difference to the import of that on which they impinge.

Q: No matter how self-sufficient or isolated, no matter how well it may be known, an occurrence may have a tonality added to it, that it could not itself have produced?

A: Yes.

Q: Phenomenologists pride themselves on their careful scrutiny of what they confront. I don't think that they have said that they have seen any emphatics. Why?

A: An emphatic is not a feature alongside others. It intrudes and it qualifies. Phenomenologists are obsessed with the visible. An emphatic does not have to be visible in order to make a difference.

Q: No matter how self-sufficient or isolated, no matter how well it may be known, an occurrence may have a tonality to it that it could not have produced? Yet, no matter how carefully something is scrutinized, one may not be aware of the emphatic that intrudes on it?

A: Yes.

Q: How, then, does one know it is there?

A: One must have a baseline in what is common, normative, matter of fact, and recognize when it is intruded on. Uniforms, medals, and titles alert even foreigners to the fact that emphatics are being used and even to the kinds of differences they make to that on which they are imposed and to those who take note of them. Many emphatics, of course, are not known to have been expressed, usually because one does not know what is normative.

Perhaps no one is aware of all the emphatics that are used even in his or her own society or of the differences that these and other emphatics make to that on which they are imposed. Some emphatics may not be identified or used unless one approaches them in a distinctive way. As was already noted, religions claim to be able to make some emphatics available that otherwise would be missed, and works of art make some emphatics evident only to those who approach them in an acceptive spirit. Some of the ontological emphatics that are examined in the following chapters not only make a difference to that on which they are imposed but reveal something about the natures and functionings of their sources.

Q: Isn't every being insistent on itself? Does every one always express an emphatic?

A: An insistence may not do anything more than thrust something away from the source of that insistence. An emphatic alters the import of that on which it intrudes.

Q: For whom?

A: It may alter its import for the source of the emphatic, for the recipient of it, or for others who are aware of either or both.

Q: Even when it is not acknowledged?

A: An emphatic makes a difference, but the difference may not be noted. A "thank you!" is an emphatic closing an exchange, but it may have such a common use that its absence also at times has the role of an emphatic.

Q: The absence of an expected emphatic is an emphatic?

A: Not necessarily. Given the normative course of an interchange, though, with some emphatics accepted and used, the absence of any may play an emphatic role. A failure to put a question mark at the end of a written question emphatically points up an error, carelessness, or ignorance.

Q: If no emphatics are intruded into the routine, will this produce its own emphatic?

A: It may, but it need not. When some emphatics are prescribed, their omission may express a different emphatic that underscores a rejection or a failure. Not to say "thank you!" is to provide an emphatic that sets one outside a particular social situation. The saying of it may also have that effect. I once heard an attendant on an international flight express a delighted astonishment when he was thanked by some passengers for carrying out an assigned service.

Once, when I was in England, having my hair cut, the barber wanted to learn only one thing from me. "Is it true," he asked, "that in the United States, if you buy something, the clerk does not say 'thank you!' when you pay?" When I told him that this often occurred, he fell silent. I refrained from adding that if you say "thank you!" to clerks in some stores, you are met with by blank stares. I also refrained from remarking that English workers show a deference, not shown elsewhere, to those with certain accents or from telling him that I was surprised to hear a greengrocer say that he expected his son to become one as well. The Japanese must be astonished when they first take note of the manners of both the English and the Americans.

The discussion that follows is primarily concerned with emphatics that originate from or terminate at singulars, ultimate conditions, or Being. Although it moves more or less progressively from an examination of the nature of others and othering to an occupation with emphatics having an ethical import, I see no great difficulty in the way of one who, with an occasional use of the index, might follow a different route.

Chapter 2

Others

F ew things seem so obvious as that this hand is other than that hand, foot, ear, nose, book, shoe, sun, indeed of anything else that there is. If one takes "other of," "other for," or "other than" to be an emphatic, "emphatic" would seem to be an odd way of referring to what was commonplace. That it is an emphatic becomes evident when it is recognized that these terms refer to what has an intrusive force, adding a new import to what is different from something else. Each entity is subject to a power that keeps it apart from every thing else. None is self-enclosed; each is with what is not itself because and so far as it is subject to an othering that both relates it and keeps it apart from some thing. The ubiquity of "other than" makes evident that the relations of diverse entities is emphatically qualified by what intrudes on them from a position different from that which is occupied by them as simply alongside one another. There are in fact a number of different kinds of otherings to which entities are subject.

1. Diverse Others

From its position, each being is *for* some other; from the position of each of the others, each is an other *of* it. If there are at least two entities, no matter what their natures and how they act, they are others of and for one another. To deal with the existence and nature of others, as though these were solely or primarily problems of how a person could come to know that there was anything in addition, is to attend to a part of a larger one. Even in the absence of persons, there are realities that are others of and for one another.

If one takes a stand anywhere—in one's mind or in some other part of one's person, such as the character, or in the lived body or organism—one would not be cut off from all else. Whether or not one understands the nature of perception or other ways of knowing or encountering anything outside oneself, one would still be with other entities, each distinct from one another and from oneself. There never could be just one entity; at the very least its possibility and what sustained and referred that possibility to it would be distinct from it. "Other than" is an emphatic, at once distinct from and separating as well as connecting termini. Neither terminus need be human; "other than" relates beings in the cosmos as well as those in nature, whether or not there are humans and whether or not these are acquainted with anything in nature. "Other of" and "other for" spell out ways that entities are other than one another; they are emphatics, the first with its source identified, the second taking note of where it terminates. Neither awaits an invitation; neither requires a human at the beginning, at the end, or in between these.

Any entities, no matter how alike or how disparate, are emphatically other than one another. Neither termini awaits an invitation, a consciousness, or a specific act for it to be related as other than everything else whatsoever. "Other than" intrudes on every relation that those termini have to one another and makes these have the role of others for and of one another, whether the fact is known or not. "Other than" is a specialized version of the Dunamic-Rational, at once intelligible and effective, and is instantiated in the specific relations of other than that connect different realities. It does not await an invitation, a consciousness, a decision, or a searching before it operates. Because of it, whatever there is will be related to everything else as a coordinate, no matter what other relations it may have to them, including "duplicate," "imitation," or "image."

2. Others of and for Persons

To be is to be "other than" something else, related to this by what identifies them as distinct from one another. The fact stands in the way of the epistemologies that have dominated modern philosophical thinking over the century. If all that one knows is in one's mind, there is evidently nothing that one can know about what is outside it. One may credit whatever has a sensed and an intelligible side as representing, or re-presenting, what occurs apart from oneself, but as long as one confessedly remains inside one's mind, one evidently cannot know what there is outside the mind and, indeed, if there is anything there.

What is outside one's mind is other than what is inside it. Each component in the one may, but need not, match what is in the other.

Whether it does or does not, the two will be related by an "other than." This intrudes on whatever specific relations they may have, and it terminates in them as together but apart, each an other of whatever else there is. Every reality, finite or not, inside the mind or outside it, is other for and of every other. If "other than" could not be traversed by what is at either end, there would never be any knowing of what occurs outside one's mind. Indeed one could not attend to anything that was in his or her mind, since the attention would require one to continue to be distinct from the mind on which he or she focused.

References to shocks, blockages, experience, falls, determinations, foundations, consistency, or combinations of these fall short of enabling one to arrive at anything. If an othering does not relate what one has in mind to what there is apart from it and conversely, one will be left with what is in one's mind, with no one to whom the fact could be conveyed and with nothing else to which this could be credited—or one will be environed by what can never be known to exist.

Knowing something that is not in one's mind requires a bridging of the gap between what is and what is not in the mind. This requires the use of the Dunamic-Rational, of which "other of" and "other for" are specializations. One does not use these; instead one submits to them as means by which one is enabled to be related to and to be in a position to end at what is distinct from what one has in mind.

"Other than" is an emphatic, expressing the governance of termini by a specialization of the Dunamic-Rational by what is distinct from them. What is external to the mind can be known by this only if there is some way in which it can be reached and the outcome known. That is but to say that what is in the mind must be brought to bear on what is outside it, that this be sustained, and that the result transferred to the mind. The "other than" that relates an independent mind and object must enable the mind to arrive at the object and the outcome to be brought back to the mind for acceptance, qualification, or use. Knowing something requires a submission to what can bridge the gap between thought and object, and conversely.

Descartes knew that he had to account for the fact that he knew some things about what was other than what he had in his mind. He also knew that the two had to be related, as other than one another, by what was distinct from both. All he had to acknowledge was an emphatic, because a specialized version of an intelligible, dynamic power was able to convey to the other that which was made available to the other. Instead he had recourse to a God, who is not the object of a clear and distinct idea, to guarantee that such ideas alone are surely true.

It is true that if I think, I am. It is also true that if I write, I am, and if I run, I am, with the "I am" used to refer not to a mind, but to an "I" which might express itself in or through a mind. Descartes needed something that would enable him to know what was outside his mind. This is nothing more than the Dunamic-Rational, which is able to relate what is in the mind to what is outside this and vice versa. If he wanted to dignify it as being due to God, it should be understood to bring what is in one's mind to what is outside it, and conversely. Descartes was content to have his God certify that clear and distinct ideas were true. He should have maintained that his God made such ideas true by bringing them to bear on what is distinct from them. He would thereby solve his problem, but only by supposing that there was a God who occupied Himself with making some of the ideas that people entertain be true of what is other than those ideas.

No one is merely or even mainly a thinking being; all have lived bodies and organisms and are again and again forced to take account of what has been emphatically brought to bear on these. Everyone is subject to conditions that bring what he or she has in mind to bear on what is outside it, and conversely.

We do not avoid or solve the problem of knowing others or what they do, simply giving up thinking and instead struggling to master what gets in our way. There is no need to struggle or master in order to know that there is a book on the desk; it suffices if we submit to the othering that connects us with the book and that enables the encountered book to provide a beginning for a move back to us as knowers.

We do, to be sure, sometimes struggle to master what defies us. The defiance is conveyed to us in the same way that its presence is— by what brings it to us as that which exists as other than ourselves. To be blocked is not yet to be defied; one is defied only if one has already insisted on oneself and thereupon has managed to arrive at what is distinct from oneself.

Othering is a component in every relation. Even identity, since it connects at least two different instances of what otherwise would be self-same, provides a place for it. One who was unable to know an other would be a forsaken monad, denied even the relation to God that Leibniz thought all monads had, the God who saw to it that changes in one self-contained monad were in consonance with changes in all the others.

To be is to be other than. "Other than" is an emphatic that each being uses to maintain itself in contradistinction to what else there is. A solitary, finite being would be other than the conditions that confine it, as well as other than Being itself. Being is other than everything else, as well as other than its own possibility, as sustained by and referred to it by the conditions that Being produced.

A person's "me" can be emphatically made into the terminus of an emphatic begun elsewhere. Were there only one person, he or she would still have a "me" at which he or she could arrive by moving to it from a position beyond it. Each person is a source of emphatics. Some of these begin at the person's "I," circle around the person, and arrive at this as a "me," owned by that person.

When we are self-conscious, we provide an affirmative answer to the question, whether or not there is a position beyond ourselves. The "me" that I know when I am self-conscious may not coincide completely with the "me" at which another terminates. Those who are concerned with discovering how one could know that there are others are occupied only with what is other than what is in their minds. They face only a part of the problem of knowing what else there is.

Each of us is—or, to speak more precisely, has—a person. Each of us also has a lived body and an organism, owns and expresses him- or herself in and through these. The most that anyone who overlooked them could rightly claim is that one is subject to emphatics that are inexplicably produced by unknown others.

In the act of accepting oneself as a "me," one subjects oneself to an emphatic "other than" everything else. Despite grammarians who are occupied with regulating the use of English—but in good accord with French usage—it is not uncommon to say, "this is me, the man from across the street," "this is me, the woman who fixed your window," and the like. The "me" here expresses the double fact that one's "I" has come to a terminus and that a place has been provided by this from which intensive moves can be made toward that "I."

Evidently "me!" has two emphatic roles. One expresses the fact that an "I" had made the "me" be the terminus of an insistence and another the fact that the "me" is arrived at as the terminus of another's approach to one's presence. One who asks the question, "Are there others?" addresses oneself as an "I," via a "me." One surely is not addressing others. Still, if one pivots on the "me," one will treat this as being other than the "I."

A person can provide a place for many imposed emphatics. Each of these is traceable to sources that may differ in nature, place, or role from any other. Did one begin with what exists apart from any and all persons, one would be in a position to arrive at a person, if one could identify the emphatics that terminate at this. Given the fact that those who take a stand at their persons and then ask if there are others, or how these could be known, often are writers and teachers of psychology or philosophy, they evidently have already answered the question before and while they express it. What they evidently are asking is not if some others are, but how one can best express the fact that this is known.

3. Others of and for Lived Bodies

We live together primarily as lived bodies, owned and used by ourselves as singular beings. Each of those bodies joins contributions from a person and an organism, relates those contributors as they are apart from one another, and interplays with other members of the humanized world. Each member of that world is an other of and for all the rest. In addition, each is with all of them because and so far as it and they are subject to the same governing conditions. As the first, each is emphatically distinguished from the others; as the second, each is emphatically related to them.

The humanized domain is different from that occupied by persons, as well as from that occupied by organisms—and from that occupied by cosmic units. Humanized realities are both apart from and together with others. If they were not apart, they would not be distinct beings. Were they not together, none would be in the same domain with others, and none would therefore be subject to the same governances.

31

The question "How does one know anything that exists outside one's mind?" is not identifiable with "How does one know what exists outside one's lived body?" A mind is not a part of a body. It cannot therefore be identified with a brain or with any part of one. It is a part of a person; a brain is part of an organism that is owned and used by an individual who also owns and uses a person and a lived body. That individual sometimes can make what is in any of the three affect what is in the others.

4. Distanced Others

An other is distinct both from that of and that from which it is an other. This may be present in a different domain. It could be an ultimate condition, or it could be Being itself. Neither of these is in any domain.

An unsustained emphatic could be nothing more than an expression, not yet freed from its source. The presence of an other would be doubtful, and perhaps mysterious, did one on arriving at something not know that what was there brought an othering to a termination. Occasionally we ask: "Is there somebody here?" and not only get no reply but discover that there are no humans there.

To know what is being terminated at is to know that something exists apart from the termination. The question that makes sense here is not "How can we know what is unreachable in any way?" but "How can we know another in a better way?" The question "Are there others?" is evidently addressed to and may be answered by the same person. If the question is raised by one in some work or discussion, some acknowledged others are evidently being asked to tell one what is already known. What one does not know is how one knows them as existing apart from oneself.

It is foolish and futile to tell others that there is no known way to attend to anything that is not in one's mind. It would be no less foolish and futile to hold that there are no minds but only brain states, apparently known by using a brain, or that there are only physical units existing in a space-time, some of which know this. It does not matter how clever one may be in designing keys. If there are no locks that they fit, they will open no doors.

5. Co-othering

As apart from one another, we sometimes function as members of the cosmos do, keeping in some accord with one another. Were the accord adventitious, it might never be repeated. Yet every reality whatsoever is other than everything else. Even Being, eternal and necessarily existing, is other than the eternal ultimate conditions that it necessarily produces. Since finite beings are Being itself as conveyed and confined within limits set by the ultimate conditions, to the degree that those conditions act independently of Being, those finite beings, too, will be other than Being.

Some co-otherings await the occurrence of something to join. Some, like those connecting Being and the ultimate conditions, are eternal. That does not preclude them from having different roles. Although "other than" is a symmetrical relation, its termini may be quite different from one another and may act in quite disparate ways.

Being is eternal and unchanging, acting in only one way. Finite beings come and go and might never have occurred; yet they are both other than one another and other than Being. The paradox that this seems to elicit vanishes with the recognition that finite beings are Being itself, as recovering the hold on the ultimate conditions that Being forgoes when and as those conditions jointly act independently of it. When and as the ultimate conditions act on their own, they enable Being, in miniaturized forms, to repossess them.

A related, apparent paradox, that finite beings can be other than one another but that one could cease to be while the others continue to exist and function, vanishes with the recognition that "other than" is a relation able to end with its own termini. When and as there is more than one entity, there is an "other than" that connects them. This does not swoop down on some item and tear it apart. Nor does it bridge an otherwise impassable gap separating disparate realities. When and as there are a number of distinct beings, there is an "other than" that relates them. Since some realities come and go, "other than" evidently is a relation that awaits occurrences that it will necessarily connect, when and as they exist.

The ultimate conditions confine what they convey. "Other than" does not do that. It connects what it does not control. Both the conditions and it are prescriptive. Both express themselves emphatically. Both are instantiated.

"Other than," since it terminates at Being and the ultimate conditions, must occur when and as they do, i.e., always. Since it also relates every reality to every other, is expressed emphatically, and is instantiated, it is easy to take it to be an ultimate condition. Nevertheless it differs from one in being dependent on the existence of distinct termini. Each of the termini has its own controlling center, to make its relation to anything else be an "other than" or a specialized version of this. Since it is their self-centeredness that sets them in opposition, evidently "other than" does not prescribe to them as a condition would. It is prescriptive, but only with reference to what already exists apart from one another and from it.

6. The Dunamic-Rational

If there are a number of domains, e.g., one occupied by persons and another by cosmic units, there would be no way in which one could pass from either to the other unless there were something that enabled what was in one domain to be joined to and perhaps be brought to bear on what is in another. The problem haunts every account that tries to explain how what is in one domain can deal with what is in another—and, of course, how one could know how what exists in one's mind could have any connection with what is outside this. Separated from the Dunamis, a vitalizing, primal power, the Rational would provide only idle, formal relations that would not enable one to pass from one item to another.

In the absence of the Dunamis, inferences, as well as passages from one domain to some other, would be impossible. One might be tempted to deny that there were any passages, but one would then be forever fixated at one position, unable to act, move, carry out an argument, correct any errors, learn, accept, or reject anything.

The Dunamic-Rational makes possible an intelligible passage from what is in one domain to what is in another. In its absence there could be only one domain, or there would be a number sealed off from one another. No human would have a body that had natural or cosmic components; nothing that happened in the cosmos or nature would affect what people could do; what was in one's person would be unrelated to what happened elsewhere, even in the lived body or in the organism.

Heraclitus and Bergson apparently rejected the conditioning role of the Rational. They could not, therefore, claim that their inferences could be assessed as being formally validated. All they could do would be to go along with the flow, no matter where this went. Whatever happens happens, they would have to say, and that is the end of the matter.

Schopenhauer, Nietzsche, and Peirce acknowledged both the Rational and the Dunamis under other headings. The first two set them in radical opposition. Peirce instead supposed that the Dunamis—he called it "Chance"—becomes more and more rigidified until it is no longer differentiated from the Rational. Were that to occur, there would be no inferences or any other kind of passage. Everything would be fixated, unable to move, No one would be able to act, carry out an argument, correct any errors, learn, accept, reject, or report what occurred.

The Dunamic-Rational makes possible an intelligible passage from what is in one domain to what is in another. In its absence there would be only one domain, or the members of one domain would be sealed off from what is in any other. "Bah!" is not a strong enough emphatic to hide, preclude, or eliminate the evidence provided by the existence of other realities.

Each of us is a singular being who is confined by and possesses boundaries in and through which one expresses oneself. We do not just terminate at the boundaries of our lived lives or organisms, keep within the limits of our persons, or some subdivision of this, such as the mind. Like all boundaries ours too face outward and inward. Our appearances, like the appearances of other realities, are the outcome of meetings of expressions of ourselves and of conditions jointly instantiated in an hierarchical order. None reveals what beings are in themselves. All, though, provide beginnings for intensive moves—into the beings—and also enable us to arrive at the conditions that, with them, constitute the appearances.

Conditions and individuals not only interplay, but may add emphatics to the result, alerting one to the fact that those conditions and individuals can be moved toward as they are apart from one another, at depths below those that they had expressed when they interplayed. Appearances are neither just what is publicly evidenced by beings, nor are they just conditions instantiated or the two placed together. They are outcomes of expressions produced by mutually supportive, distinct conditions and individuals.

When we accept some appearances as familiar and commonplace, we tend to ignore their two sources. Usually we take only unexpected or novel appearances to be emphatically produced, either by the conditions or by the beings to whom the appearances are attributed. Although we usually speak of appearances as if they were idle attenuations of the beings to which they are credited, we do sometimes recognize them to set limits within which realities exist. When we begin at appearances in adumbrative and discerning moves into the singulars that sustain the appearances they helped constitute, we find the appearances to be more and more subjected to and transformed by their possessors, until they become indistinguishable from them and from one another.

Dealt with from the position of conditions, an appearance is a qualified limit of what appears. Dealt with from the position of what owns it, it is an expression qualified by instantiated conditions. Constituted by both, it has a nature of its own.

8. The Constant and Variable Otherness of Beings

Although Being is single and undivided, it is an other of and for finite beings in two ways. Being is other of finite realities that those conditions confine. It also is an eternal excellence in which each being participates to some degree, without affecting it.

Jews have their ritualists as well as their Hasids, each focusing on a confessedly unknowable, unnameable God. What the one may take to be an objective matter of fact about the nature and demands of the divine, the other takes to be specialized emphatics that are due to the divine, the neglect of which will reveal one to be an atheist or a heathen.

Question: I would prefer to begin our discussion by proceeding from the beginning of the chapter to the end. At the end, though, you make a number of statements about Being that no one—even one who had read your previous writings, or even only *Being and Other*

Realities, could have anticipated. It sounds as if you accepted a Roman Catholic theology and secularized it to make it appropriate to Being.

Answer: I have here moved beyond the position I had arrived at in that book. That was to be expected, unless I was trying to become my own disciple. Reflecting on the ways that others have tried to arrive at a final being, becoming more and more aware of the participation in Being that mystics have always emphasized, I have come to see that each being not only presupposes Being but participates in its excellence. This supplemented a previous awareness that the Hegelian dialectic operated within the confines of Being and needed to be matched with an understanding of Being as other than whatever else there was. Both Being and finite beings would be torn asunder were it not for the fact that both are realities that express themselves in two ways.

I know that it shocks some to hear that one has gone beyond the position that one had previously ended with. Some think that the previous account is thereupon invalidated, that a number of different systems have been advanced, or that the entire project has been revealed to be not worth carrying out. A creative, systematic philosopher is somewhat like a poet rewriting a long poem, preserving some parts of earlier versions in later ones. What had been done is not invalidated, but moved beyond. Indeed it could as well be noted that some themes—e.g., the need and outcome of intensive moves, the recognition of the existence of a number of domains, the presence of ultimate conditions, the interconnection of epistemology and ontology, and the complex nature of persons—have been persistently acknowledged by me over many decades.

Too many treat philosophic accounts as fortresses within which one must always remain and from there fire shots, somewhat at random, that keep all others at bay. Efforts to be comprehensive, an acknowledgment of errors, and advances into new territories are disdained. It is, though, hard to find any serious thinker who has not discarded or modified positions once held without denying that they had some merit.

Today philosophy for many is nothing more than an academic discipline to be set alongside others. Efforts to be comprehensive, acknowledgments of errors, and advances into new territories are disdained. Yet, often enough, nothing much more is done than to expand, subtletize, and enrich what has been achieved, to challenge and curtail precipitate moves, and to take advantage of what has been done in order to gain new insights. As has already been noted, the idea of emphatics was in the offing once the depths of beings were recognized and the converse of adumbrations and discernments considered. Again and again, as one engages in frontier thinking, one is forced to reassess what had been maintained and to probe areas newly opened up.

Q: You seem to recommend that one should read only an author's last book, presumably when that author is dead.

A: No. Much of what had been maintained in the past may be sound. Later discussions may provide it with new settings, raise new questions, and point toward better answers. One thing is sure: a philosopher who defines him- or herself to be an "-ist" has stopped too soon and too short.

Only recently have poets and novelists had important academic posts. Only recently, too, have creative thinkers found that they are not as welcome as they had been in previous centuries. Epistemology, particularly if it plays variations on the position maintained by Locke and is backed by little more than an analysis of linguistic expressions, is the preferred subject, perhaps because it allows endless play with the variations.

Q: You sound bitter.

A: I am not. I have not been badly treated. I am expressing a concern about the way philosophy is being arbitrarily confined today and the way that it is required by so many, in important positions, to follow some rigid method or is allowed to deal only with some special subjects and denied the right to examine what is. I welcome those who are interested in understanding what has been neglected, particularly if it promises to enhance our understanding of primary truths.

There is no one solid rock on which everything rests. Even Being, which necessarily is, and to which nothing can be added and from which nothing can be taken away, is related to what is other than it.

Epistemology is a reputable subject. Since it is pursued by real beings, and is occupied with showing how these can know what is other than themselves, it cannot be cut off from ontology. Ontology, in turn, since it is occupied with knowing what is real, cannot be cut off from epistemology. In each, it will be found that there are occurrences involved with one another. This thesis, incidentally, was stated some six decades ago, and has never been abandoned.

Q: Being, you maintain, is other than everything else. Is it also intruded on?

A: Yes. It is intruded on by references to it by the ultimate conditions it produces, and it is intruded on by itself as conveyed and confined by instantiations of those conditions.

Q: Are the termini of an othering sustained?

A: As that which in fact occurs, the termini of an othering are sustained by distinct realities. These are able to do other things as well.

Q: "Other than" is an emphatic?

A: Yes.

Q: What is its source?

A: The Dunamic-Rational as made relevant to entities that exist and function independently of one another.

Q: Doesn't the multitude of otherings make othering a commonplace, precluding it from being an emphatic?

A: The otherings differ in kind and in termini.

Q: If Being is other than everything else, will it not be subject to emphatics due to them? Will Being not then be subject to qualifications by them and, so far, be altered?

A: The emphatics to which Being is subject are produced by what Being produced to do that. We do something like this when we look at ourselves in a mirror and are affected by what we see.

Q: Why use the term "emphatic" to refer both to what is produced and to what intrudes on something else?

A: Because they are identical. It is a produced emphatic that is intruded on something else. It is not possible to ask or to answer a question about others, or how these could be known, unless there were others and something about them was known.

It is at once amusing and saddening to hear Humeans tell others that there is no way to acknowledge anything other than what is one's mind. Rorty has recently enjoyed himself in making the fact evident, but he asks one to pay the price of acknowledging a "language of mankind," about whose vocabulary, references, and practitioners nothing is said.

Q: You do maintain that Being and beings exist apart from one another?

A: Yes. Otherwise they would not be other than one another.

Q: Does each have its own center and ways of acting?

A: Yes.

Q: Are they then not unrelated, not other of or for anything else?

A: Each is a source of an emphatic "other for."

Q: Would an atomist find any warrant for supposing that there were emphatics?

A: He or she would not. That is why he or she never can claim that there is more than one self-enclosed unit—him- or herself. There is, for the atomist, no one to whom he or she could report the supposed discovery.

Q: If Being and beings exist outside all relations, will that not preclude their having the status of others of and for one another, and therefore also of their being known?

A: The emphatics that Being and being express, as well as those that they sustain, provide passages from and to them. To know any reality, it is necessary to reach it as what is other than oneself. When one moves intensively into any to some degree, one's contributions become more and more subjected to and unified by them.

Q: When I come to a wall, I am not just stopped from going further, but what I present is affected and could perhaps be stopped by the wall?

A: No. A wall is not a singular being; at best it is a plurality of joined units.

Q: It is different from other walls. It is more than what it is seen to be. It blocks us and other things. It can be graceful, strong, and owned, and it can have been there for a long time.

A: One cannot carry out intensive acts into it.

Q: You may not be able to do so. Do you deny that a poet might?

A: A poet might treat the wall in many ways. He or she could view it as an emphatic, underscoring a separation between lovers, enemies, the elements, and the like. He or she could use it to express a warning, a challenge, or a claim. If it is a work of art, it will emphatically express the fact that it protects and limits, and perhaps emphatically warns others to respect it.

Q: A weak wall, having considerable artistic merit, will express or sustain an emphatic, but a strong wall, brute and ugly, will not?

A: I am beginning to waver. If a strong wall makes its resistance evident, perhaps by its massiveness or the nature of its material, that resistance apparently will be emphatically expressed. A wall that is the outcome of creative work invites an acceptance of it both as a barrier against what is alien and as a protection for what is cherished.

Q: Would a broken wall, one that was left standing after a storm or a battle, be an emphatic?

A: Yes and no. If could be an emphatic that was traceable to its source, but it would not, of course, be a wall that was emphatically protective. Ruins are often read as emphatics that had sources in the past.

Q: Might not all realities be the same at root, expressed in a plurality of oppositional terms that at best are just alongside one another?

A: No. There never could be only one reality. Being that necessarily is also necessarily produces the ultimate conditions that it needs in order to have its possibility sustained and referred to it.

Q: You hold that the question "Do you know others?" would not be raised and could not be answered, if all that one knew were confined within oneself. May I not imaginatively place something emphatically before me?

A: Yes. If what you accept is resisted by you, there will be an opposition between you as receptive and you as insistent, with respect to the same object. You would then be an other of and for yourself.

Q: You refer to an "othering" and also to the Dunamic-Rational as enabling you to be related to something distinct from what is in your mind. Aren't these known and therefore in the mind?

A: They are insistent, intrusive, compelling. We are related to them even when we do not know them.

Q: Isn't this what is maintained by those who hold that we know the outcome of transformations that physical stimuli or sense impressions undergo when they impinge on us?

A: No. They suppose that we transform what is physical, sensed, or somehow affects or resists us into what is in the mind, but they cannot explain how or why this occurs or how one knows that it does.

Q: You deny that we are receptive to photons and other physical entities and transform them into ideas?

A: I do not deny that they may impinge on us. I do not, though, grant that they are transformed into our ideas or that they enable us to look back in time and see their sources. I will later have an occasion to examine the problem of perception and our knowledge of what had once occurred. For the moment it may suffice to note that what is perceived could not be apart from a perceiver unless it were sustained by some reality different from was able to perceive it.

Q: Might not all realities be one at root, expressed in a plurality of ways?

A: No. Even Being is faced with what is different from it. The ultimate conditions are produced by it, when and as it is, and always remain distinct from it.

Whitehead is one of a small number of recent philosophers who recognized the reality of Being—he called it "God" but did not claim it was an object of worship or that it ever produced anything other than lures that atomic temporalized units accept on their own terms. Whitehead never did show why or how such temporal atoms exist or even that there was a God who adopted what these provided and converted them into lures for succeeding atoms. Nor did he account for, or even provide for, responsibilities, accountabilities, or long-range pursuits. He provided no explanations for the existence of any finite reality, nor offered warrants for the supposition that they do what he said they do. Unlike his contemporaries, though, he knew that it was one of the tasks of a philosophy to produce an ontology, and he opened up the subject in arresting ways.

It is never enough to offer a set of descriptions and an account of a semicircle in which atomic, temporal units and a final Being are able to take account of the immediate predecessors of those units and in which the Being in addition could provide lures that enabled the successors of those units to be better than their predecessors. At the very least one should show why there are any contingent beings, why the supposed God must be, and that, if He exists, He does what He is said to do. One might claim that the acceptance of the supposition makes it possible to understand what otherwise would remain obscure, e.g., the role that "God" or Being plays in the cosmos, but that alone does not enable one to understand what persons, humanized beings, natural objects are or to understand the instantiations of the ultimates that confine and are used by finite beings. If it is maintained that there are contingently existing finite beings, their presence should be accounted for.

To ask if there is an other is at least to ask about what is other than oneself or what one is focusing on. The vagueness of the question should alert us to the likelihood that it may have multiple answers. A final answer, that there are many ways in which realities are related to one another and many others in which relations are themselves related, is abbreviated when one attends only to others and otherings.

A satisfactory account of what there is will not stop with the understanding of the ways in which different kinds of beings are related to one another. It will also attend to other major connections. One of these is provided by signs.

Chapter 3

Signs

A sign is an emphatic. Like "other than," it interrelates distinct entities. Unlike this, it relates what is at one position to what is at
another, connecting an "other of" to what is an "other for" it. The
overcast sky is identified as a sign of an incipient, inclement weather
when it is taken to relate the present weather to what will soon occur.
"Me" is a sign used by the "I" to refer to itself as a terminus.

1. The Emphatic Nature of Signs

A sign exists only when used by someone to refer to something that
thereby becomes an object for that user. Were the overcast sky not
used as a sign, it and the inclement weather that might follow would
so far be just occurrences.

The growing interest in the nature of signs today was awakened by
Peirce's studies of the subject. He thought, though, that there had to
be two distinct entities, a sign and an object, and that the result needed
an interpretant before the sign function could be completed. No user
of a sign, apparently, was needed. Nothing, though, is a sign if it is
not used. It will then terminate at an object. No interpretant is
needed.

A sign without an object is at best a signal, something used that
awaits a terminus. A sign without a user is at best a designator, something that may be pointed at something else, but not terminating at it.
No interpretant is needed at either time.

A sign may have no affect on its user, but it makes a difference to
its terminus, turning this into an object-for-a-user of that sign. In the
absence of either a terminus or a user, what would have been a sign
would instead be something that could be used as one. Its use need
not be accompanied by any particular attitude, bodily function,
thought, or desire; it suffices if it mediates a user and a terminus.

The same entity may be used as a sign by different beings and
terminate in different objects. A thermometer may be used by

someone as a sign of an interest in the fluctuations of a fluid in a tube or to convey an elementary scientific knowledge about a relation between pressure and temperature. Someone could also use it as just a tube with something unidentified in it, marked with numerals placed in an accepted order. It would be a sign, though, only if and when it was used by that person or someone else to refer to something.

Sometimes a "House for Sale" is not taken down immediately after its sale is completed. Sometimes an "Elect Brown as Mayor" remains fastened to a post long after an election is over and the ballots counted. Evidently, what could have been used as a sign at some earlier time may not be able to be used in the same way at a later time. Hung up in a dormitory, it does not function as a sign, lacking as it does a user and perhaps even an object.

A dedicated battlefield and a celebration of a historical event refer to what is no longer. A purported deconstruction of what is now available takes place over an ongoing time; instead of enabling one to get to or recover what had occurred, it takes us further and further away from it. It therefore does what all historic references do—use a sign that does not, indeed could not, arrive at what had once occurred. A record and a report are signs when used by someone in the present to refer to a coherent account about the ways pivotal events may have occurred.

Since a signal does not require an object at which it terminates, it may remain a signal even when not heeded or even if there is nothing at which it is to terminate. If something functions as an appropriate terminus, the signal becomes a sign of this. A signal also could be turned into a sign of its source by one who uses it to terminate at that source. A lost wanderer may set up signals that no one notices or heeds. If someone uses the signal as that which had been provided by that wanderer, the user will turn the signal into a sign of the wanderer. The user may know nothing more about the wanderer than that he or she has lost the way or needs food, help, or something else that one who took account of the signal may be able to provide.

Something may be identified as having a relation to something else and may be used as a designator of this. It would not achieve the status of a sign if no one used it to terminate in what was so designated. Without a user, it could be said to point toward what a user might be able to terminate at as the object of a sign. Every sign allows for a distinction between a signalizing and a designator, the one lacking an object, the other a user. It does not result from a union of the two. A sign is a mediator between a user and an object. It does not add a signalizing to a designating. These, though, can be distinguished within it.

A sign is a specialized version of "other than," emphatically relating a user and object as of and for one another. It may relate a thought, a belief, or an appetite to an object. Conversely it may relate an object to any one of these. Since a sign is never without a user and an object, a letter sent over a distance must, to be a sign, relate sender and designated recipient over the entire journey or must achieve the status of a sign only when received or read. A written will is a sign that may relate the representative of one now dead to those who are alive or who may represent those yet to be born. Even as joined to something by means of laws, rules, or customs, what is used by no one must so far await use before it is able to be a sign.

The arm bands that the Nazis compelled Jews to wear were signs of degenerate humans only or mainly for the Nazis. For some others they were signals asking for help that, too many—even those who were opposed to the Nazis—ignored.

Moanings and groanings sometimes provide signals about the distress of those who are unaware that they are signaling. If a terminus is accepted by the user of a signal, the signal becomes a sign of that terminus. A sign consequently can be taken to be produced simply by someone using something as an emphatic that is sustained. In the absence of a sustainer, what may have been a sign could be no more than a signal awaiting a referent.

It is not easy to determine the degree to which a person makes use of the lived body as a sign for that person or for the organism or instead is used by an individual owner to act in this way. An individual may make personal use of the lived body as a sign of something in the humanized world or the organism. A person may also enable the organism to use the lived body as a sign of what occurs in the person. This is what apparently occurs when an injury to the organism is felt as pain.

2. Human Signs

"What distinguishes a man from a word? . . . It may be said that a man is conscious, while a word is not. But consciousness is a very vague term. . . . The man-sign acquires information . . . so do words. Man makes the word, and the word means nothing which the man has not made it to mean, and then only to some man . . . man can think only by means of words or other external symbols. . . ."

". . . The word or sign which man uses *is* the man himself . . . my language is the sum total of myself, for the man Is the thought."

Collected Papers of Charles S. Peirce, 5.313, 5.314; edited by Charles Hartshorne and Paul Weiss

These striking and perplexing comments, particularly the claim that man is a sign, do not fit in neatly with Peirce's systematic studies of the nature of signs. They do, though, point up the need to look at signs in a fresh way. It is hard to determine the degree to which a person makes his or her lived body a sign of something else in the humanized world or to be sure whether or not one had that use in mind. It would also be difficult to show that an organism does or could make use of a lived sign of a person, particularly if this requires an inexplicable loss of physical units and energy similar to that which is entailed by references to trips supposedly made by some to an unlocateable heaven or netherworld.

A pain in one's finger is a personally undergone, organic disturbance. One may identify a pain as a pain in the left thumb or in some other distinguishable part of one's organism. It could also be identified as a felt pain, used as a sign of something that is occurring elsewhere in the person. It is its occurrence in the lived body to which one refers to when one speaks to a physician about one's pain. What a patient wants to know is not how severe the felt pain is—he or she knows that already—but where a disturbance in the organism could be controlled and perhaps blocked or overcome.

Since there are no signs if nothing is used to end at termini, to make use of Peirce's theory of signs, we would have to say that signs not only have users but also have objects. He slighted the role of users and needlessly supposed that there had to be one or a series of interpretants.

Signs intrude on objects. Distinct from the beings that use them, they have emphatic roles only when used and therefore only when they in fact terminate at something. There are emphatics in addition to these. These may do no more than make themselves available in various objects without necessarily affecting them. To be made that at which a sign terminates, nothing more need be done than to terminate at it. Since the object of a sign may be in some other domain than that in which the user is, evidently a sign must be a specialized version of the Dunamic-Rational. This alone is able to connect what is in one domain with what is in another.

Question: Peirce understood "symbols" in a way that few others do. The term has a long-entrenched, well-understood role in theology, where little or no attention is paid to users and attention is paid mainly or only to a distinctive kind of reality to which these refer. When theologians speak of "symbols," they refer to what is authoritatively endorsed as providing appropriate ways of referring to God or to those who are able to intercede for those who wish to elicit His help. Neville underscores the fact that they are "broken," not necessarily terminating in a determinate outcome. You, a nontheologian, are claiming, against their understanding of what the pious use in their references to God, that the religious do not use symbols and instead are occupied with using emphatics that are divinely intruded into objects, and are available for use by those who deal with those objects in a   proper spirit. You know, better than they, what the pious do and can do?

Answer: I am trying to make evident that there is a good, established, usable way to understand the nature of signs and what they do. What interests the theologians are not signs, but emphatics, some of which they take to be available in quite mundane objects, did one but attend to these in designated ways. Signs, or "symbols," terminate at objects. What the religious want to learn is how emphatics having a divine origin can become available and are to be used. Theologians are too ready to accept the classifications and distinctions of traditional philosophies. Sometimes they profess to accept some more modern view, but they rarely allow it to impinge on what has been traditionally accepted. It will take a long time, I think, before they will give up speaking of symbols, when what concerns them are emphatics, some of which are expressed in signs that enable believers to arrive at the supposed divine source of those emphatics.

Nothing artificial, as a symbol is, could be counted on to take one to what is eternal and perfect. At the root of every religion is the claim that it has ways of making divinely produced emphatics available in a manner and to a degree not otherwise possible.

Q: Does the acceptance of an emphatic, as being due to God, provide a premise for a proof that God exists?

A: No. A proof has two parts, one connecting a premise with a formally necessitated conclusion and the other connecting a beginning to what is certified by the premise, a movement from this to an outcome, and the certification of this by the necessitated conclusion. There are no "proofs" of God that meet these demands. Thomas Aquinas offered five proofs of God, but none of them withstands critical examination. The only proofs that are needed involve the use—not of symbols or any other signs—but of emphatics that were produced by God and could be traced back to Him.

Those who are skeptical, or who deny that there is a God, identify no emphatic as having a divine origin. There is no way to show that they are wrong, since there is no way to show that this or that object, or every one of them, is where a God has made Himself available. Religions must be content to maintain that they provide effective means for making divinely produced emphatics available for use as beginnings of moves to the divine.

Sacred objects may function as signs, if and so far as they connect their users to termini. Anything sanctioned for use in an act of worship, therefore, may have the double role of providing a sign of the divine and of an emphatic that one could presumably use to begin a move back to Him as its source. References to religious symbols confusingly blur the two.

Q: In one of your books, decades ago, you offered an astonishing number of proofs of God. Now you say there are none.

A: I have again and again said that I erred, in part because I followed the lead of Aristotle, Descartes, Leibniz, and Whitehead, among others. What I there dealt with did not refer to what was beyond Being or to what was an object of faith. I did not then understand the nature of Being, nor the fact that a reference to God would best begin by finding emphatics that could function as signs that have Him as their terminus.

Q: May you not here have committed similar, regrettable errors?

A: Yes, though I hope that none is as serious. One of reasons for this exchange is to help me and others uncover faults and errors that would otherwise be overlooked.

Q: You acknowledge only those errors that were made by you in the past.

A: Of course. When I discovered that I had erred, I went back over what I thought had led me to the errors. Sometimes that required me to rethink what I had maintained. All my works—including this—have been rewritten many times. After able thinkers criticized a manuscript that they had scrutinized with care, I published it, only to find that I had to make corrections in what I had published, to yield outcomes that would not, I think, have been discovered otherwise. Some of my copies of published works contain changes I would like new editions to incorporate. I doubt that there are any philosophic studies of book length about which something similar could not be said.

Q: Aren't there many signs—red lights on empty streets, the ring of a telephone when one is not present, e.g.—that are not used?

A: They are not signs, but they could be used as signs. It would be amusing to see someone in a shop lowering his or her voice when he or she saw "Quiet!" on one of the placards that was being sold for use in a library. One may ignore a legally placed road sign, refusing to treat it as a sign. It would still be a sign in the context of enforceable laws that assign users and referents for it.

There are laws that define the users of public signs. An adult who did not use them would be equated with one who refused to use them. An infant is not expected to obey signs that demand "Keep to the Right" or "Danger."

Q: Adults who refuse to use a road sign are nevertheless users of it?

A: They are legally defined by laws or customs to be such users and are subject to admonishments, fines, or punishments because they did not make a required use of them.

Q: A nonuser of a sign can, by law or custom, be or be made into a user?

A Not made into one, but be defined by law or custom to be one.

Q: There are two kinds of users of signs—those who make use of them and those who are dealt with as making use of them?

A: Yes.

Q: Could anything be used as a sign?

A: No. No one could use Being as a sign.

Q: It has been said that each human embryo, even if it has a terribly defective organism, is a sign of God's benevolence and love.

A: They think the God of whom they speak could be reached in an act of faith. A religious person identifies some things to have been affected by emphatics produced by God or by some agent that God uses. One who does not have that faith knows no such divinely produced emphatic. That does not, of course, prevent him or her from understanding the religious to claim that the presence of divinely produced emphatics has been assured by some authority or sacred work and that under their guidance or auspices one would find those emphatics available and be able to use them to move toward their source.

Q: If I broke a window in an aimless throw of a ball, would that ball be a sign of the broken window?

A: Not unless it were used to enable someone to attend to that outcome.

Q Could objects in nature or the cosmos provide termini for signs used by humans?

A Yes. Signs instantiate the Dunamic-Rational, and therefore they are able to relate what is in one domain to what is in another.

Q: There are many emphatics awaiting acknowledgment?

A: —and use. Yes. Truth, the topic of the next chapter, is an emphatic that sometimes awaits the one and sometimes the other.

Q: In a rebellion, or when disinterested, don't some use old signs in new ways?

A: They could. In effect, they will then make use of the same objects as new signs, connecting different users and objects.

Q: Do subhumans use signs? Don't some of them use smell and sounds as signs?

A: They seem to do so.

Q: You do not accept Peirce's three-fold ways of dealing with signs?

A: Yes and no. There are important triads deserving study. Users of signs, signs, and objects of signs could be classified as Peircean firsts, thirds, and seconds, or as firsts, seconds, and thirds, but without our gaining any insight into them or into what they do. A classification such as Mendeleev's provided a presentation of the chemical elements that is eminently desirable since it allows one to compare elements in ways that lead to major discoveries. Peirce's does not seem to be able to do that.

Q: Could objects in nature or the cosmos provide signs used by humans?

A: Yes. Those signs instantiate the Dunamic-Rational and can therefore relate what is in one domain to what is in another.

Q: Is there anything that could not be involved in some sign situation?

A: I do not know of any. Indeed, to know one is to make it be the object of a sign that relates it and the user of that sign.

Q: Surely, not everything is now known? How can you speak so confidently about that which you do not know?

A: I am, of course, not acquainted with everything, but that does not mean that I cannot know the nature of pivotal realities, how they are interrelated, their major subdivisions, and what they must and could do. The fact that something is known to be a subject or an object for a sign does not mean that it is completely understood.

Chapter 4

Versions of Truth

In contrast with the treatment of a cause as a source, an origin, or a precondition for an effect, truth is credited to a claim that is upheld. Where a cause functions as though it were prescriptive, a truth is an emphatic that both enriches a claim and is sanctioned by what sustains this. If x is true of y, x is enriched by "true!" The y of which x is true sanctions it and will be sustained a z that enables the y to be apart from the x.

Some versions of truth take it to depend for its presence on a claim or a claimant. Others take it to depend on what occurs apart from any claims. A number of versions seem to have such evident warrants that almost everyone takes some use of them, even though explicit acknowledgment may be made of only one. Five versions are in fairly common use; a fact not acknowledged by any of them. Subtending these, it will become evident, are still other kinds of truths, rarely noticed but presupposed by the five.

1. The Correspondence Version of Truth

Apparently the most familiar as well as the most commonly used and endorsed warrant for crediting something as true, the correspondence version, has not received the close examination that it deserves. It credits something that occurs apart from what is entertained with the ability to impose the emphatic "true!" on this, because and so far as there is a desirable matching of the two. It may be taken to hold between ideas, beliefs, diagrams, maps, sentences, formulae, hypotheses or words and what occurs apart from one or more of these. The matchings may be confined to what occurs at the beginnings or endings of both, to their pacings, to their subdivisions, or to anything in them that may be in accord in some way. Some users of this version of truth concentrate on one or the other of these correspondences; others accept a number. It is not often, though, that these different kinds of correspondence are distinguished or any reason given for preferring one over another.

The correspondence theory takes as primary what occurs apart from what is taken to be true. "True!," for it, is an emphatic acquired by what one entertains, because and so far as this matches what occurs apart from it, in the mind, a language, or elsewhere. Even skeptics start with the acknowledgment of something—usually a supposedly truthful report of what others supposedly maintain, thereby revealing an absolute skepticism to be self-defeating, since it must, after all, deal with a true version of what it criticizes.

In all its variants the correspondence version of truth takes what is said, believed, hoped for, predicted, or otherwise maintained, to be unimpeachably warranted by what exists apart from one or a number of these, because the two are matched in some way. Most users of this version seem to be interested only in those matchings that hold between structures, divisions, pacings, or rhythms and what occurs somewhere else—usually in something outside one's mind or outside some language. Even skeptics start with the acknowledgment of something—usually a supposedly truthful report of what others claim—and thereby reveal that an absolute skepticism is self-defeating, since it too must deal with a true account of what it criticizes.

It is to be expected that the defenders of this version of truth will disagree with one another, with some allowing and others excluding the acknowledgment of correspondences between emotionally toned expressions and commonplace occurrences or between some other parts. In all cases something entertained in some way will be matched with what occurs independently of it, with the latter emphatically adding "true!" to the former. There are some, though, who ignore the independently existing sources of emphatics and take a claim to be true if and only if it is stated precisely and, presumably, has units that match those in an ideal language.

A comprehensive and neutral account of the correspondence version of truth focuses on the matching of what is entertained with that which makes it be true. It will, of course, presuppose that one has some knowledge of what exists apart from what is being entertained, or it will have to be content to make a blunt, uncertifiable claim that there is something distinct from what is being entertained, enabling this to be true of it.

Conceivably one might advance a variant of the correspondence version that requires no accord between what is entertained and what occurs but simply defines the entertained to be true of that to which it is referred, perhaps because it is entertained by someone who has an authoritative position. A dictator may take him- or herself to warrant such and such expressions to be true. In the name of functioning as one who will preserve or enhance the state, he or she may then take some postures, speech, songs, and acts by others to certify that what is expressed in these claims are truths.

Variants of this form of the correspondence version of truth are used by positivism, a once flourishing but now almost vanished philosophy, bound to reappear with the acceptance of some great scientific revolution in cosmology. It too presupposes that one has some knowledge about what exists apart from what one entertains, but it does not show how it knows this.

Conceivably one might advance a version of the correspondence version of truth that requires no accord between what is entertained and what occurs but that simply defines the entertained as being true of that to which it is referred, perhaps because it is entertained by an authoritative figure. A dictator may warrant such and such expressions to be true because he or she believes that they are justified by what occurs in fact. No neat matching of what is entertained and what supposedly justifies this is required; it is said to exist and therefore to warrant taking the entertained to be true.

In some way and in some form, the correspondence version of truth takes some claim to be true because it matches and thereupon is warranted by what occurs apart from the claim. There is an air of impersonality and objectivity to the claim that makes it appealing, particularly to those who wish to free themselves from an overoccupation with themselves, their needs, hopes, and fears. Unfortunately it defeats itself in its demand that something over which it has no control and of which it has no sure knowledge be taken to determine whether or not what is entertained is true, false, or doubtful. Confident that it alone is sound, defenders and users of this version of truth ignore the assumptions that they make, the most glaring of which is that they know what is not being entertained and can use this to determine whether what is entertained is true. It is to be expected that its claims, range, and use will be challenged by other versions of truth.

Again and again one takes some claim to be true, only to find that what encouraged one to do so is not trustworthy. We think that what we maintained had been substantiated, only to find that, when we try to act in the light of this, we cannot, primarily because it requires us to say or do irrelevant things or because what we had maintained cannot be relied on. We belatedly find that the needed corresponding occurrence on which we had apparently relied is not what it seemed to be. That finding, of course, like the acknowledgment of what matches what we entertain and supposedly take to be true, would not be possible did we not have direct access to what is outside our minds. We do have such access, but of this the correspondence version of truth knows nothing.

The correspondence version of truth quietly acknowledges an emphatic "appropriate!" as having been imposed on what is confronted, but it provides no account of the source or use of that emphatic. The embarrassment is sometimes called "epistemological" and identified as marking a place where much needed work is to be done. If, though, there is no way of knowing what could make one's claims be true, the work will be antecedently defined to end in failure or to lead one over an infinitude of steps, looking for what could be acknowledged, without making use of the correspondence theory of truth.

The distinctions and connections that a common language permits or demands are crudely made. Sometimes they reflect practices that have been long established. For any of its units and expressions to be subject to the emphatic "true!," it is not necessary to have them match what occurs in fact. Sometimes this may prove to be undesirable. Some of the details in what occurs may have no relevance to what is said of it.

The precise distinctions made in an artificial language may satisfy the needs of analysts or lawyers, but it will not necessarily express all that is true of what elicited those distinctions. Appealing to those who wish to be free from preoccupation with themselves, their needs, desires, hopes, and fears, the correspondence view makes too many unexamined assumptions to permit a careful thinker to accept it without question. Confident that it is sound, one may ignore the assumptions that it makes, but does not justify, only to find that even then its range and use will be seriously challenged by other versions of truth.

One could take scientists to be making good use of the correspondence version of truth, having refined the ways in which truths are to be expressed. One would then suppose that the scientists not only know what occurs, but that this makes, what they entertain, be true. Again and again everyone takes some claim to be true. Were it instead supposed that one begins with hypotheses and then tries to learn under what circumstances these are confirmed by what happens in fact, one would take them to carry out a different, prescriptive use of the emphatic "true." The claim that scientists, or anyone else, will or must alight on what somehow matches a hypothesis in structure, divisions, or pace could then be ignored, for all that would be required would be that what is terminated at be able to make the hypothesis somehow and in some way be true by it.

"Confirmation of hypotheses" has become one of the most casually used expressions in supposedly rigorous studies of the acquisition of knowledge. Too often, it makes use of some other version of truth—often the inductive, crediting future events with the ability to make that which had been previously maintained become true.

The correspondence version of truth is not presupposed by every other. Nor does it take adequate account of all the roles that "truth" has, even in scientific theory. Northrop and Popper noted that hypotheses can be disconfirmed but never fully confirmed, since they have a generality that no facts could ever match. Evidently they supposed that hypotheses could be characterized as inadequate, mistaken, false, and the like. They accepted the correspondence version of truth to account for the subjection of an hypotheses to an emphatic "false!," "mistaken!," "inadequate!," and the like. That kind of substitution could be carried further, with "plausible!" and "doubtful!" replacing "true!" and "false!"

Exactly what corresponds to what is not readily, and perhaps could never be, known by anyone who does not have a knowledge of what somehow matches what is entertained. The defenders of the correspondence version of truth are ominously silent about the nature of the matchings required and particularly about which ones are to be ignored or rejected.

A number of different usages of the correspondence version of truth may be accepted when dealing with some issue. When Einstein held that the path of light would swerve near the sun, he used the idea of correspondence in two different ways. One dealt with the correspondence between his theory and what could be observed about the light and the sun; the other dealt with the correspondence between what was observed and what occurred. The second was simply assumed to hold. Were it not for the independent, successful use of the second, though, there would be no warrant for taking what was observed to provide a confirmation of his theory.

A good use of the correspondence version of truth is made by judges, guides, and mechanics. Other uses of it are made in daily conversations, sometimes expressed by carrying out various acts. Sometimes these lead one to attend to different sources. "Guilty!," i.e., "this state, in accord with its laws and the evidence that has been made available, has concluded that you committed the crime for which you are charged," affects various officials, the accused, and others in different ways.

Truths that are supposed to hold for all time are sometimes assumed to match the parts of precise expressions with essential parts of what exists. It is not always necessary, though, nor is it common, to take all of the parts of a true expression to match every part of that which makes it true. Usually truths and that to which they correspond have different careers and associates.

The ready and widespread acceptance of the correspondence version of truth makes evident that there are common, acceptable ways to pair claims and occurrences. It should also alert us to the fact that there is a mediator, distinct from both, that enables what one has in mind to be connected with what occurs apart from it, and conversely. Other versions of truth, the following discussion will make evident, are also dependent on mediators and, like the correspondence version, fail to account for them. Eventually we will be forced to attend to a version of truth that alone can and does provide for what is needed.

Sometimes it is maintained that different communities not only have different language systems, but that one can imagine some to be so self-enclosed that they are beyond the reach or comprehension of anyone outside those communities. The view gets in its own way since it tacitly claims to know truly that these could be known to have languages incommensurable with its own. One can, of course, categorically state that there could be such a language, but one could not justifiably hold that it has parts or usages that do not correspond to one's own. The most that we could maintain is that we do not know what versions of truth they might use or how they might use them. The same claim can be made about the versions of truth that are used in parts of our own society.

We cannot consistently hold that other societies are impenetrable and also that they do or could make use of the correspondence theory of truth, or some other, in ways that we cannot understand. We certainly cannot properly use our idea of what they might be doing as a means to learn what truths we can or cannot affirm in our own society. Even there we may not know what is the intended counterpart of what we are saying. If I say "girl" in my society when I watch someone run, no one else can be sure whether or not I am referring to the gender of a young person or to a supposed girl's way of running, and/or am approving, disapproving, or having other thoughts.

The Wittgensteinean idea that one can so refine language that what is said matches something else not only accepts an unjustified and unexamined idea of some kind of correspondence, but makes the unexplained supposition that one does know truths about some items because they correspond to the outcomes of rigorous analyses of one's language. Quine, following Tarski, says that the [true? correct? only?] meaning of "x is y" is the statement that x is y, where x and y are words, not anything else. The correspondence version of truth is here confined to a matching of linguistic expressions inside quotation marks with them as not confined by these. Both Tarski and Quine accept a correspondence version of truth but give it a not-justified limited range.

Matching expressions inside quotation marks with those without them makes use of the correspondence version of truth. Confining this within narrow limits does not obliterate its faults. The quotation marks are provided with no counterparts; yet they emphatically join what a supposed replacement of an expression does not. Tarski and Quine should have said that x-is-y is the meaning of "x is y," since the "is" here has an indispensable unifying role. That would, of course, still be far from showing that no other correspondences are possible or desirable.

Did those in some community of which we are not members say $1+1=3$, that would not mean that they had an arithmetic that was different from ours. The "3" might be understood by them to mean "2" with a "1" quietly added for getting the right answer, or for any one of a number of reasons that those outside that community could not know. Were the community sealed off from ours, we obviously could not warrantedly say anything about what occurs there, any more than we could say what occurs outside our minds or our language if whatever we maintain is wholly inside it.

It is one of the correspondence's strengths that no one could criticize it unless one's idea of it corresponded to it. That, though, will not prevent others from subjecting it to strong, even unanswerable criticisms and from offering useful and tenable alternatives to it.

In some places, in order to realize some particular purpose, it may be desirable to skip over niceties in speech. A mechanic tells his young assistant to get the big wrench, expecting him to know that this is not the biggest wrench in the shop, but the one suited to the job. Here the primary correspondence is between what is needed and what will meet the need. The request is for what will provide a solution to the difficulty; if properly met, it will end in a correspondence of the use of an instrument and a difficulty that this could help one overcome.

The ways in which thoughts or expressions follow one another may not be in accord with the ways in which their counterparts do, even when subjected to the same laws. Conceivably a logic or a mathematics, some force or power, might affect our claims as well as what is affirmed elsewhere. Conceivably we might be assured that what once had been in accord will continue to do so. There would then be something that compelled or at least allowed for a continuation of whatever kind of correspondence had previously occurred. If we are then to avoid an infinite regress, we must sooner or later speak correctly of what is apart from us, without having to use the correspondence version of truth.

2. The Assessive Version of Truth

Everyone, at some time or other, takes truth to characterize certain claims that prescribe to what occurs. The most obvious are those certified by mathematics, logic, and religions. Others express an authority's conviction or demand, a clairvoyant's claims, or a gambler's hunch. All express an emphatic "true!" about what may have little or nothing in common with that to which the emphatic supposedly terminates at. One may be justified in saying that what is happening may cause a fire, even without knowing how it could or what the fire's strength or length will be. In effect, on this view, to say what is true is to add the emphatic "true!" to something that is entertained or claimed to be sustained by something else in some way, at some time. There may be nothing in the one that is matched by anything in the other; the "true!" here is a shortened way of saying, "it must be true!" or "it will be true!" No claim is made that there is a matching of parts, subdivisions, or anything else in what is affirmed and what occurs.

Two radically opposed groups subscribe to this view. Mathematically guided scientists are in the one, personalists in the other. The first find some expressions to have an intrinsic clarity or structure that emphatically legitimizes whatever sustains those expressions. The second instead take some expressions to be authenticated by the individual who produced them. Where the one holds that some claims express root truths that function as endorsements of what accommodates or replicates the claims, the other takes only those that reveal or express oneself to be true. Opposed to one another, both take the correspondence view to be dependent on the endorsement of something exterior to its user, of which little or nothing is known. "Truth!" here is an emphatic that is not dependent for its certification on what exists apart from it.

Conceivably one might do no more than accept as true only whatever sustains those expressions, instead of taking them to be authenticated by the individual who legitimizes those expressions. One instead could take some expressions to be authenticated by the individual who produced them. Where the one holds that some claims express what legitimizes that which sustains the expressions, the other takes some expressions to be authenticated by the individual who produced them. Where the one holds that some claims express root truths that function as endorsements of what accommodates or replicates the claims, the other takes only those that reveal or express oneself to be true. Opposed to one another, both take the correspondence version of truth to be dependent on the endorsement of something exterior to its user, of which little or nothing is known. Instead they take "truth!" to be an emphatic that does not depend for its certification on something that exists apart from it.

Conceivably those who accept this version of truth might do no more than accept as true only what those who accept the correspondence version do. They will do this, though, for a different reason; they never look to something, other than the claimant, for something to warrant what is accepted. So-called brute facts, for the defender, are no more than unanalyzed items, abstractions, torn away from a primary assessing power. Errors, falsehoods, or mistakes that are made by its defenders are taken to be distortions, both hiding and pointing to a truth that never could be gainsaid because it is grounded in oneself beyond the reach of any rejection by anyone else.

This version of truth could be understood to endorse any claim because and so far as it is certified by oneself as a person. Never allowing itself to be defeated, even if it seems not to be upheld by any other person, it always find a complete warrant in its being accepted by one who affirms it. References may, of course, be made in some other ways in and through which an individual may express him- or herself, but one will then use a different version of truth.

The assessive version of truth can also be, and often is, misused. Shown that the object of condemnation is worthy of the greatest respect and honor, a defender of this version may maintain that he or she was carrying out a more deeply grounded assessment than that which is usually provided. Or, when rejecting what others accept and perhaps even endorse, the defender may maintain that he or she was attending to a deeper fault than that which had been noted by others. Rulers sometimes have recourse to that device when getting rid of those on whom they had relied or when justifying their rejection or destruction of those who may even have been major causes for the ruler's achievement or good reputation.

It is difficult to see how those who hold this view could account for errors or falsehoods, since its claims are taken to be so imperious that nothing else could possibly void them. It cannot explain why or how anything could be strong enough to get in the way of its claims. Since what would be said to do this is antecedently defined to be false or inane, what the holders of this view take to be truths would not be subject to an acceptable denial.

Galileo destroyed the Aristotelian view that heavier bodies fall faster than light ones (in a vacuum). Although he did not take himself to be using an assessive version of truth, he made use of it when he made evident how the rate at which different bodies would fall in a place where none was in. He argued that if two bodies of different weights were tied together, they would, on Aristotle's view, fall at different rates at the same time—at the rate of the two, at the rate at which each falls, and at a rate between the two. Galileo's supposed dropping of bodies the short distance from the top to the bottom of a small building without making use of well-calibrated chronometers at the top and the bottom is an obvious myth. In any case, the experiment was not needed.

The price that the Hobbsean savage paid in order to live in peace with others was to submit to a sovereign's edicts. The savage would, at least tacitly, begin by endorsing the sovereign rule as just or as right. Hobbes wanted the savage to act obediently, but the savage's transformation into a subject ready to obey had, of course, to precede doing what a sovereign decrees for his or her subjects. A savage who is ready to be subservient to a ruler must provide a personalized emphatic, expressing a willingness to obey.

"Truth" is only one kind of endorsing emphatic. If it is warranted because it is produced by a person, there would be no reason why "Good!," "Beautiful!," "Splendid!," or "Bad!," "Ugly!," "Defective!" should not have a similar warrant. One who uses the assessive version of truth, or variations of it appropriate to those other emphatics, does not so far know that there is anyone other than oneself to talk to, or anything other to talk about. Thus one may attend to logical necessities and mathematical truths or to anxieties and fears, and another may claim that what is affirmed holds for everyone but still not have allowed for a place other than the mind, person, or being in which to locate the necessities and supposed truths.

To know that we, or anyone else, provides an undeniable warrant for an emphatic truth, we must be able to move beyond its expression toward the truth by carrying out a convergent, intensive move. A defender of the assessive version of truth tacitly assumes that this has been done, not by accepting something as possibly true and then looking for what would make it true in fact, but by identifying "true!" as an emphatic that is expressed by or through an unimpeachable act of the person or the mind. It makes other things acceptable, not the other way around, as the correspondence version of truth does with its dependence on the existence of something else to certify that what is being maintained is true of this.

Since the assessive version of truth allows for no defeat, its advocates will take truth to be grounded at a deep level of themselves, beyond the reach of any rejection, though presumably also able to be withdrawn or altered, if they think this desirable. If frustrated, bewildered, overwhelmed, blocked at every turn, one who accepts this view of truth will treat what fails to sustain it as being irrelevant or superficial and will suppose that its warrant could be found by carrying out an intensive, convergent, discerning move into its claimant.

We can get to know another by moving from a truth that the other emphatically maintains toward the provider of it. Even when humans view one another with distaste, they move intensively into them as sources of emphatic truths. A marriage can be maintained by means of an anger that starts with either the husband or the wife and that ends deeply within the other, thereby making possible an awareness of a truth that is being expressed, half-hidden though it be by the emotionally toned overlays.

We would not be functioning comembers of a society, nor could we know what is other than what is in our minds or is expressed in our language, if we did not both know what is apart from these and used "true!" in ways that others do. If we assumed that they used a correspondence version of truth, we would also assume that what they took to be truths were personally assumed by them to match, in some way, what is apart from them and that they used the equivalent of "true!" on similar occasions and for similar reasons.

3. The Community Version of Truth

Each person makes assessments, sometimes without being aware that this is being done. That person and others may agree on what they take to be true, but the agreement might not be known by any of them. If one takes a stand apart from all others, one can claim but cannot show that what is affirmed is likewise affirmed by others as well or is justifiable on other grounds that one should accept. It cannot even be shown that it would be right to do this. One of the claims of the community version of truth is that it can meet such challenges successfully.

In recent times the view has been refined by some pragmatists. Stated somewhat independently by Peirce and James, it has been subtletized and developed by Dewey. All three were influenced by the idea that a community spirit pervades scientific studies and that this spirit is exhibited in all successful living and thinking. Due mainly to Dewey, the view is today widely accepted, though mainly in the United States. Most take this community view of truth to provide a means not only for presenting, but for obtaining truths that need no other sanction than that they are the outcomes of successful struggles to live in an otherwise alien world

Dewey backed his account with the claim that he was trying to deal with real problems, not with those posed by academics and mainly addressed to one another, by making use of a method he supposed was followed by all scientists. He skipped over the fact that the methods followed in astronomy, geology, archaeology, chemistry, and biology are distinctive. Although he made frequent references to nature, he was primarily concerned with humans as living together in the humanized world, where all things are viewed in terms of their bearing on human affairs. Nature and the cosmos, the ultimate conditions, and Being, as apart from the humanized world, dealt with in humanly relevant terms, do not have humanly relevant foregrounds and innocuous backgrounds. Santayana, in a criticism that Dewey never adequately answered, made the point when discussing Dewey's view of nature; the criticism deserves to be extended to cover any attempt to view any domain as though it were in fact subdivided into a humanly relevant and a humanly irrelevant part.

When we are concerned primarily with what is relevant to human welfare, something like the Deweyean approach is desirable. It is not to be ontologized, to make the cosmos, or anything in fact, be subdivided in light of humanity's needs or interests. Those needs and interests do make some things attractive, some unattractive, some of no interest, and some of great importance. The fact points up our special needs and concerns, but it also shows that any reality may be broken into parts, one relevant to human concerns and the other not.

Freed from this limitation but interested in a humanized world where everything can be envisaged as having some relevance to our encounters, needs, and uses, something like the Deweyean approach will be preferable to others. It also will enable one to avoid both the impersonal acceptance of whatever occurs, which the correspondence version of truth permits, and the claim for unimpeachable justification that is tacitly made by the users of the assessive version of truth. Truth for it is an emphatic, crowning an achievement in living well in the humanized world by overcoming obstacles and difficulties. Occurrences in other domains are ignored or are interpreted as though they were in the humanized world. It also leaves the existence of the obstacles unexplained. Not only are these unaccounted for, they are presupposed if truth is to be achieved.

If there is no way to know what provokes and contributes to a struggle, there is no way to know if there is anything more than what is being struggled with. That could be something that one had unknowingly placed in one's own path. A blockage provides no evidence of the nature, place, status, or power of what plays that role. To know that, one must know the source of the blockage, a source able to do other things as well. What is in one's way, at the very least, has a reality of its own, interplays with other realities, and is subject to common laws. It both presupposes Being and participates in its excellence. To take as true only what reflects the overcoming of obstacles is to preclude truths about what does this. It should also be noted that there are no less than two struggles, one carried out by a member of a community and another by what is being mastered.

Pragmatism, as now understood, attends to emphatics that are expressed when difficulties are presented by occurrences in the humanized world, with each contestant insisting on him- or herself and resisting the other. Other beings can coexist with many others to whom they are indifferent and/or who might get in their way. By the time we come to the end of this work, it will become evident that pragmatism has a large number of forms, expressing a single program which in turn specializes a more primary endeavor instanced in many other ways as well.

Those who study animals in the wild sometimes maintain that these make their own kinds of emphatics, expressed in animals' attitudes, preparations, and acts. In effect, the animals are taken to be pragmatists with distinctive skills and to be occupied with doing a number of limited things. It would be more reasonable to hold that those naturalists are primarily occupied with a study of emphatics other than "truth!" or some cognate and that these apply not just to what humans maintain but to what animals and even lesser living beings, severally and together, struggle with, accept, or reject.

Considerable justice to the spirit of pragmatism would perhaps be done were one to hold that each living being is prepared to express emphatics when faced with obstacles, that it will favor those that are relevant to its success in overcoming these, and that it may also express others that underscore the fact that it is succeeding or failing. That would reveal this version of truth to offer but one of a number of types of emphatics.

Truths about what occurs in the humanized world might refer not to the outcomes of single, successful struggles, but to those that are carried out by a member or a representative of a group or even of humanity. In each, beings would be affiliated with others, most of which would not be known. Were there no condition uniting them and defining the limits within which this version of truth were applicable, there would, of course, be no way to know if and when it played a role.

A confinement of the community version of truth to the humanized world points up the need to deal in other ways with what occurs in nature and the cosmos, as well as in individuals and ultimate conditions. If a member of one domain is to be related to what is in some other, a mediator will be needed. Such a mediator is also needed by any version of truth, so far as this takes what exists, apart from what is claimed, to be the source of the emphatic truth that characterizes what is claimed.

The Dunamic-Rational enables what is in one domain to be related to what is in another, for acceptance, rejection, or modification. It need not be thought about before it is utilized. When and as anything is in one domain, it is available for others in another domain. Its absence would preclude a twofold interrelation of what exists in different domains and would prevent a theory of knowledge from doing anything more than to presuppose that some way of expressing what is claimed is somehow warranted by what occurs apart from it. The fact has a singular bearing on the centuries-old problem of perception.

There are no less than three irreconcilable facts that a satisfactory theory of perception must somehow accommodate:

A. what one knows is in one's mind;

B. occurrences at a distance take time before they arrive at one who is able to perceive it;

C. what is perceived is in the present.

A. A mind is one subdivision of a person. It is used by an individual who owns and can express him- or herself in it. No matter how carefully the "brain" or other parts of a body are examined, no trace of that mind, or of any other part of a person, will be found. If it is held that what is in the mind is primitive, irreducible, obstinate, coherent, plausible, useful, logically certified, or mathematically expressed, one will still be left with something that does not yet show that it refers to some matter of fact. One could, of course, claim that certain ideas in the mind—those that are clear and distinct or have some other virtues—are guaranteed to be true, but one could not then know if there were any such guarantee or even if there were any being that could provide it. To claim, with Descartes, that clear and distinct ideas are certified by God to be true is to presuppose one has a true, and therefore presumably a clear and distinct, idea of God and presumably of what He does. There is no way that one who self-confessedly is trapped inside a mind can find a way to know anything outside it and therefore that this or that idea or combination of ideas has a counterpart elsewhere.

B. We see the sun, which is at a distance. We can shout and later hear an echo. We have come to know the speed of light and sound and have learned how waves and particles that began a long time ago arrive here where we now are. Impinged upon, we are immediately related to the sources of those waves and particles. That does not mean that we are then immediately related to the sources of those waves and particles. We cannot, here and now, see or hear what has long passed away. There is no escaping the present and arriving at what is no longer. No one can look back and see what happened in a room a minute ago. It is no more plausible to say that we could look up and see a star that had long been extinguished. The particles that are assumed to have set out on a long journey some time ago do not have tags on them, telling those who are hit in the eye by them just which ones originated when and where.

C. What anyone perceives, even if it is at a great distance, is perceived when he or she perceives it. What is perceived, the perceptual object, did not travel from the distant and remote past to arrive at a perceiver. If it did, anyone now existing could be acquainted with what had occurred centuries ago but never with anything present.

The stars I see are not stars that once existed and may exist no longer. I am not at the corner of a cone in the present looking into a past radiating out backwards and presumably endlessly. At best I see appearances of stars. These may be seen in many places at the same time, e.g., in the water, viewed through a telescope, or by looking up at them. Appearances of past objects are perceived by many beings in the present. Here and now I am therefore perceivable from every position at some time but not by any contemporary. Each of us is a being who is alone, cut off from all else, but perceivable by what may exist when we are no longer.

Neither this nor the other views offers a satisfactory answer to the problem of perception. Each, though, contributes to the solution. This takes the reality of a being, in contrast with what is perceived, to be apart from the perceiver and also to be intelligibly related to other realities, one of which is a reality that is able to know. Although I perceive only what is present, the act of perception is elicited when I am impinged on by whatever agents were produced by the reality that is perceived.

Photons and the like do not produce percepts, but they may arouse some to engage in perceptual acts that terminate in the appearances of the sources. What I perceive is in my mind as that which is also intelligibly related to what is both externally related to it and confronted as an appearance. The impingement of physical entities on my organic body elicit the use of my mind to use my lived body to act as a perceiver of an appearance of what is real apart from myself as a reality. When I perceive, my mind is intelligibly related to a distant reality; my body functions as a perceiver that is enabled to be coexistent with the appearance of the reality; and that appearance is intelligibly related to that reality. The perceived and the perceiver are contemporaries; each depends for its presence on a reality—the one on the reality of the object perceived and the other on the reality of the being who perceives. My mind is intelligibly related to the reality of what appears, and it is the source of myself as a perceiver.

Some time may pass before another reality or my mind expresses itself, the one in appearances, the other in a perceiver. Nothing physical acts on my mind; this is intelligibly related to other realities. Nothing perceived acts on anything; the perceived is provided by a reality and is faced as a correlate by the perceiver, There is a time lapse before the perceived and perceiver become correlates, but no time lapse before one reality is intelligibly related to others.

There might never have been any perceivers. That would not preclude realities from expressing themselves in appearances. The appearances are always available, but it requires a distinctive kind of being, one with a mind, to be able to perceive the appearances as coexistent, though distant, owing their presence to the act of a reality that is intelligibly related to others who are able to provide perceivers.

Realities and minds are rationally joined; the perceived and perceivers are correlates. The relation of the first pair to the second is that of source to what is interrelated in another way. The two pairs are related somewhat as a logical necessity is related to an inference carried out within the limits within which the necessity operates, though there need be no reference of the perceived or the perceiver to their sources.

When one perceives, one is at once faced with the perceived as distinct in being and location from oneself. In the absence of a perceiver there will be realities that are making themselves manifest in multiple ways while they are intelligibly related to one another. Perception is the outcome of an act by what is intelligibly related to other realities that provide a correlative for what those realities make available. Perception gets no further than to what other realities make available.

When one perceives, one is at once faced with the perceived as distinct in being and location, is intelligibly related to the source of the perceived, and is stimulated to perceive what that source makes available somewhere and at some time. The perceiving is prompted by stimuli that cause one to express oneself in an act that takes what other realities produce to be correlates. Without stimuli there would be no prompting of the mind to express itself as a perceiver.

It takes time for what is distant to arrive at and to stimulate beings who are able to perceive, all the while that those beings are intelligibly related to the sources of those stimuli. When the stimulation occurs, the beings are enabled to perceive. Though the perceiving does not move back in time, it arrives at what took time to appear. Perceiver and perceived, though existing at the same time, come to be only as a result of activities that take time. Stimuli, the mind, the source of what is perceived, perceiver and perceived—all are needed if there is to be a perception of what is not just in our minds, not just a combination of stimuli and reactions, or in a past time and in a remote place.

The perceived is an appearance; the perceiver is a subdivision of a person who is using his or her mind. In the absence of a mind that could have stimulated one to engage in a perceptual act, there would only be impingements on the body that affect the body's functioning. Although able to act in additional ways, the mind, as involved in perception, is related to appearances that coexist with but are apart from it. From the standpoint of a perceiving person's mind, the perceived is an emphatic that a reality has made available. That reality can be known by attending to the process by which the reality produced the perceived appearance and thereupon can arrive at what is also intelligibly related to a source of that perceptual act.

This account of perception, if correct, must be accommodated by all versions of truth, so far as they are occupied with knowing what is perceived as existing outside the being who perceives. The community view takes for granted that one perceives what one struggles with but ignores the question of how perception of anything occurs. A demonstration that some other view is not tenable does not suffice to show that the community view is sound. The fact that one may not be able to proceed smoothly at all times does not mean that one is acquainted with what is outside oneself, but only that one has not yet accepted, accommodated, or rejected it.

The beginning and ending of a struggle are part of it. To get to what provides the beginning and ending, one must know what exists. Deweyean pragmatists somehow supposedly know that they are being blocked by what exists apart from them. Their acknowledgment of the blockings, in fact, expresses a tacit acknowledgment of the presence of obstinate, independent occurrences as not yet worthy of being honored by being made the locus of some such emphatic truth as "In my way!" An obstacle to be overcome is an obstacle credited with the ability to be related to what one intends. It is identified not by using a community version of truth, but some other—most likely, the correspondence or even the personalized version.

Did one wish to extend the use of emphatic truth to cover all cases where success had been achieved in the satisfying of expectations, justifying fears, or promoting a good life, one would have to credit bees with embodying or somehow making use of truths. The fact that a bee found something that brought its search to an end, and even enabled it to send others on a similar, successful flight, does not justify speaking of bees as if they were in search of what makes some entertained claim worthy of being honored, for providing an equivalent of an emphatic "true!"

An appropriate or helpful act need not back any claims. What is prompted or directed does not necessarily cover all cases where success has been or will be achieved in ways that satisfy expectations, justify fears, or promote a good life. Although it is not unreasonable to maintain that beings other than humans make no use of an equivalent of "true!," it is arbitrary to claim that they make no use of emphatics that overlap this in various ways. Their cries, songs, pawings, sudden rigidities, alerted ears, flights, and scurryings alert other members of their kind not only to possible threats and dangers, but sometimes to the fact that something is wanted or needed. Animals' emphatics are expressed in acts that punctuate otherwise routine activities, sometimes alerting others to a need to attend or act.

The continuance or improvement of a successful inquiry or of a hearty, successful life, and indeed of any activity, from sport to science, could conceivably be taken to be superior to others, did we have a sound measure that applies to all ventures, or at best to all uses of an emphatic "true!" The fact that the expression of an emphatic may await the successful completion of a struggle points up the need to make use of another version of truth, the inductive. This awaits the arrival of something before it could be completed. Until this arrives, a truth will not be credited to a claim, unless it is qualified by an expression of one's expectation or by a numerical value that expresses the likelihood that the truth will be sustained.

4. Induction

None of the preceding view of truth takes much, if any, notice of the time that joins what is maintained to something else yet to be reached and that will sustain, qualify, or reject it. Yet they all begin at temporal positions that are different from those where they end.

A process has a distinguishable beginning and ending, with the ending providing a termination for the beginning. Until the termination is reached, the beginning may be credited with a "true!," having a probability value that is to be replaced in the future with a simple "true!" or "false! Although any face of a perfect die thrown at random may have only a probability value of $1/6$ before it is thrown, at the end of any throw the claim that a specified face has or has not turned up will be unequivocally true or false. In other cases the alternatives will not be so clearly distinguished, and the assigned probability value may express nothing more than one's confidence in the nature of the outcome. "True!" will then be presented in the form of a fraction that expresses the likelihood that what is attached to this will be exhibited in a possibly infinite long run in which all alternatives are realized in their proper, mathematically determined proportions. If one demanded that a perfect die thrown at random have a three turn up on one die and a five on another, the probability of that eight would be no greater than the probability of an alternative selection.

On the basis of what had been learned in the past, one may inductively infer that some other occurrence will take place at some other time. Until this is arrived at, the emphatic will not be expressed. When it is arrived at, the probability value will be replaced by an expression of a certainty that is provided by what sustains it. A claim has a probability value only with reference to alternatives that could have been realized instead.

Since we make decisions whose consequences we try to envisage, we inevitably concern ourselves with providing and accepting inductively reached outcomes that at the time could be true elsewhere only under certain circumstances. Since, too, what one person takes to be reasonable, another does not, inductions will sometimes be hard to distinguish from confident guesses. To avoid that outcome, refuge is sometimes taken with formulae that provide inductive values for equally possible alternatives over "a long run." That run has no determinable end. There is no time long enough in which it could be completed. If after some thirty random throws every side of a die, no matter close to perfection it be, were to turn up five times. we would find our mathematical calculations satisfied. If instead one side turned up thirty times, we would have to look to further throws in which the other sides came up that many times. There is nothing amiss if one side of a perfect die, thrown at random, turned up *n* times, no matter how large the *n* is, before any of the other sides turn up. A mathematical formulation of probability values deals with ideal objects, in ideal situations, occurring in an ideal long run. Its actual use requires qualifications, if it is to be pertinent to what occurs.

When we make decisions whose consequences we try to envisage, we try to provide or to accept outcomes that are inductively reached but which could not have been known at the time that the decisions were made. When they in fact occur, those consequences have no probability value less than 1. Any other values refer only to a presumed likelihood of their occurrence. What is said in advance about the likelihood expresses nothing more than one's degree of confidence. Stated in numbers, this gives some a sense of certainty that expresses what must occur in the long run, in which all possibilities are realized in strict accord with their numerical values.

Interested in anticipating what may be learned about what is at another place or time as a result of the operation of some cause or as the outcome of random activity, one will be prone to qualify other versions of truth by what one inductively infers will occur. Most of the time the qualifications will not be quantified or even mentioned but instead will be expressed in preparations made for dealing with the prospect when it is realized.

Tradition and both individual and common experience affect our practices, dictating where, and to what extent, it is reasonable to expect that an emphatic truth will be sustained. Since there also is an anticipatory component in whatever is said or done, no claim—even one that will be sustained—could at the time that it is entertained be more than probably true.

What is known to have been repeated a great number of times may not occur again or ever be distributed as it had been. We have only a limited assurance that future occurrences will be more or less like what had occurred at previous times and then only so far as they conform to the same laws in similar circumstances. An induction that is upheld is qualified by them. The emphatic truth that is thereupon provided will, as a consequence, have to accept another version of truth as an instance of itself. This reciprocates, expressing a correspondence, personalized demands, or the practical uses of which the induction may make use.

A stock market is one place where many different inductions compete as predictions. No one knows which, if any, will be upheld—neither those that have been upheld in the past nor those made by watchers of stock market swings. Some who invest in the market make wild guesses; others base theirs on careful studies of performances, trends, and actions of the issuers of the stocks, on governmental reports, on what occurs in other markets, or on the kinds of relations one's government has with others, but no one knows all the causes that make a market rise or fall or the effect it has on other economic and noneconomic interests and involvements, or conversely. Not only are there many independent variables and multiple ways in which these may affect one another, but there is no knowing just when future radical fluctuations will in fact occur.

A promising use of the inductive version of truth projects into the near future what had been recently learned about the distribution of different occurrences in the recent past, cushioned by a memory of what followed this—some knowledge of causes and effects in the marketplace, of the weaknesses and expectations of pivotal figures and institutions, and of changes in governments, employment rates, natural resources, and controls. If we seek certainty, there will be no escaping the need to master all of them, to understand how they affect one another, and to know what the likelihood is that they will do so adversely. The judgments of those who spend most of their time trying to understand the course and strength of economic trends is likely to be more reliable than the judgments of those who pay less attention, but it does not assure that they will not make poor predictions. Twist and turn as we like, we cannot turn inductions into deductions.

An induction is involved in every claim. What satisfies its claim occurs elsewhere; it is not deducible, since it is always subject to multiple causes whose separate and joint effectiveness are not well understood. No induction can be warrantedly accepted as true. It is, therefore, to be expected that those who take their stand with some other version of truth will, at least tacitly, suppose that the inductive version uses theirs in inappropriate ways. At most they might agree that inductions could tell us about what is likely to occur, but "likely" is such a sinuous term that no one knows when it turns into "unlikely."

The inductive version of truth is a claim made about a possibility that is to be realized in a determinate future that does not yet exist. In the meantime it will try to express a truth tied to a likelihood that its claims will be sustained. Bolstered by a hope it cannot defend, it may nevertheless be upheld here and there, now and then. The fact sustains the gambler. The rest of us, too, though over a wider range and with many hedges, focus on likelihoods and expect that equally weighted alternatives will occur in equal numbers in a finite time.

Overlooking details and minor variations, under the guidance of those who have lived more or less successful lives and keeping within the limits of established practices, most of us manage to make many successful inductions. We find that we can count on many things to act in the same ways and to have the same kinds of effectiveness again and again, but we do not know whether or not, or for how long, they will continue to do so. Our successes and our failures are usually not spectacular. Our rough-hewn inductions, since they do not demand precise confirmations, can be confirmed to a degree that other versions of truth cannot be. Everyone makes use of such inductions, for all make claims about what takes time to arrive at. Even the personalistic version will take time to come to an end, where it completes its claim to be true.

There are no substitutes for inductive truths any more than there are substitutes for the other versions of truth. All have uses. All are desirable. None suffices, nor is any in a position to determine the merits of the others, except in question-begging terms. While rejecting the idea that theirs should be eliminated or superseded, the defenders of each take note of the fact that the others often make use of it.

Inductions never do more than provide suggestions of what it is reasonable for one to expect. Since there always is an anticipatory component in much of what one says or does, one will inevitably deal inductively with what is not yet encountered. Since matchings, prescriptions, and adjustments will also be required, the other versions of truth will also play some role in the use of any one. Sometimes the inductive version of truth will be taken to override or to disqualify even what one takes to hold in the humanized world. Both daring and restrained in a way that other versions of truth are not, the inductive version of truth always refers to what is not yet available. The probability value of surmises and predictions are partly expressed in preparatory acts. What is accepted is only probably true, even when it is personally insisted on.

The inductive version of truth presents it as an emphatic that awaits a sustaining elsewhere. Whatever probability values are associated with it refer to the likelihood that the sustaining will be provided. The knowledge that it will be provided, though, requires that some other version of truth be brought into play. The formal version of truth supposedly meets that demand.

5. The Formal Version of Truth

What is intrinsically intelligible and fixed, expressed in contentless terms, and instantiated by everything is held by some to be the subject matter of mathematics and logic and to be necessarily true because of its structure. Supposedly completely intelligible, alone acceptable to a clear mind, it takes what is not reduced to its truth to be improperly expressed and therefore not really a limitation. Somehow a devil in the guise of a sloppy use of language keeps one from what is unmistakable and beyond denial, leaving it to analysts first to exorcise the devil and then to reorder language so that the devil has no place where reentry is possible. Truth is here understood to be an emphatic that never could be gainsaid, despite all the confusion and errors that seem to stand in its way.

Those who hold this version of truth do not stop to tell one how the confused or false could have occurred or how it could play any role. Nor is it shown how it is to be used to guide, clarify, or control what may be maintained for other reasons. Their presence, as well as confusions and errors, become mysteries or are attributed to powers that are nevertheless too weak to stand in the way of what supposedly brooks neither limitation nor denial. A special case of that emphatic, called the "clear and distinct," takes everything to be the Rational in a more or less evident form. It and other variants make use of a version of truth that would be beyond the power of its defenders to understand, were they not able to attend to it with error-free minds. To be able to speak of errors and confusions as being the result of using improper or inadequate ideas, words, or grammar is to leave unanswered the question of how these could have possibly been able to get in the way of what is clear, distinct, and necessary, which presumably are beyond the reach of any defeat or denial. The defeats could, of course, be defined to be impossible, but that will not prevent denials from being present, obdurate, and perhaps even impossible to overcome. Strictly speaking, anyone who held this view would have to treat whatever doubts and questions are raised about it as being no more than inadequate ways in which it is reinstated. That would still leave the occurrence of the doubtful and questionable an inexplicable mystery. The formal version of truth is caught up in the paradox that if it could not possibly be opposed it has nothing to overcome.

What is formally necessary can be taken to be the source of an emphatic "true!" that could be used by one with a clear mind. When what seems to defy or deny it is taken to be inchoate or overcompressed, it will then be supposed that this needs only to be analyzed in order to make evident how the truth is to be sustained. The Rational would then be taken to provide an emphatic that intrudes everywhere, though perhaps not always readily identifiable or discoverable.

The supposed universality of a formal truth not only needs an inexplicable source, but requires something other than itself to enable it to be instantiated. It and other variants, at least tacitly, must acknowledge the Dunamis to be interinvolved with the Rational or else leave its sustaining to beings that exist only contingently and therefore could conceivably be unalterable for a while, then change or disappear.

Schopenhauer identified the Dunamis with a primal will; Nietzsche identified it with a Dionysian vitality, inseparable from an Apollonian rationality. It would be hard to distinguish it from an Heracleitean flux, a Bergsonian elan vital, or a Peircean chance, were it not for the fact that it is not only inseparable from the Rational, but expresses itself through this. With the Rational it relates what is in one domain to what is in some other. In its absence there would be no knowing anything outside one's mind, no nature distinguished from but related to the cosmos, no humanized world produced after nature, and no persons existing together in a domain of their own.

Existentialism bypasses the Dunamic-Rational as too impersonal. Pragmatism tacitly rejects it as at once too fluid and static to be relevant to the kind of causation that is exhibited when people act purposively and effectively to overcome what is in the way of their prosperity. Naturalism implicitly criticizes it for its inability to account for the different times through which the beings in nature exist, the spaces which these occupy and in which they are related, and the causes they initiate and to which they are subject. In their different ways, the three find it to be too austere and detached to be able to do anything more than enable one to present what is otherwise known and understood in a universally acceptable form.

Despite its cold objectivity and great range, despite the fact that it has no particular relevance to what occurs in just one domain, the Dunamic-Rational provides an emphatic truth, connecting what would otherwise be unrelated. It does not, though, reject any of the other versions of truth. It takes them to be so many providers of terms for it to connect, while allowing them to have roles in limited areas. Not only do they reject that concession, but they take it to be not worth treating seriously by anyone who is concerned with knowing particular truths about what in fact occurs.

Inflexible, pertinent only to structures and units that these connect, the Rational is a condition outside all passages, the sensuous, the brute, and the idiosyncratic. Cut off from the Dunamis, there would be no necessary relation that inferences had to formal necessities. Reciprocally, were the Dunamis to function in the absence of any constraints provided by the Rational, inferences could properly end anywhere. Legitimate inferences have beginnings and endings that match the antecedents and consequences of what is rationally joined.

The Dunamis never allows the Rational to be as unruffled as formalism takes it to be. Nor is it outside the reach of understanding, as vitalism supposes. Acting independently of the Rational, it connects whatever this begins with and that with which it ends. Joined to the Dunamis, the Rational makes it possible to relate all the previously examined versions of truth as having distinctive, legitimate ranges. One who accepts the two as distinct but joined is not only able to pass from any item to any other in all the previously examined versions of truth, but can certify all of them as having distinctive, legitimate, though limited applications and ranges. One who accepts the two as so joined not only is able to pass from any item to any other in any domain, but is in a position to examine all of the others versions in a neutral spirit. Evidently the preceding examination of these presupposed its use.

Kant's references to "syntheses" as involved in all additions offered a signal way to alert one to the neglected but inescapable, effective role of the Dunamis. He did not take express note of it, contenting himself with the use of the term "synthetic," which contrasted with the accepted views that his predecessors thought sufficed to explain mathematical operations. We can—and we do—make use of rules in which antecedents are in fixed, formal relations to consequents. To get to a conclusion, though, we must carry out an activity and therefore make some use of the Dunamis.

Although the Rational is an ultimate condition alongside the others, it is realized in a way that is different from theirs. The Dunamis, to which it is joined, is unlike the individual units in it, which express themselves in and through it when they interplay with the ultimate conditions. A formula in which x necessitates y, even if y is identifiable as "x or non-x," would have nothing to begin at or end with, were the x and y not dunamically related apart from, though within the compass of the necessity. We can and we do ignore dunamic connections when we attend to laws and prescriptions expressing necessities, but these, as well as their termini, are qualified by what is different from those connections. As will become evident in the next chapter, the existence of individuals and the inescapable presence and irreducibility of universals are essential, supplementary parts of a single view.

The Dunamic-Rational and its version of truth are not alongside the four that have been examined. Instead it provides a general form that each specializes in a distinctive way. Were no use made of it, there would be no knowing the others in an unbiased way, as alongside one another. Never competing with any of them, the Dunamic-Rational allows a place for each, once they have been stated clearly, i.e., restated in accord with its demands.

The defenders of the other views are not disturbed. All, at least tacitly, reject the supposition that they are rightly dealt with as one of a number. Since the Dunamic-Rational version of truth does not allow them to make their claims to being superior to their rivals, it and the other versions will remain at an impasse, unless some other position can be taken that allows one to determine the merits and ranges of all of them.

A nonprejudgmental survey of the five foregoing versions of truth would set them alongside one another without denying that the fifth appropriately determines the legitimacy and ranges of the other four. No one of them could rightly determine the merits of the others. None is sacrosanct, but not until they are set alongside one another is one in a position to understand their legitimate ranges and limits of any of them.

6. A Disjunction of Claimants

Each of the first four versions of truth tacitly makes the double claim that it is relevant to what actually occurs and that it can never be replaced. The fifth, justified by the Dunamic-Rational, has too great a range for them. It also seems unable to exclude anything short of the self-contradictory and cannot allow either for what is absolutely fixed or fluid. They, unlike it, attend to matters of fact; it, unlike them, determines the ranges and justifications of all of them and does so from a position that is biased toward none. Also, unlike them, it respects the practices and satisfies the demands of mathematicians and logicians.

Paying no attention to contingencies and having no way to refer to some matter of fact that might warrant a truth, this version must be content to acknowledge and evaluate the others when these accept some claims as true. It tacitly assumes that the others were initially, though not expressly, taken to deal with the warrant for a truth claim from a neutral position when, in fact, they are biased toward those that are sanctioned in special ways. Even if there were a preferential position that one of them might enjoy, it would not have been dealt with properly were it not seen to be but one of a number. Each should be viewed as one of a set of five, if one is not to view them without an antecedent bias favoring one or the other of them.

If metaphysics is understood to be the subject that, among other things, attends to those ultimate conditions that are instantiated in what does or will occur, we will take a firm step into it when we acknowledge not only that there is more than one version of truth, but that they are competitors. Before the different versions of truth could be properly set in opposition to one another, however, they have to be seen together and therefore to be envisageable from a position distinct from those that each occupies.

The acknowledgment of the five versions of truth, no matter which one may be favored or used, offers a confirmation and a reaffirmation of the claim that there are five primary, ultimate conditions. Conceivably there might have been more or fewer than five conditions, and these might have been different from what they in fact are. Whatever their number and kind, they are always subtended by another that envisages them as making competing claims about what can rightly be credited with the emphatic, "true!" One escapes the war of each of the five against all the others, by envisaging them from a sixth position that sets them alongside one another.

Were the ultimate conditions different in nature from what they are, the five versions of truth that have here been distinguished would be different for each condition. The Assessor, the Affiliator, the Extensional, the Coordinator, and the Dunamic-Rational underwrite distinctive versions. To allow for all five versions, if only to determine their ranges and warrants, is to make use of a sixth.

The sixth version of truth takes the other five to be making claims that deserve to dealt with. The fifth, though not itself alongside the other four, is viewed by the sixth as but one of five, each making a distinctive claim to identify a distinctive, legitimate version of truth. It does not evaluate the others but instead expresses the truth that they make competing claims to define when the emphatic "true!" is justifiably expressed.

7. A Fixed Truth

That there are just so many versions of truth, when there could have been more or fewer, makes evident that those already dealt with are envisaged from another position that is not subject to that criticism. Being, as that which is perfect and eternal and does only what it must, provides what is needed.

Always self-same, Being makes no claims. Nor does it depend for its reality or excellence on anything else. All it does is produce what can both sustain its possibility and refer to it and, so far, have the status of a genuine reality defining its own kind of truth. "True!" here is one with "real!, an emphatic that Being bestows on whatever it, directly or indirectly, makes be and which participates in Being's excellence to some degree. In the absence of Being there would be no warrant for holding that the ultimate conditions and finite beings were more than imaginaries.

Finite realities, and what they separately and jointly do, have natures and careers of their own. Each is enhanced to the degree that it participates in Being's excellence; each also remains distinct from Being, because and so far as it presupposes Being as other than it.

The other versions of "true," already noted, have origins and references different from any that are attributable to Being. Yet nothing seems so remote and effete, so empty of content, as Being. Few ever refer to it, and most of those who do refer to it identify it with a God who is beyond anyone's ability to know or even to understand and who in the end is reachable, if at all, only by making use of emphatics that He supposedly made available in ordinary objects and that can be used on special occasions to move to Him.

Forced conversions into some religion can result in people being compelled to carry out various practices, but they fall short of enabling the converted to make use of the supposed available emphatics that would enable one to move toward, or at least attend to, their divine source. Rituals and other religious practices could conceivably enable one to use some objects on some occasions as effective and ready ways to be alert to and to use emphatics, due to the divine, but no one else can know if they do or do not succeed.

It has been the unfortunate practice of some philosophers to use "God" where it would have been more correct to use "Being." (For a while, I thoughtlessly followed that practice. I now use "God" as most religious persons and theologians seem to do, to name an object of faith and worship who is beyond understanding but who could be approached and perhaps reached through the use of an emphatic that He presumably made available.) "Being," even when participated in as excellent, is not interchangeable with "God." This refers to what is beyond anyone's ability to know, or even to understand, and does not do only what it must.

Presupposed by everything else, Being provides a "true!" that intrudes on them. All other versions of truth apply to what is within its compass. It is necessary in itself and is both presupposed and shared in by every other reality. The ultimate conditions are necessarily produced by it, to sustain and refer its possibility to it. In their absence there would be only a possibility of God, i.e., a possibility that was a subordinate part of Him—but was no possibility for Him—that could be sustained apart from and referred to Him.

Whatever conditions there are, are instantiated in every being, with a different condition dominant in whatever domain the being is in. Those conditions, like the individual beings that they confine, depend on Being for their presence. The different versions of truth that they warrant are certified by it. One is inclined to rest with that fact since there is nothing more basic than Being of which we have any knowledge. Yet, though whatever else there is depends either directly or indirectly for its existence on Being, that does not compromise the act that there are many beings with realities and natures of their own.

8. Individualized Truth

Since each individual is a being, both self-centered and able to own and express itself in and through the ultimate conditions that confine it, each can, does, and must deal with all else—and therefore with all other versions of truth—from its own position. A person offers just one of a number of ways in which specialized versions of such an individualized truth can be qualified and expressed. A lived body and an organism are two others. An individual owns and expresses itself through all three.

No matter how accurate and complete the knowledge and how sure and unqualified the reference to other sources of emphatic truth is, everyone of us still remains a distinct reality, apart from all others. Providing the kind of single base that Being does, in terms of which all others can be dealt with neutrally, none competes with Being. Being subtends coordinate claimants, where an individual faces them as different from itself.

No matter what version of truth that one may acknowledge or use, it will depend on one's presence and acts as an individual. Although Being and other realities exist and act independently of any individual, it takes an individual to acknowledge the fact. That acknowledgment, whether expressed through and qualified by the person, lived body, or organism, is individually produced and maintained.

A neglect or distortion of the individual's role, as a neutral arbiter of different competing claims to provide emphatic truths, will force one to maintain that the claims are made only by persons, lived bodies, or organisms, each with its characteristic limitations and biases. The acknowledgment of the indispensable role of individuals in the sustaining and use of emphatic truths, though, does not compromise the independent warrant for the truths that the ultimate conditions or Being already provide.

Despite the insistence and acceptance of other versions of truth, each individual consistenly warrants truths from a deeper level. There each provides a steady source of an emphatic that expresses his or her acts as final determinants of what is true, whether this be expressed in and through the person or in some other way. Whatever the person, lived body, or organism may do and whatever claims may be made by other realities, an individual adds a distinct emphatic endorsement to them as that which is other than the individual. That endorsement is not identifiable with what a person might provide. A person is a subdivision of the individual, owned and used but having a distinct nature and way of functioning.

An individual is able to provide a version of truth that the person, lived body, or organism, or any subdivision of these, cannot. Every endorsement of truths that any of these may provide is tacitly qualified by the individual, who need not endorse whatever the others endorse; sometimes an individual treats what they accept or reject as failing to take account of what is required.

The truth that Being provides expresses a neutral position from which the others are faced as distinct claimants able to express it in only limited ways. Like that truth, this individualized version of truth does not make or endorse any claim, but like Being, it provides a standpoint from which all other versions are faced in a neutral way.

9. Disjoined Eternal Truths

Being and the ultimate conditions necessarily exist, the one in and of itself, the other because Being makes them be when and as it is, so that its possibility is sustained and referred back to it. There might not be anything other than Being, its possibility, and the ultimate conditions that sustain this and refer it to Being. Nor is there any lapse of time here; when and as Being is, there are ultimate conditions that sustain and refer Being's possibility to Being.

Whether or not there is anything else, Being and the ultimate conditions always are. Each expresses a truth about the other—Being expressing one that is beyond the reach of any denial, the other characterizing Being as possible. Those truths are emphatics imposed on and sustained by one another. Neither, of course, is affirmed, maintained, or claimed. Being and the ultimate conditions necessarily intrude on one another, the first endorsing the second as its agent, the second accepting the first as its final terminus.

It is always true that Being is presented with its possibility by the ultimate conditions and always true that the ultimate conditions make Being the terminus of the possibility they sustain. When and as Being is, it is possible in two ways: it has its possibility within it as a subdivision, and it is the terminus of the possibility as that which is sustained and referred to Being. These are not truths that are affirmed or defended. They do no more than express the fact that, despite their independent natures and functionings, Being and the ultimate conditions need and are satisfied by one another.

An account that acknowledges only eternal truths tells us nothing except what these necessitate. At the very least, these would have to hurl sustainers before themselves in order to provide the truths with opportunities to be true. Unlike the necessary truths that are affirmed in mathematics and logic and that presumably hold in a world controlled by one or the other or both, the truths that Being and the ultimate conditions intrude on one another have no bearing on anything else.

10. Truths Together

The different versions of truth that have now been noted present it as an emphatic. They differ in their understanding of its warrant, justification, and range. If what is here said of them is correct, must it not also be said that they form a single disjunctive set of truths? Will that set not express a single truth that none of them can encompass? Unless we are caught in an infinite regress, must that truth not be one beyond which there could be no others? These questions haunt every account of truth that allows for more than one kind, since it supposedly deals with them from the position of another, and so on and on, apparently endlessly.

One answer: there is one final truth that exists only in the form of a disjunction of all the others. It could be displayed, but the display could not be set in contradistinction to them. Conversely, they could be disjoined, but there is no final disjunction that is then used. "Disjunction" would here be a radically indeterminate term, finding determination only in an actual disjunction of limited entities. There would then be no actual disjunction of the previously examined versions of truth. Yet there are, as we have already seen, a number of versions of truth, each with its own source and scope, able to be set alongside the others.

A satisfactory answer will not overlook the fact that three different kinds of connections are here expressed by the apparently innocuous "together with"—one connecting the first five versions of truth, a second connecting conditions and whatever they govern, and a third expressing the subordination of whatever there is to Being. The final answer, expressing a truth that cannot be gainsaid, is provided in a disjunction of all of them, each offering a limited version of it. Even in the absence of all finite beings, a disjunction of a truth with a place the ultimate conditions and whatever these might confine overlooks the fact that the togetherness is inescapably oriented toward Being. Being is together with whatever else there is, in a unique way. The personal version of truth mimics the one that Being provides, differing from it mainly as the unnecessary and dependent differs from the intrinsically necessary that is dependent on nothing but that which it itself provides—the ultimate conditions that sustain and refer its possibility to it.

A refusal to ask if something crucial is being overlooked, instead of making anything vanish, leaves one's account open to challenges and qualifications that may seriously affect what had been maintained. When process philosophy rests with the claim that there are transient, contingently existing atomic occurrences and that that is the end of the matter, what in effect is maintained is that it cannot account for the presence of what need not have occurred. No one can compel it to provide an explanation—but also no one can compel someone else from maintaining, with equal obstinacy, that there are no contingent occurrences anywhere.

Different versions of truth are together. All are subject to Being. This is an other for them in a way that they cannot be for it. Although both severally and jointly other than Being and, so far, symmetrically related to it, Being has an insistence that nothing else has. The "other than" that relates Being with whatever else there is has only one primary, fixed end, which could not have been different from what it is.

These conclusions apply to whatever one takes to be or that would be provided. Being, it must therefore be said, despite its independent, eternal existence, is not only always accompanied by the ultimate conditions that sustain and refer its possibility to it, but necessarily expresses one kind of truth, with another kind expressed by the ultimate conditions, and other kinds by whatever finite beings there are. This is but to say that truth is an emphatic that is not only expressed by Being but is present whenever and wherever anything else is.

Question: An unheard number of versions of "true!" Why not just one, sixty-four, or ten thousand?

Answer: I do not care how many there are. I have come to the present conclusion, guided by my discovery over the years, that there are four distinct domains, each under the dominant control of a distinct ultimate conditions, that the domains are connected by means of the Dunamic-Rational, and that beyond these there is a necessarily existing Being that is the source of all else.

The most basic emphatic "true!," like all other emphatics, has a source, and awaits a sustaining. It is sustained by Being, the ultimate conditions, finite beings, or subdivisions of them. It shows all the other versions of truth to be together, each with a distinctive range.

Q: Conceivably someone might find a good reason for adding other claimants to truth to your list?

A: I do not see how this could be done or even what would prompt one to try. Nor do I now see how or why the number could be reduced or decreased. I suppose combinations of some of them might be used to express additional versions of truth, but I do not see any reason for holding that they are needed. Still, this is a new study, and much that is now said should be refined and made more evident. More likely than not, important distinctions and connections have been overlooked. It would indeed be astonishing if refinements were not needed and introduced. An account might be sound on the whole, and essential components noted, but it may need to have its range increased or contracted. A systematic, comprehensive philosophic account invites critical examination and prepares the way for others that not only do justice to its claims, but add some that might otherwise not have been envisaged.

Q: Does your account have the same relation to predecessors that you think it may have for successors?

A: Perhaps. Despite, or perhaps because of its claim to comprehensiveness and completeness, it should promote fresh ways of probing, just as it has been here promoted by reflections on what was offered in *Being and Other Realities* as a systematic study of the major realities and their relationship to one another. That work failed to take account of emphatics and therefore could not do full justice to some important ways that realities insistently intrude on one another to give them a new import. As will become evident toward the end of this work, a new area of investigation will be opened up, itself prompting another. Like this, it will explore areas that are neglected as long as attention is not paid to what exists below the surface of things, making a difference to what is commonly acknowledged.

Q: Although they may not use "true!" explicitly, aren't various professions, such as medicine, law, education, and perhaps also governance, warfare, and the markets occupied primarily with occasions when they express emphatics?

A: I took note of some of them in the first chapter. Again and again we use "true!" explicitly, or some variant of this, without remarking on the fact. We are usually alert to emphatics that are expressed in the signing of a lease, the presenting of a diagnosis, the double locking of a door, uniforms, prisons, the conferring of honors, and what must be expressed in civil intercourse, but each of us tends to ignore many others that are expressed and well understood by most.

Q: It seemed, at first, that you held that emphatics, particularly "true!," were intrusive into the uninteresting, the banal, the unimportant, or routine. Aren't you on the verge of saying that it is the commonplace that is emphatically distinguished from whatever else we say or do?

A: The longer we attend to the study of emphatics, the more surely will we take the commonplace to be distinctive.

Q: Present you with a number of alternatives, and there you are, able to know their different merits and defects. Did you not in fact start out with a knowledge of many of them?

A: "Knowledge" is too strong a term to be used here. As I have already noticed, I followed leads provided by an already acknowledged Being, ultimate conditions, and beings, as apart from and as interinvolved with one another.

Q: Yet somehow you seem to have a surer knowledge of the disjunction of the kinds of truths than you are of any of them. Paradoxically you seem unable to state that fact as clearly as you do the nature and limitations of all the others. Would it not be better to state the final version of truth as nothing more or less than the disjunction of the other nine?

A: Yes.

Q: Yet few, if any, other than you, refer to it or take a stand on it. Also defenders of any of the other versions of truth will treat your final kind as just a competitor whose merits they will judge from their own distinctive and presumably impregnable positions.

A: That is to be expected. Competitors must submit to impartial determinations of the merits of one another's assessments. The submission, if not voluntary, will have to be forcefully elicited or be the outcome of the compulsion to which a comprehensive view subjects them. It is conceivable that someone might deny or dismiss "if p and q is true, then p or q is true," but that will not jeopardize it.

Q: Would it not be more modest, more reasonable, and more helpful to focus on truths that have been dealt with by great minds and then go on to provide a position from which all of them could be dealt with splendidly?

A: Having had Gilson as a teacher, I have great admiration for, am even in awe of, the range, care, and knowledge that a great historian of philosophic thought possesses. The history of philosophy, though, does not seem to provide good examples of all the versions of truth. Whether it did so or not, the need to allow for all the primary cases in order to determine the merits and ranges of each is not to be ignored, particularly when one seeks to explore what seems to be untrodden territory.

Q: You say nothing about competence, care, or integrity. Yet these are indispensable if one is to succeed in carrying out any difficult work.

A: They are always needed. One must take account of them if one is to know what is operative and what controls.

Q: You leave the question, of the proper use of the various versions of truth, if and when they are appropriate, for others to deal with, or even for yourself at a later time?

A: Yes. I have tried to focus on pivotal factors and issues.

Q: Are those factors or those issues of equal importance?

A: Yes and no. The first five versions of truth are frequently used. Initially they are faced as equals. From the standpoint of each, the other four are defective. In some situations it is nevertheless desirable to use one of them rather than any of the others. All the while there will be others presupposed by them. No one has the time, energy, opportunity, or perhaps even an interest to deal well with all.

No one method will enable anyone to make great contributions to all the arts and sciences, build a noble character, raise a family, lift enormous weights, master every sport, and govern a state at the same time over a lifetime. The supposition that a single practice or method is alone trustworthy is based on the unwarranted assumption that all other ones are properly or best dealt with in only one way.

Q: You have been using a number of methods?

A: Under the guidance of an adventurous effort to understand the natures and major interrelations of primary, pivotal realities.

Q Does each method make use of a distinctive set of emphatics?

A: Yes. That, though, does not preclude a common use of some. The paths of different disciplines occasionally criss-cross, and sometimes the same objects are dealt with by a number of them in emphatic and nonemphatic ways.

Q: Do prayer and other religious acts use divinely instituted emphatics to arrive at their source?

A: That is what a religion, at least tacitly, claims to do. Religions differ from one another in what they take to be the loci of divinely expressed emphatics. It is not uncommon for a religion and its defenders to deny that those who use the agencies that are sanctioned by other religions could use emphatics that were divinely produced.

Since one who does not acknowledge anything that a religion might take to be a place where a divinely expressed emphatic has been made available may still respect the belief and practices of those who do, he or she could be more respectful of each than any of the other religions are.

A religion could of course, allow for others and even treat them with respect. None, though, takes any of the others to have the kind of access to the divine that it professes to have. If one wanted a quick course on how to become an atheist, one need do nothing more than listen to the criticisms that the advocates of some religious practices make of the others. Even those who speak courteously and do not try to make converts are confident that they make the best identifications of divinely instituted emphatics. One who engages in no religious practices differs from those who allow for only one set, disagreeing with all instead of with all but one.

Q: How does a prayer differ from an induction claiming that a number of well-balanced heads and tails thrown at random in a sealed-off chamber will be equal after a certain number of throws?

A: An induction claims to be sustained at some future time.

Q: A mother prays for her child not to die, and the child recovers from a serious illness. A group prays for rain, and the rain comes.

A: If one counts only those prayers that are followed by desired outcomes, all prayers are answered. If one counts only those that are not followed by desired outcomes, none are answered.

Q: Again and again, inexplicable events occur.

A: They are not accounted for by referring to the inexplicable acts of an object of worship. Faith always passes beyond the reach of understanding.

Q: You offer a general account of each of the various versions of truth and leave the detailed examination of them, as actually used, to those who are interested in special endeavors?

A: Yes.

Q: Being provides the only single, final, intelligible position where all conflicts resolved?

A: No. The final, tenth position is where Being, the ultimate conditions, and beings are at once distinct from one another and inter-related.

Q: Hurrah! In one way or another, a long-sought universal solvent has been found.

A: Nothing is dissolved. At the end a final position, in terms of which all alternatives can be faced without antecedent bias, is identified.

Q: Might not one propose some such version of truth as "Whatever I say on Thursdays is true?"

A: It could most conveniently be identified as using the personalized version of truth. It is to be rejected as untenable because it can provide no explanation for the occurrence of the needed emphatic on that date.

Q: Do emphatics need any other warrant than that they are insisted on and that they find a sustainer?

A: No.

Q: Are there emphatics marking off holidays, holy days, birthdays, anniversaries, and the like?

A: Yes. Sometimes emphatics, coming from opposing positions, intrude on what the sources of those emphatics produced. As I will later try to make evident, present moments of time may be emphatically charged by the contributors to the constitution of those moments.

Q: If I say "Good morning!" and my greeting is ignored, or, more pointedly, if I say with Hobbes "I have squared the circle" and nobody agrees, does that mean that I have not expressed an emphatic?

A: You have expressed one, but like an induction about the state of the cosmos in the future, you must wait for an acceptance or rejection of it. There is a refutation of the squaring of the circle available in mathematics, but one may still want to have it made available in other ways.

Q: You, like the rest of us, are fallible. May you not have misconstrued what you take to be the different versions of truth and their relations to one another?

A: Of course.

Q: After you have finally come to the end of the study of the emphatic use of "true!" or of any of its cognates, might not the whole account be subject to a new emphatic, perhaps even the emphatic "false!"?

A: Yes.

Q: You offer a general account of the different versions of truth and leave the detailed examination of them, as actually used, to those who are interested in special endeavors?

A: When a new field of inquiry is opened, one will undoubtedly skip over some important issues and misconstrue a great deal. As I will try to make evident, the present study of emphatics should alert one to the existence of another, opened up by Peirce and effectively replaced by another explored by Dewey. There is a universal pragmatic program that pragmatists have ignored and therefore have failed to see that they were occupied with specialized versions of this.

Chapter 5

Particulars

When we are confronted with what seems to be an irreconcilable conflict, it is desirable to attend to what the opponents might compatibly constitute, then distinguish those contributions, and finally show how they could function together. The claims made by the defenders of the rejected positions can then be replaced by what shows them to be playing supplementary roles. Until it is discovered that this is not possible, one should look for that replacement. At the very least, it must be said that their joint envisagement shows them to be together. Contradictories defy all unions.

1. The Issue

The conflict between those who hold that universals and those who hold that singulars are the only, the major, or the primary realities, although not as bloody as those that have been carried out on behalf of sovereignties, conquests, or freedom, have lasted longer. It could be brought to an end by rejecting the claims of only one of them or by showing that they are compatible, perhaps if they limited their claims. It would be begging the question to reject the claims of either by refusing to attend to them. As a matter of fact, we usually begin our examination of competing claims by envisaging them as together in some fashion, perhaps as occupied with achieving the same goal but playing supplementary roles. If what was sought was the annihilation of the other, the conflict would still be one in which, for a time, they were compatible in some way. The conflict could then be understood to involve an overstress on unduly limited views that, in fact, are meshed by rules of law, rights, and the conflict itself, while allowing for independent, even oppositional acts in a common setting.

"This blue" refers neither to what is just a universal nor to a singular. It refers to a particular. Particulars are where universals and

95

singulars are interinvolved with one another and subordinated to the result. Neither a mask nor an irrelevance, this unites the two, thereby making it possible to carry out moves into the one or the other.

Many particulars are commonplace, familiar, unemphasized outcomes of the interplays of conditions and singulars. Some particulars are also intruded upon by emphatics stemming from one or the other of the contributors to the constitution of those particulars. As existing neutrally between sources of their interinvolved and submerged components, those particulars may still be subject to emphatics that instantiate a universal or that make evident that they are expressed by an individual.

The view that we do, or should, begin in doubt and do, or should, think only when our courses are blocked takes account of the fact that we are involved with beings that resist us, sometimes so effectively that we are or should be forced back into ourselves to find better beginnings to other routes. It is matched by the view that we should begin with what is intelligible. A Cartesian will maintain that we start with the confused but should move to what is clear and distinct as alone fully intelligible. He or she does not say whether or not the move is necessarily flawless.

Although there are many situations that we are forced to work over and through, many are accepted as backgrounds and contexts in which appreciative and constructive acts are carried out. Again and again, we begin below the surfaces that we present or confront, and we may then move toward the singulars that had helped constitute them.

A phenomenon is an appearance of a singular that is cut off from what enabled the appearance to be one of a kind. Since one is stopped by that which provides what one is stopped with, no matter how much we would like to focus on phenomena, we cannot free them from the appearances of which they are components. No decision, no abstracting, no bracketing, no concentration on what is before one, could sever all connections with what owns and expresses itself through this. Once one has defined oneself to be alone and unequipped inside a box without openings, it is foolish to try to address someone else, even if one wanted to do nothing more than tell about the discovery. Existentialism, like a reductionism that denies that there are any minds, is unable to find anyone to whom to report its supposed achievements.

2. Particulars

We become most evidently aware of what is below the surface of what we initially confront when we carry out discerning acts of sympathy, admiration, suspicion, and love or a sequence of adumbrative, intensive, converging moves that a discernment carries out in a single step. Usually we do not pass far beyond the surface of what is confronted, but if we know that it is a surface, we know it to be what is being passed beyond. An emphatic may have traversed that route in the opposite direction.

Particulars result from a meeting of conditions and singulars. Either or both of these may add emphatics to what they had jointly constituted. Disputes between nominalists and realists usually result from the fact that both ignore the particulars that their acknowledged singulars and universals jointly constitute and on which they may intrude with emphatics. "Now!," "Here!," and "Special!" are emphatics that either one or both of the contributors to a moment of time, a region of space, or a causal action could impose on what they jointly constitute. If we are to understand singulars as they exist apart from universals, we must see them as uninvolved with one another. To allow for only the one or the other of them is to rest with expressions that have nothing with which to interplay.

Universals are a result of limited versions of conditions; appearances have singular sources. Particulars are neither universals nor appearances; they are the outcome of the unions of these. Both nominalists and realists, like the rest of us, begin their inquiries by attending to the existence, natures, and roles of particulars. Then, unlike the rest of us, each moves steadfastly in only one direction. to end with only one of the contributors to the constitution of those particulars.

Universals are instantiated conditions; appearances are expressions of singulars. Particulars are neither. They are the outcome of the interplay of the conditions and singulars and can be qualified by both of them as well by emphatics that may be expressed by either and imposed on what they had jointly constituted. Those conditions and singulars can be reached by starting from the particulars, by moving toward the source of one of the constituents of these, and, sometimes, by attending to the emphatics that these may have intruded on the particulars they had jointly constituted.

Elementary texts in logic have sometimes begun their teachings of the syllogism with the blunt assertion: "All humans are mortal." No one who read this could know that it was true. Indeed it has been maintained in a supposed trustworthy book that it is not true of Elijah who, though neither a god nor an angel, is said not to have died, as the rest of men do. What apparently is intended by the use of "all" in "all humans are mortal" is a reference to humans taken one by one, with no exceptions allowed, even for Elijah or any other humans. No reference to a collective death is intended, though it is not precluded. Each individual subjects a common "mortality" to a distinctive singularization.

3. The Reality of Universals and Singulars

Universals do not exist at some distance from us in upper space. Singulars do not exist in subterranean caverns. Both are realities, distinguishable from their expressions and what these jointly constitute. They are apart from one another, not as residents of different places in a common time or space, but as distinct, insistent realities. When those who are religious bow, face some holy place, raise their arms, or roll their eyes upward, they must be understood not as addressing some reality existing at some distant place, but as trying to avoid locating it anywhere in space.

Ultimate conditions exist eternally. Other universals specialize them. Some of these interplay with singulars, and then only for a while. There is no need to suppose that there is a universal "human," waiting patiently for evolution to arrive at a certain stage, an "airplaneness" or a "computerosity" waiting for someone to make something and then swoop down to dignify the result. When the first human, airplane, or computer appeared, universals were instantiated together with expressions of singular occurrences. There are universals, and they exist in the absence of any occasion for them to be realized, but those universals are so indeterminate in nature and range that we can say no more about them than that they are not identifiable apart from their unions with the expressions of singulars.

Were singulars detached from all universals, they would be no more than positions in the Dunamis. And were universals unable to be

98

instantiated, they would be unlocated eternities. Without losing their independence, singulars and universals interplay and thereupon constitute particulars. No one who knows only universals or who takes only individuals to be real could know the difference both may make to the same outcome of their interinvolvements with one another.

Able to interplay with universal conditions, singulars are able to present themselves in generalized forms. Each also progressively unites and singularizes it. No one who knew only a universal or a singular would ever know what they jointly produce. A Platonist might disdain an acknowledgment of a contribution by a singular, just as a nominalist might disdain any acknowledgment of any universal. Nevertheless both begin by taking account of particulars and then attend primarily to only one of their essential components, with realists content to dismiss the other as innocuous and irrelevant and nominalists treating what the realists focus on as verbiage. Individuals express themselves in generalized ways, and both progressively unite and singularize what is made available to them. Behaviorism has no way to refer to what supposedly turns "inputs" into "outputs," but nominalists think that they know it to be an unduplicable singular. Realists, in contrast with both, acknowledge only universals but, like the rest of us, initially face particulars where instantiations of these are united with expressions by singular beings. Were those particulars ignored, there would be no place where one could begin a move either to a condition or to a singular.

To know another human is to know his or her "me," and perhaps something of his or her habits, character, and being. To say that beauty is only skin deep is to betray a failure to recognize that even one's skin is at the forefront of an intensive depth from which a singularizing has already been manifested. Did we not end our references in what is more unified and absorptive, we would not have a warrant for taking what we ostensibly terminate at to be more than what we terminate with.

It is one of the virtues of existentialism—a nominalism in modern dress—that it is alert to the reality of singulars, though it unduly focuses only on those that are human and then only as expressing themselves in limited, personalized forms. Opposed to it are the views of analysts and logicians, who attend to universals but fail to acknowledge any that interplay with singulars to constitute particulars.

Hume was not radical enough, since he credited his mind—he confessedly knew of no other—with the ability to associate disparate items. Initially taking his mind to be a singular, he had no way of knowing whether or not there was anyone to whom he could report his supposed discovery. Even his own mind, that supposedly associated different items, was confessedly outside the reach of his view.

Phenomenologists are not Humeans but, like them, tacitly admit that they know nothing of what carries on the work of describing and reporting what they claim to know. Nor is it enough to remark that, if acknowledged items are found to be subject to determinations, these must be due to what exists beyond them, for if the determinations are not known to allow for a continuance into realities that own them, they could conceivably be determinations that had some other source—perhaps in one who said that they had no knowable source. If one remains in the self, there is nothing external from which what one has in it is to be set apart. Nor is there anything gained if one insists on oneself but does not take account of the limits within which one is confined.

An epistemologist, no matter how skeptical or occupied with descriptions of what he or she envisages, does not confront detached appearances. Appearances are "appearances of." One might be able to isolate them and then study them with care, but if the insistent, universalizing presence of singulars or the constraining and confining presence of universals is ignored, both the study and the care will stop short of the contributions that the universals and the singulars make to the constitution of the appearances. Well before, and all the while that one is trying to explain how one knows anything about the world about one, one is confronted with what one had helped constitute and on which one could intrude emphatics.

Before the attempt is made to provide a theory of knowledge, one should identify what the theory is to accomplish. If there is nothing that could be known to exist apart from the knower, no theory of knowledge will be needed. If something is known, the problem of knowing it has been solved and needs only to be re-presented so that the answer can be grasped, refined, and its implications made evident. A theory of knowledge should start with the known and then make evident what this is and how it came to be. If it starts with words, ideas, or categories, it will still have to account for the presence and the knowledge of that to which these apply.

To know how and what is known, one must begin with what is already known—at the very least with what one daily uses and understands. Its essential components are then to be distinguished and what is due to the knower and the known traced back to them. One defeats oneself if nothing is initially acknowledged but what is in one's mind. There is no more warrant for ignoring the "of" in "appearance of" than there is for ignoring the appearance.

Once appearances are acknowledged, one is in a position to know what constitutes them and therefore is ready to know both universals and singulars. If that acknowledgment is preceded by the entertainment of something in one's mind, they would have to be related to what is acknowledged. That relation cannot be provided by either the mind or the object. To arrive at appearances—or anything else existing outside one's mind, this would have to be related to what is acknowledged. That relation cannot be provided either by the mind or the object. One must yield to the mediating power of the Dunamic-Rational, since this alone connects what is in one domain to what is in another—here, what is in a person to what exists apart from this.

No matter how alike or unalike different items may be, they can be jointly subjected to unifying singularizations. Even a contradiction in terms, "a square with no corners," could be singularized as an expression of a confused mind, used by someone to convey some truth. Rules and programs have singular sources. Accepted in different ways, they are merged with other universals and are subject to singularizations by that to which they are applied.

Evaluations, utilizations—indeed any individual or personal set of acts—could be accompanied by distinctive movements in the brain. Those movements follow one after the other, but they provide no evidence of a guiding goal. An effective purpose is outside the scope of what does no more than one thing after another. A gun could be mechanically aimed and made to fire, but the aiming and the firing are not prospects that the gun seeks to realize. Were a target the object of a purpose, it still would have to wait for an act that would make it an actual target.

If the entertainment of a purpose were always accompanied by a distinctive movement in the brain, even if this persisted until the purpose were realized, the realization would not be achieved by the brain. Nor can a replacement of a mind by a brain be made either by a mind or a brain. It can be made only by a person or some subdivision of this other than the mind that can relate the mind to the brain. This does nothing in order to have some prospective be realized.

Conceivably every thought could be accompanied by some movement in the brain, and that movement could be expressed in a distinctive set of zeros and ones, or closed and open electric circuits, and sent over the world at great speed. No truths will then have been captured or produced though ways will have been provided for restating and transmitting what is used to express them. The truth that two and two are four is not conveyed from one place to another, though it may be provided with a multiplicity of sustainers at the same time or at other places and times.

A singular owns what confines it. It also unifies what impinges on it, subjugating this within its irreducible reality. Computers are not singulars. At best they are pluralities of distinct, complex parts, so harnessed that they function in prescribed ways. What they produce is singularized by the users at depths in these below where they are initially received and where no computer exists. Although each of a computer's parts may embrace a plurality of others and although each combination may function in harmonious ways, no computer is ever more than an aggregate of distinct parts, yoked together. Granted that a brain is a complex mechanism that functions in somewhat the same way that a well-made computer does—a fashionable but still dubious idea—it still remains true that it is the brain of an individual who owns and uses it as a part of a lived or organic body. A brain that acted as a computer does would not be accompanied with a consciousness, nor would its activities be affected by purposes. Brains have no desires, knowledge, or objectives. They do not hope, fear, dream, or know. They have no responsibilities, though they may be held accountable for whatever they do and even for some of the outcomes of their activities.

Individuals express themselves in and through their characters, habits, and appearances and as others of and for one another, the ultimate conditions, and Being. They also share in Being's excellence and, with other beings, are subject to governing laws and other conditions. They do more than speak a common language or attend to what is inside their brains. Knowledge is "knowledge of," a bringing what is entertained to bear on what sustains, qualifies, or rejects this. It may be enriched by emphatics that stem from either individuals or conditions, or from both.

It takes a while before one is able to reach the stage where one can express oneself in a plurality of readily understandable ways. To speak of a knowledge of others, particularly of humans, as though it were the outcome of an accumulation of facts, experiences, words, sense data, or satisfactions and disappointments is to attend to outcomes, or to abstractions from these, while ignoring their sources.

The failure to deal with "is" and cognate terms as both distinct from and progressively merging what they connect is not uncommon. Hegel provides a signal instance of a great thinker who did not know how what is duplicable could be singularized by finite beings. Acknowledging only one true singular—his final, eternal, absolute Spirit, or Mind—he took every other reality to be in this as a delimited version of it. They are there, but they are also outside it, facing it as other than themselves. It is because finite beings are related to Being in two ways, as that which is always presupposed and as that in whose perfection they participate to some degree, that they are able to be distinct from and to interplay with one another.

Twins, even Siamese twins, are not interchangeable. Humans, having the same status and doing similar things, are and continue to be distinct beings. All humans are "created" equal in the sense that each is a unique being, always presupposing Being, always participating in it to some degree, and always involved with other finite beings. None can be pulled inside universals or language. Indeed the effort to do so would have to be made by singulars acting in accord with what one intends to have them do. What they produce is singularized by the users, at depths in which they maintain themselves apart from one another.

It is not correct to say that we begin with something experienced, for we are initially involved with what confronts and interacts with us in ways and from depths we hardly notice. A good account of knowing cannot be built on the idea that we are surrounded by unsupported surfaces.

One of the great difficulties in understanding the claims made by particle physics is the inability to know whether or not what is being referred to by it are unit beings or just expressions of these. It is difficult, too, to determine the accuracy of claims made by some that they make good use of discerning moves into their pets or into some animals they have studied with care. It would be better to say, since we are never sure just how far our discerning moves do go, that there is no known limit beyond which these cannot pass.

"Evolution" is not to be identified with "progress." A radical change in temperature or terrain requires changes and acts that may have less scope or flexibility and an outcome inferior to what had been possible before. Darwin made an unjustified jump when he identified an ape's quiet gaze at the setting sun as a primitive form of prayer. To assume the posture that the English exhibit when they pray is not yet to have made evident that one is praying. We rightly refuse to take someone who picks up a painter's brush to be one who intends to or could paint. It should not be supposed that the assumption of a posture expresses this or that intent, particularly if we are attending to an animal.

~ ~ ~

Question: You attend to what you take to be a conflict between rationalists or formalists, and nominalists or individualists, but deny that either view can be maintained?

Answer: Yes and no. That to which they severally refer is to be acknowledged, but their rejections of one another's claims cannot be sustained.

Q: Is it your claim that the two defend what are compatible views, if these are understood to be sources of the constituents of particulars?

A: Yes.

Q: Does your answer provide a model for a solution of all conflicts?

A: No. Not every conflict exhibits an opposition between claims that could be resolved by finding a result where they are interinvolved. There are no desirable intermediates between good and bad, right and wrong, truth and falsehood.

Q: There is no one method for resolving all conflicts?

A: Why should there be? Oppositions are of many different kinds and have many degrees. Some may be resolved by each making concessions, some by granting the contenders separate provenances, some by allowing each to dominate for a while in distinctive places, and some by compensating one and penalizing the other, and so on.

Q: You do try to provide a single systematic account that encompasses all realities and that presumably overcomes any radical exclusion of one kind by others?

A: That oversimplifies what is attempted and perhaps achieved. A philosophic, systematic account is produced somewhat as a novel, a painting, a play, and an exploration are. It is the outcome of a multiplicity of separate adventures, advances, and retreats.

Q: There is no set of categories, no guide lines, no distinctive practice that can be imitated, reported, and taught, enabling the young to master the subject?

A: No. Masters of the subject open up and explore fields that others are to traverse in their own ways and on their own terms.

Q: Surely the self-criticisms, the insights, even the pivotal points that leaders exhibit, should be respected?

A: Yes, but not as the tenets of some school.

Q: You are not saying that philosophers should not teach?

A: No. I am saying that they should teach others how to philosophize, not how to carry on the work of some school or how to defend some doctrine. They should show others how to think freshly and critically, by presenting what has been discovered and learned in such a way that others can use it, presumably to make new advances.

Q: No discovered truths are to be presented, no methods are to be taught?

A: They are to be studied in histories of philosophy or in examinations of the thought of great figures. If one is concerned with enabling others to learn what has been discovered, the whole must be gone over again, with each step presented in such a way that those others are both challenged and enabled to clarify, modify, perhaps discard, and possibly open up new areas.

Sometimes one arrives at an account in which all imagined oppositions have apparently been overcome, only to find somewhat later, when looking at issues from other positions, that some crucial matters have been overlooked or distorted. The idea that a philosopher, unlike any other inquirer, must not correct, replace, or modify what he or she had once supposed, affirmed, or denied is childish. Nothing that he or she affirms is sacrosanct or is to be accepted passively. To call oneself an "-ist" is to confess that one has stopped adventuring beyond preset borders.

Q: Why, then, should one accept what a philosopher maintains at any time?

A: Because it has improved on what had been maintained before, by that individual or by others, particularly if it has sustained severe criticisms.

Q: Might it still not be defective, inadequate, in error, or confused?

A: Yes. That, in fact, is not an unusual discovery. We have learned to accept various suppositions or achievements in science and logic that contravene what had been maintained by eminent thinkers and stoutly defended by their disciples. Fault will eventually be found with some current scientific and social views, just as fault has been found with Newton's and Einstein's views, with the acceptance of slavery, and the denial of rights to women.

Q: There is no view that will always be sustained?

A: There may be any number of them, but we do not know if there are any or how long any will continue to be accepted. Some branches of mathematics seem to have been developed without any detectable flaws, but some, like Euclidean geometry, have been found to have many and to have only a limited range.

Philosophy is one with the sciences in refusing to accept answers dogmatically affirmed. It attends to singulars, universals, Being, and their interinvolvements in speculative ventures that cannot be properly end until major realities are acknowledged, and their major interrelations understood. It seeks to know what does not need the backing of authorities, tradition, or the use of a method presumably followed in other areas where other objectives are pursued. Radically unhindered by institutions or accepted practices, it is carried out by individuals who may, but need not, attend to what many at the time take to be what alone is permissible. I have lived long enough to see objective idealism, positivism, phenomenology, existentialism, and deconstructionism catch the attention of many, only to vanish almost overnight when their flaws and inability to correct them became painfully evident.

Q: What one would like to know is not what has been poorly done, but how someone who has devoted a life to philosophic inquiry carries out the work, and to hear good reasons for agreeing. So far, you have not made evident whether or not you follow any well-defined procedure that others could also use or how you arrive at your final answers.

A: I start with my common daily knowledge, refine this by an acknowledgement of myself as a singular, having a person, a lived body, and organism, existing together with others in a common domain, then try to determine what these acceptances presuppose, affect, and are affected by, to end with an account that tries to answer every question I can raise about what is being acknowledged, assumed, and foreshadowed.

In recent years I have kept in mind the fact that there are four domains, one containing persons, a second a humanized world, a third nature, and a fourth a cosmos. I have understood each to be primarily governed by a distinct ultimate condition, that the conditions are necessarily produced by Being in order that its possibility be sustained and referred to it, and that Being is both presupposed by and participated in by every being. Some of these ideas have been previously explored, but others have only recently come to the fore. Each was only tentatively accepted, until I thought I was able to show that it was unavoidable, if what had already been acknowledged was to be well understood. Movements forward were countered by movements backward, affirmations challenged by denials, and denials confronted with counter-claims. No answer was antecedently cherished; doubts and rejections were advanced, and their grounds and possible warrants were examined. I came to an end when I reached what I thought justified what I thought was an unavoidable beginning.

Starting with myself as a member of a common humanized world, I moved back toward myself as a singular and then forward to what was in nature and the cosmos, to what governed these, and finally to Being as the primal reality, presupposed by everything else and in whose excellence all participate more or less. This quick summary should not be allowed to hide the fact that the steps were initially tentative and the results were unclear and that it required much rethinking and rewriting before I was confident that I was able to communicate what I thought.

Dimly aware that there are singulars toward which one can move in intensive convergent moves, that those singulars express themselves in and through confining limits determined by common conditions, and that those conditions, though eternal, had to be accounted for, I eventually came to see the status that Being had relative to what else there was. Questions and apparent inexplicables forced me back again and again to reexamine what I had thought I had well understood. Hesitancy and dubiety were dealt with as warnings that something had not been well mastered; confidence was viewed with suspicion. Not until I could see what each pivotal reality was by itself and in relation to others was I satisfied that the major, indispensable factors had been dealt with.

Q: Should everyone do this?

A: No. There are many routes that one might traverse, beginning with irreducible truths about oneself as a person and as one involved with what occurs elsewhere, terminating in Being, and then moving back to the initial starting point. If no account is taken of singulars, particulars, universals, ultimate conditions, and Being, one will find oneself faced with inexplicables again and again.

Q: If this is what a philosopher should do, there are few who even try to be philosophers and fewer who go far along the way, aware that there are basic questions that have not been faced or answered?

A: Yes. Strictly speaking, no one is fully successful, in part because a complete account takes us into uncharted territory, armed with an insufficient number of questions and tests. A philosophical adventure is carried out by making advances into unprobed territory, followed by radical criticisms and possible retreats, new explorations, rectifications, and groundings.

Q: How could one know what should be doubted, amended, rejected, or accepted?

A: Every claim should be doubted and, if found wanting, should be amended or rejected. What is accepted is what has, so far, not been found wanting, all the while that it is open to a critical examination. At every crucial point one should stop and ask if one's answer lives up to its promise to face and overcome difficulties and to make evident what must be affirmed. What stands in the way of knowing what is real, without raising other problems that cannot be solved without making radical changes, must be faced and answered.

The idea of emphatics was already on the fringe of what was claimed decades ago about adumbrations, since some of emphatics start from where those adumbrations move toward. It is to be expected that there will be other discoveries made when one examines the present view from new angles and in new ways. This is but to say that it shares in the spirit that is characteristic of scientific inquiry without following its method or restricting itself to what this deals with.

Q: Here, where you deal with the conflict between those who take their stand with universals and those who take their stand with singulars, you find an answer in a reference to particulars. Would either of the contenders accept that answer?

A: Not, of course, if they were concerned only with the maintenance of the positions they initially hold. Yes, if they wanted to understand the strength and weaknesses of their views. We have no right to suppose that they could not be persuaded to give up their claims, once these have been shown to be untenable.

Q: Do you know any singulars?

A: Yes, but I know none as it is in itself; I know it only as the unity in which all that it accepts are united and submerged. It takes a great, never entirely successfully act of discernment to reach a singular; yet this is always effectively present in what it owns and controls and in what is evidently focused on. It also takes a great and never entirely successful effort to stop at a sheer surface.

Q: Do you know your own being?

A: I know myself as a singular by carrying out an intensive move that is sometimes more penetrative than any I make into others.

Q: Tyrants, the bigoted, the causal, and the indifferent all make intensive moves into those they maltreat?

A: If they do not, they are not aware that those they deal with are individuals. Usually they allow the achievement of some objective to get in the way of a focused acknowledgment of the singularity of those whom they injure or destroy.

Q: As not expressed, does a singular have any reality?

A: Yes. It is a positioned unit in the Dunamis.

Q: No one is immortal?

A: No one, as owning and expressing him- or herself in and through the person, lived body, or organism.

Q: What kind of reality do the ultimate conditions have? Are they beings?

A: The question has long troubled me. I have wobbled on the issue and have not yet been able to come to a sure conclusion. They are realities, able to sustain and refer Being's possibility to it, conveying, confining, owned, and used to the very extent that they act independently of Being. I do not now know how to determine whether or not they have interiors that could be moved into by carrying out intensive moves.

Q: Is every finite being an individual?

A: Yes, but only humans express themselves in and through their characters, persons, lived bodies, and organisms.

Q: Are human sperm and unfertilized eggs individuals?

A: They are not human beings, but they are singulars. Every finite entity, even the smallest of physical particles, is a singular.

Q: A singular sperm and a singular egg may join and thereupon produce a singular embryonic being?

A: The two singulars are in the Dunamis, with this owning and expressing itself through them, as well as in other ways.

Q: Do adumbrations and discernments enable one to move convergently and intensively into beings, beyond any preassignable point?

A: An emphatic—such as an "oh!"—may be intruded on some being below the point where adumbrations and even discernments usually stop. There are unpredictable degrees of penetration into others as having depths that we had not previously acknowledged.

Q: Is every finite being an individual?

A: "Individual" has too many long-entrenched associations with humans to make it a safe term to use when referring to those beings that express themselves only in the cosmos or only in nature. Each, though, is a unique being.

Q: Are the appearances of beings particulars?

A: Yes and no. They are particulars-as-owned-and-biased-toward-singulars and particulars-as-instantiating-conditions. A mere particular is neither owned by or biased toward a singular or a condition.

Q: Would there be any appearances were there no one to whom they appeared?

A: Yes and no. Until someone or some condition ended of them, there are only appearings. These do not provide either resting places or transmissions for the insistence of others.

Q: If the Rational and the Dunamis are always interinvolved, must an individual not be involved with the Rational, even when he or she does not express him- or herself in any domain?

A: Yes, but he or she is then rationally joined to every other unit that is in the Dunamis.

Q: If no one, or only an odd figure here or there, agreed with you, would that not make your view suspect?

A: Yes, but that does not mean that it is not right or well justified. A philosopher is a radically self-critical thinker; so is every good reader of the philosopher's work.

The quarrel between the realists and nominalists would never have lasted long had they both recognized that they, like the rest of us, begin in and, for the most part, attend to particulars. These are never entirely sundered from the universals and singulars that constitute them. It is sad to see accounts built on uncritical acceptances of what had been heard about science and its achievements or to watch acute thinkers' trying to understand all else from the position of logic or language.

Q: Are these remarks not tinged with bitterness, perhaps contempt?

A: Neither. I am, though, occasionally surprised and sometimes perplexed, wondering why anyone would want to spend a philosophic life on what evidently is a tiny part of reality. I do not belittle the lifework of those who struggle to master some limited field, but I am underscoring the fact that a philosopher cannot properly stop short of trying to understand the natures and interinvolvements of the major kinds of reality. There is not much to choose between those who think that nothing can be rightly maintained if it conflicts with some dogma or is outside the concern of some specialized inquiry and those who just ignore what is presented after critical issues have been critically examined, separately and together.

Q: Couldn't there be a plurality of unrelated entities? Might the end result not be the acknowledgment of impenetrable areas?

A: Yes and no. We can consider any number of unrelated items, but they will necessarily be part of a single set, if only in the sense that they are being considered together.

Q: At best we can see a plurality of intrusive items becoming more and more unified, but we cannot get to any singular being that is able to do this?

A: We are acquainted with singulars, but never as cut off from all their expressions.

Q: There are hypocrites, masterly liars, confidence artists, and politicians who speak and act in ways that deceive many of us. Don't the deceived adumbrate and discern those who mislead them?

A: They may, but they also take misdirections to provide good beginnings for the kind of intensive moves that are carried out on other occasions. Those who are not deceived may not be more perceptive than the others. They may not do more than refuse to follow misdirections, without knowing why. Some are able to recognize attempts to deceive in expressions that others accept at face value. The avoidance of the deceptions may sometimes require better focused and more penetrating discernments than are usually carried out.

Q: Are words universals, singulars, or particulars?

A: We initially identify singulars by using universals and add emphatics that are sustained by words. Each word is a universal, instantiatable many times.

Q: No singular can be named or identified?

A: Yes and no. We initially name and identify singulars by using universals at the beginning of intensive, converging moves toward those singulars.

Q: When one refers to "the members of the United States Senate," is that reference accommodated by each member? They may not know that they are being referred to, and they may be in many different places. Isn't it true that most of our references are to that which could not know that references are being made to them? Isn't it true that many references are not at the beginning of adumbrations or discernments?

A: Yes. Many serve to mark off something from neighbors or to fixate what could be made subject to an adumbration or discernment.

There is no preestablished, specifiable point at which any one, or any number, must begin or end.

Q: When I walk across a room it makes sense to say that my body occupies different places at different times. Do I, as its singular owner, move along when and where that body does?

A: Your expressions, your lived body, and your organism will be located at different places, but neither you nor your person will be located at any of them, at any time.

Q: It is not correct to say, "I am speaking to you, as we walk down the street?"

A: It is correct. References that end at different places and times are accepted by individuals who are not at any place at any time. We may and we do, of course, use emphatics to affect what is in time. As will become evident when we examine the nature of time, conditions also not only help constitute present moments but may and do add emphatics to them.

Q: Some expressions do not seem to have any singularizations. A mother cries out to her child: "Robert Thomas, where are you?" He answers "Here!" The answer is correct but uninformative. Does the mother know that the "Here!" is being singularly expressed?

A: She does. She recognizes the child's voice, may note the place from where it comes, but may not know just where it is being expressed.

Q: Why aren't individuals crushed beneath all the qualifications that the ultimate conditions provide?

A: Individuals own and express themselves through what confines them.

Q: I am not aware that I own and express myself through any.

A: The fact, though, does not await that awareness. If you are speaking to me, even if only to express a disagreement, you express yourself in what you do and say. This may be quickly overlaid with common social amenities that provide emphatics which hide what is meant.

Q: Must one know the ultimate conditions, if one is to understand any finite being?

A: Yes and no. We are usually content to know what members of other domains do and could do, but if we wish to have a good understanding of them, we must know their constitutions. That will inevitably require us to attend to ultimate conditions.

Q: Do we have to attend to particulars before we attend to individuals?

A: In acts of fear, sympathy, and love, we may pass immediately toward an individual, hardly noticing any particular, but we will in fact have begun at one.

Q: Why is it not sufficient to account for me or any other finite being as the outcome of antecedent causes?

A: A sequence of these, no one of which might have been, leaves one faced with the question of why it occurs. The answer is provided in part by taking account of the functioning of constant, universal conditions.

Q: Could there then be anything novel? Could there be conflicts, struggles, surprises, defeats, or victories?

A These surely occur. Much that is unpredictable about them, though, occurs within the context of what is constant. In every ongoing present, a prospect is realized in ways that are then and there determined. Although we may know the nature of realities and their relations to one another, the conditions with which they interplay, the particulars that result, and the emphatics that those realities and conditions may intrude on their joint product, we find ourselves faced again and again with the unexpected. Not only do we not have a sure understanding of the governing laws, but we do not know how causal acts will in fact be carried out, since we do not know all the factors that may be involved.

Q: In your first book, *Reality,* you claimed that epistemology and ontology were inseparable parts of a circle. Do you still hold that view?

A: Yes and no. A sound epistemology depends on a sound ontology, and conversely. One could, though, formulate a good account of what is real but stop short of producing a satisfactory account of how or what one knows. One could also produce a good account of how one knows, but not provide a satisfactory account of the primary kinds of reality.

Q: Surely there are realities not yet known. Shouldn't we be content to form hypotheses that could be falsified but are never confirmed? Aren't hypotheses formulated in general forms that no multitude of confirmations could exhaust but that one failure could hobble or destroy? Could we ever show that any hypothesis about what there is in any domain, or how it functions, warrants it in its full generality? Presumably you are not offering hypotheses but are making claims about finite beings that apply to all of them, both those that had expressed themselves but no longer do and those that have not yet expressed themselves but may do so at some future time?

A: I am not offering hypotheses about what will happen at this or that place or time. Instead I am trying to understand essential truths about primary kinds of realities and their interinvolvements. The fact will become more and more evident as we proceed. To speak of hypotheses as able to be falsified but never fully confirmed is not only to set nontemporalized universals in opposition to particulars, but to pay no attention to singulars. One will not consequently be able to say anything warranted about why or how falsifications occur.

Q: One should, from now on, accept what you say about adumbration, discernment, emphatics, singulars, universals and particulars?

A: Not "accept," but seriously examine the claims made on their behalf. Conceivably what has been maintained may have to be subtletized, qualified, supplemented, and revised, with basic questions about the existence and natures of different kinds of beings faced and answered in additional ways. The fact that no one who ignores the mediating, effective role of the Dunamic-Rational has been able to show that he or she knows anything other than what is in the mind or language must be set before anyone who offers an account that seems to be both all-comprehensive and sound but who refuses to endorse it as final and complete.

Q: You can't have it both ways. If you have a sound account, say so; if you think there may be serious flaws, omissions, or unjustified claims in it, say so.

A: I am offering what I think is a sound, comprehensive account. That does not preclude a reflection on the fallibility of humans, of myself in particular, or the fact that no discipline can rightly be denied a future where it may be found to need correction. If I must make a flat-footed claim about the correctness of the view that is being presented, I can do so, but I must then put aside my knowledge of failures and limitations of great works of the past and the errors and omissions that characterize what I had previously claimed.

Every systematic inquirer—even one who attends to what is always presupposed and acknowledges only what else there had to be, as well as some realities, such as him- or herself, who are but might never have been—acknowledges the major pivots of a comprehensive view. He or she knows that there are particulars as well as singulars and that there are conditions and a Being that necessarily is. One may misconstrue them and their activities, but I don't think it possible for a systematic inquirer to show that they do not exist or that major truths about them for him or her are not now known.

Nothing is to be just accepted; it is to be mastered and then passed beyond. We should ask of every view: does it live up to its promise to face, examine, and overcome inescapable problems and to solve those that stand in the way of knowing what is real, without raising others that could not be solved or without making radical changes in what is maintained?

Chapter 6

Time, Space, and Causality

There are three kinds of extensions—temporal, spatial, and causal. Each of these is a specialized version of a primal ultimate condition, extensionality. The temporal adds a directionality, the spatial adds a plurality of symmetrical connections, and the causal adds a thrust that is instantiated. None of these need occur. Their instantiation is one with their interinvolvement with singulars; apart from these the extensions would at most be achievable.

I will here focus mainly on the nature of time and the temporality and beings that constitute it. Not only is there a passage of time in persons, where there may be no space and no causal action, but even when it is interinvolved with either or both of these, it retains a constant nature. Everywhere, it is exhibited in a sequence of present moments, in each of which a determinate beginning is used throughout by temporality and beings together to make a prospective end of a moment become determinate and thereupon provide a beginning for the next present moment. An actual space and a causality will, in contrast, depend on the interplay of beings with other facets of extensionality.

The outcomes of interplays of beings with different dimensions of extensionality are open to emphatics, some of which will be distinctive because they result from different specialized versions of extensionality while allowing for others. A present moment, a place, and a causal process could be emphatically qualified by the temporality, spatiality, or causality and/or the beings that help constitute that moment, place, or process.

1. Present Moments

Each present moment of time, no matter in what domain it occurs, is the outcome of an interplay of beings and temporality. The two make more and more effective use of the determinate beginning of a moment to enable the prospective end of the moment to become more and more determinate until it is completely determinate and thereupon available for use both to begin and to be used throughout the next present moment.

There is a vast difference between a present moment and any other moment that is then past or future. A present moment is begun, progressively constituted, and completed; a past moment is a rigid stretch between fixed points; a future moment has no end that is being made determinate. Nothing occurs in a moment that is past or future. The one is a sheer determinate extension that is occupied by nothing while the other is an indeterminate prospect for which no determination is being made available.

One moment of the past is distinguishable from the moment that preceded it, in having that with which this ended provide it with a beginning. One moment in the future is distinguishable from what follows it in having an end that—while still indeterminate—can serve as the beginning of what follows it. Past moments are contentless, determinate extensions, in an order of earlier and later; future moments are also contentless but indeterminate and in an order of before and after.

A time, encompassing a past, present, and future as subdivisions, is at best an inert condition, abstractable from any moment of present time. This has a relevant but contentless, determinate, sequentially ordered antecedent, divisible into a sequence of empty units. Nothing happens there; the only ongoing time occurs in the present. This is never wholly determinate nor wholly indeterminate, since it begins with and uses a just achieved determinate outcome to make its prospect become fully determinate. The manner and outcome of that determination is worked out over the course of the present. Each present moment is new, no matter how monotonous the time and how similar one moment's end may be to another. Each moment is also different from its predecessor and from its successor since the one is already completed and the other has not yet begun.

There is some similarity between the atomic view of time, shared by Whitehead and process philosophers and by Russell and other analysts, and the present view, since with each the present moment begins and ends with what is determinate, bounding it off from what precedes and succeeds it. None of the others, though, can explain how anything could be credited with a career, grow old, decay, or be accountable, since each moment and its content for them is both fresh and complete. Even if, as with the process philosophers, one took a moment to begin by somehow reaching into the past and pulling this inside itself and is able to attend to a prospect that a supposed God set before it as a lure, each present would still be atomic. Even if one supposed that moments were sealed off from one another, one would somehow have to escape a present to be able to show that it was closed off from other moments.

There are different kinds of time in different domains. The time that is personally lived through is not identifiable with the times that occur in the humanized world, nature, and the cosmos. All of them, though, instantiate the same temporality, but in different ways. Poems, plays, and even sporting events are carried out within specified times marked off by conventional timepieces but nevertheless occupying distinctive times. They combine personal and humanized ones to produce times that are unlike either.

The time that interests cosmologists is different from the time that occurs in persons, in the humanized world, or in nature. Astrologists claim to be able to translate cosmic times into personal times; seers claim to be able to translate times pertinent to nature or the cosmos into those pertinent to what occurs in the humanized world. Sometimes some try to carry out translations moving in the opposite way, to translate what occurs in the personalized time of dreams into what will occur in the humanized world, nature, or the cosmos. The issue has not been dealt with in other areas with the independence and perceptiveness that Freud exhibited when he sought for the kernel of truth in works devoted to the interpretations of dreams that others had dismissed with a shrug. No one knows whether or not there ever will be a sound way to translate every occurrence in one domain into some other, but that does not warrant the supposition that there are no good ways to do so or even that it is not worth trying to discover what these might be.

One thing is evident, neglected though it usually is: there are a number of different times, each with its own distinctive beginnings, transitions, and endings. The time lived through by a person in dreams, hopes, fears, or ruminations is not the time lived through by the lived body or organism. Sharing some general features, the times have different lengths and tonalities and may be qualified by different emphatics.

Spaces and causal processes, too, have diverse forms in different domains—sometimes even in one domain. One's child at the other end of the room is closer than the chair in which one is comfortably seated. A book two feet above one's head is more distant than the book that is two feet away. Indeed we do not know if any two spaces are equal, since we do not know if the measuring of the one is duplicated in the measuring of the other. The difficulty of carrying out a task in a given place or time also makes one causal process differ from another that could have occurred in the same place and time. We do not know if any two spaces in any domain are equal, since we do not know if the measuring of the one is contracted or expanded when we measure the other.

Emphatics are added to dates when wars are signalized as having been won, though the victories may in fact have been achieved a while back. Novels, plays, concerts, and dances build on what was done, what is expected, and what the beginning and ending do to one another.

To understand time, space, or causation, one must give up the long-established practice of dealing with them as if they were self-same everywhere or as if some one version of them is paradigmatic and all the others are more or less distorted forms of it. There must, of course, be something in common to all the different kinds if they are to be properly dealt with under one heading, but that commonality could be a universal, differently instantiated in each, and/or enabling one to interrelate them. As they occur, involved with the same beings in multiple ways and with different beings in different ways, space and causality, as well as time, present a problem too complex to deal with as though they were monotoned, controlling conditions, instanced in persons, the humanized world, nature, and the cosmos in the same ways and with the same subdivisions.

Present moments differ in content and range. So do spatial regions and causal processes. Nevertheless we can and we do take different moments to be equal, subject different spatial regions to the same measuring devices, and assume that different causal processes have comparable causes. All variations in them may be taken to reflect the intrusion of qualifications either by singulars or by a conditioning extensionality. One will fail to achieve a good understanding of the emphatics that are introduced into time, if attention is paid only to those that are caused by persons.

There is no personalized space, though it is not unusual for some to refer to the space in which their personal interests are expressed as a "personal space." Although persons may express themselves in and through acts that are carried out in space, the occupation of the space by a human requires the use of the lived body or the organism.

Acts of will have an evident causal efficacy. Other acts of the person apparently make a difference to one another. As a result there is a kind of causality in persons that, unlike any other, traverses no space. We do imagine spaces and dream of objects in space, but the spaces, even when imagined to be traversed, are traversed by no one. Also a person may make a difference to the way the humanized body or organism functions. That difference is produced without covering any spatial distance.

Time, space, and causality, when they actually occur, may be subject to distinctive emphatics, originating with either or both the singulars and the extensional conditions that constitute them. Every moment, region, or causal act may be characterized as having the same nature as all the others and could be overlaid with emphatics that reflect an additional insistence by either or both of its sources.

Space seems to be a fixity whose presence needs to be accounted for just once, while allowing for variations in its contours. Causality, often enough, ends in brute occurrences that show the effects of actions begun earlier. Passing time is more perplexing, consisting as it does of a series of present moments that seem to replace one another without leaving any evidences that they had done so. The understanding of it, nevertheless, helps one understand both space and causality, the one as divisible into traversable, distinguishable parts, and the other as that in which time always plays a role.

A moment that had just been completed ends with a prospective terminus made determinate through the use of what had been made determinate at the end of a preceding moment. That end is used by both temporality and a singular to make the prospective end of an ongoing present become more and more determinate and be available for use throughout the next present moment. Each moment is freshly constituted, beginning with a fully determinate outcome with which the preceding moment ended.

The fact that the same or a different prospect might be envisaged in successive moments seems to justify Russell's claim that time could have begun and could have ended in the present moment, but only if one ignores the question of what could have provided a determinate beginning for the moment or for the progressive determination of that with which the moment ends.

2. Personalized Extensions

If a present moment is envisaged as a line connecting two distinct positions in one direction, no account will have been given of the fact that a moment not only begins with a just-achieved determinate content, but continues until the prospective end of that moment is made determinate and is thereupon made available for use throughout the next moment. From beginning to end the process exhibits the outcome and the interplay of two distinct kinds of reality, a conditioning temporality and a singular.

There are no present moments that precede or succeed one that is in the process of becoming. To be a present moment is to have a determinate beginning and a gradually achieved, determinate end. Temporality and singulars jointly use the beginning to produce that end, which then becomes an available beginning for a subsequent moment. A present lasts as long as it takes for temporality and a being together to make its prospective end determinate.

In each domain different kinds of moments occur. Those moments would be incomparable in length, content, and rhythm if they did not share a common nature. All of them, too, may be qualified by the same emphatics, originating from either the conditions, the singulars, or both.

Every moment can have a "now!" intruded into it by the temporality that contributed to its constitution. A different "now!" could be intruded by the singular that had shared in the constituting of that present moment. Together they produce a "now!" that is different from what either could have produced alone. A state holiday is an instance of the first; a difficult task just completed is an instance of the second; a wedding anniversary is an instance of the third.

An account of time that ignores emphatics bypasses the fact that the temporality and beings, either separately or jointly, may produce emphatics, thereby adding a distinctive tonality to that on which they intrude. Alike in their constitution, one present will therefore not only differ from those that had been and from those that will be in being progressively made determinate, but it may also be qualified by emphatics that are introduced from deeper depths in temporality and/or beings. We know that we express ourselves from positions below the point where the expressions are manifested. We discover that temporality also does this, because we sometimes become aware that this is the source of emphatics intruded into what the temporality had helped constitute.

3. Now!

It is not evident whether or not Einstein, when he said to the positivist Carnap that he was troubled by the "now!," was referring to an emphatic that was being sustained in humanized, personalized, or some other time. Given their common interest in cosmological physics, one could reasonably suppose that Einstein was referring to the time that occurred in the cosmos. Given the fact that they were conversing in a common, humanized time, it would also be reasonable to suppose that Einstein was referring to an emphatic introduced into that time. Shimony, who reported the story about Einstein and Carnap, seems to suppose that it is to the latter that Einstein was referring. Since Carnap allowed for no occurrences that were outside the interests of science or psychology, he and Einstein were evidently talking at cross-purposes.

A present moment of time is subject to an intrusion of an emphatic "now!" by either or both of the realities that constitute that moment. Even if there were one time that was pertinent only to persons, another pertinent only to what is in the humanized world, nature, or the cosmos, the presents in each would be qualified by distinctive, emphatic "now!s," produced by a conditioning temporality and singulars jointly, or by one or the other.

A "now!" that was intruded into a present by a singular and/or temporality spreads over the entire length of a present moment, though we may sometimes try to speak of it as though it referred to some subdivision of this, particularly since there is no accepted way for determining the length of any present or the spread of the "now!" It is most convenient to take it to occupy an entire present, making it stand out against other presents that had been and those that will be. The "now!" is in an ongoing present constituted, sustained, and perhaps underscored by a singular and temporality. The moments that have passed away and those that are still to come are not sustained by anything in the past or the future. One cannot get into the past or future by perceiving, imagining, or deconstructing the present or future.

What we affirm of the past is a reconstruction that we produce over the course of a sequence of presents by imagining plausible antecedents of what we now know. No one could possibly carry out a reconstruction in an ongoing time that will enable him or her to become better acquainted with the past. One gains a knowledge of the past by making use of present evidences; the act requires us to move further and further away from the past as it had in fact occurred. If one holds that we necessarily overlay what was in the past, by what we do or suppose in the present, we will never be able to discover that past or know the overlay except by entering the future and there presumably producing still other overlays. The prejudgments we make in trying to understand the past can never be wiped out; the most that we can do is move further into the future, expressing new ideas about what had once been.

Each present moment is new, differing from all others that preceded it and all those that may follow. It is constituted through the persistent imposition of a just-achieved past on an indeterminate, prospective end of that present. The end that is reached may fall short of what one sought. Just what it will be can never be fully known in advance. A determinate end is gradually determined over the course of a present moment.

What is emphatically introduced into a present moment makes itself known by the qualifications that it adds to what is there. Subdivisions of a person, such as a mind or a will, may provide a "Q.E.D.!," a "Yes!," a "No!," or an "Alas!" qualifying what is present. Other emphatics, due to temporality, are harder to detect, though the occurrence of a scheduled holiday may evidence an emphatic that is traceable to temporality, below that expressed in the constituting of a passing moment.

Emphatics, introduced by the mind or will into what a person had helped constitute, change the tonality of a moment. The qualifications that an individual introduces into what either helped constitute changes its import. "I mean it!" is an emphatic that a person may introduce into the outcome of an individual being's involvement with temporality. It can occur either when some other emphatic is or is not being introduced by the temporality or the individual.

"I am!" is an emphatic that Descartes, as an individual, introduced into a passing moment that was the outcome of the interplay of temporality with his personalized thinking. He did not ask himself what difference there was between such a personalized, present moment and a personalized causal act. He also credited his God with the ability to add an emphatic "true!" to every one of people's ideas that were clear and distinct. That God presumably could have added other emphatics but apparently did not, for unknown reasons, or did so in ways and for reasons we have still to discover.

We can try to calibrate our distinct personal times or our personal causal acts with the time and causation that are operative in the humanized world, by taking one or the other as a standard, by focusing on what is common to all of them, or by looking to the Dunamic-Rational to provide a warranted translation of any into any other. The result need not necessarily compromise the different times and causal processes through which persons and humanized objects pass.

4. Humanized Extensions

Pragmatism, as it is understood today, is committed to the acknowledgment only of what occurs in the humanized world. There, common measures of units, or of periods of time, may be imposed on all occurrences, no matter how diverse or how quick or sluggish they may be. The moments will vary in thickness and may be connected with some or all the others in many ways. In all, occurrences will be at spatial distances from one another. Also causal processes, which are begun in the same way, may be interinvolved with diverse materials and could be said to be distortions of some normative versions.

Artists are acutely aware of the distinctive nature of humanized spaces, times, or actions. Although a play, a concert, or a dance is performed within limits that are presumably measured in a monotonous clock time that is acceptable in the humanized world, the performances

125

themselves exhibit different kinds of space, time, and causality, with distinctive lengths, dictating the ways in which various moments will be clustered together or set apart from one another.

Try as we may, focused perhaps on a personalized time or causality, impressed with scientific accounts of the nature of time and its presumed inseparability from space, we continue to be interested mainly in what occurs in the humanized world, where we live together with others. The reports of what supposedly occurs in a cosmic space, time, and causation are written and discussed in humanized time. They then do no more than mark the beginnings, endings, and high points of such occurrences.

Pragmatism, particularly as explored by Dewey has, to its credit, insisted on the integrity and importance of the humanized world. The fact that it cannot do justice to persons, natural beings, and cosmic units or to the nature of mathematics and the laws that govern it makes evident that, even when given the widest possible range, it can be accepted as sound only within limits. That, though, is also to be said about any view that acknowledges what occurs in only one domain. Even then, as will become evident at the end of this work, it deals only with a fraction of what it could and should; a pragmatism that is not arbitrarily limited in range will, at the very least, allow for the replacement of anything anywhere in a person by what is in the humanized world.

The kind of interinvolvement of space and time that cosmic physics endorses is different from that which occurs in nature or the humanized world. The first provides mathematical ways to relate units that accompany measures of both. The second relates units that are qualitatively different from one another.

We express our persons in and through our humanized bodies; these are extended in space and enable us to carry out causal acts. They provide a warrant for taking the humanized world to present evident instances of the presence of time, space, and causality. The claim is not accepted by those who take their stand with what occurs only in persons, the cosmos, or nature.

5. Natural Extensions

Painters and poets of nature, geologists, naturalists, ecologists, and explorers not only agree in believing that nature is a domain that exists in contradistinction to all others, but also in holding that one can understand what is in it, as existing there apart from what is in other domains. Evolution, though, is thought by some to allow no real distinction to be made between what occurs there and what occurs in the humanized world. Darwin tried to make this evident in his *Descent of Man,* a work lacking the cold objectivity of its justly famous predecessor. The domain of nature existed before there were humans existing in a domain of their own. It continues to do so.

The time that occurs in nature has a quite different punctuation from that which occurs in the humanized world. The seasons in that world do not match the seasons as they occur in nature. Spring, summer, fall, and winter do not in fact begin on the days we have marked off on our calendars. We may plant, cultivate, stunt, or kill trees, vegetables, and fruits just as we may fish and hunt in seasons whose beginnings and endings we define but of which nature knows nothing. We know much about what is in nature; we may and we do use, mutilate, protect, and destroy what is there. All the while, what is in nature continues to be interrelated and to function inside extensions that are different from those persons, lived bodies, or organisms. If humans had humanoid ancestors, these would not be humans in even a limited form if they did not own and express themselves through persons as well as through lived bodies or organisms and if they did not relate these to one another. Similarities and analogues between humanoid skulls or bones fall short of showing that humans are or ever were beings in nature. It is unfortunate that Darwin was opposed by clerics who backed unsubstantiated claims about nature and its ways. Huxley made evident how weak their opposition was. That, though, was not sufficient to show that humans are subject to the same conditions that govern the continuance of and changes in natural beings or the groups they form.

We have no warrant for taking the predecessors of humans, as we know them to be today, to be humans, unless we also can show that they had persons in and through which they expressed themselves, that they had lived bodies that could be used as signs by their persons and organisms, and that they could produce some of the emphatics that we now do. Humans live together in a humanized world that is both bounded off from nature and related to it by means of the Dunamic-Rational. The understanding of the relation of the humanized domain to nature depends on our ability to know just how the Dunamic-Rational connects them. This is what an evolutionary theory that seeks to move from nature to the humanized domain should provide.

As embryos, none of us has a clearly defined person, lived body, or organism. Presumably each of us, before we were born, passed from that embryonic stage through a number of other stages to that in which we now are, but we do not know how or when this occurred. Freud thought we began life as polymorphously perverse, but only so far as we were persons, apparently without having any affect on the lived body or the organism.

Neither the lived body nor the organism of a human could be well understood if no account is taken of the person and of the individual who owns and expresses him- or herself through all three and who sometimes uses them as relevant to one another and sometimes expresses him- or herself mainly through one or two of them.

6. Cosmic Extensions

It is a common practice today to take the latest reports of cosmological physicists to state the only tenable views about the nature of extensions in the cosmos. Some go further. They treat them as the only views that should be accepted, despite their evident inapplicability to what is personalized, humanized, or in nature and despite the fact that the cosmos is occupied only by unit and complex bodies.

What is in the cosmos is subject to the outcome of ultimate conditions and realities. It differs from what is in other domains in containing distinct, irreducible unit beings not controlled by any more basic reality. It is not evident whether or not those beings come to be or pass away in time, causally affect one another, or pulsate in some accord in a common place.

The extensions in nature, in the humanized world, and in persons are different from those that are in the cosmos. Some cosmic objects may exist for just one moment and may be expressly replaced by others that are possibly enhanced versions of themselves. Some may pulsate in a position for a while or even endlessly.

A cosmological account should acknowledge a plurality of units that are distanced from one another in space but may have no ability to act on one another. Conceivably, then, it might find no need to acknowledge any causal process. Each unit could conceivably exist in its own time. This could be in consonance with the times in which other units occur. Each unit is distanced from the others in a common space, but it may do no more than pulsate in a common time and be involved in similar kinds of causal acts.

Einstein's supposition that cosmic space and time are inseparable, with their units matched, may or may not withstand the next paradigmatic change in cosmological physical theory. All that can now be safely maintained is that there is a cosmological space and time and that there may also be a cosmological type of causation, with each cosmic unit having its own nature and punctuations, all interrelated over the course of cosmic time.

It would not be wise to abandon or to alter what we know about extensions in the humanized world because of what cosmologists today find is useful to assume about a domain into which they, like the rest of us, cannot enter. They can try to account for both minute and great occurrences by envisaging ways in which successful predictions about cosmic occurrences could be made, but only if the extensions in the humanized world are qualified in ways that are not appropriate to that world.

Where in most other inquiries expectations are built on a knowledge of what the passage of time, the traversal of space, and causal activities end at, cosmologies take the outcomes of experimentation and observation to provide warrants for understanding extensions as having this or that nature, role, and interinvolvement. Whatever the conclusions, their accounts will be abandoned or qualified if a simpler, more comprehensive, and more reliable characterization of time, space, and causality is provided, just as careful inquirers into the natures and activities of persons, lived bodies, organisms, and what is in nature will alter their accounts to make possible a better mastery of them.

A philosophical cosmology can never be fully in accord with one favored by scientists, in part because it maintains that there are other domains in which extensions have different natures and roles from those that they have in the cosmos and that there is just as much or as little warrant for taking any to be variants of or inexplicable deviations from some other.

Cosmologists who refer to an original "big bang," or a first moment in creation, think of a moment of time as occurring independently of space and causation. Those who hold that nothing other than vibrations in place occur think of time as uninvolved with causation, while those who acknowledge nothing but atomic units take space to be no more than the outcome of an overlapping of reciprocal times and treat causation as an expression of a final reality, occupied with adjusting other beings to one another or with extracting from them whatever good they contain.

Unit beings in the cosmos are coexistents that conceivably could have had temporal spans and causal powers other than those they now have. Although the spans of those beings could have been different in character and length and their powers could have been exercised in different ways on different occasions, only some of them might interest cosmologists. What is needed is a single account in which the cosmos is so understood that it does not preclude the reality of persons, humanized beings, natural, or cosmological occurrences that current cosmologies not only do not but cannot acknowledge.

There is no one privileged way to learn about what occurs in any domain. In the end, what is known must be set alongside what else there is in the domains of persons, humanized beings, natural beings, and cosmic units, each subject to the same set of ultimate conditions, but ordered in different ways in each domain. We know crucial truths about the natures and functionings of persons, humanized beings, organic bodies, and natural beings but very little about cosmological units.

It is odd to be presented with a cosmological account by those who, with process philosophers, make no allowance for the existence of themselves and others as persons or for any humanized or natural beings. It is no less odd, of course, to be offered accounts by materialists, skeptics, Humeans, and existentialists who have no way to acknowledge the existence of any other beings, to whom they are presumably speaking.

Where, in most other inquiries, expectations are built on a knowledge of what the passage of time, the traversal of space, and/or causal activities end at in the humanized world, the outcomes of observation and experimentation in that world are today taken to provide warrants for claims about the spans of those extensions as they occur in every domain. One of the important virtues of a view that acknowledges a plurality of domains is that it stands in the way of attempts to understand persons, humanized realities, natural beings, and cosmic units as though each was a special case of one of the others. It is a danger that one is faced with whenever a great advance is made in cosmology or in the understanding of nature.

Those cosmologists who hold that vibration in place is all that occurs in the cosmos think of time as uninvolved with causation. Those who acknowledge nothing but atomic units not only take space to be no more than the outcome of overlapping reciprocal times but treat causation as an expression of a final reality, occupied with adjusting other things to one another or with extracting from them whatever good they contain.

Leibnizians favor the idea that unit cosmic beings vibrate in place; Whiteheadeans take a final reality to utilize what had just been achieved and to produce an inviting prospect for use at the next moment. Neither acknowledges any emphatics. Conceivably the God each speaks about but does not take to be an object of worship might produce emphatics. The luring prospect that Whitehead thought that God set before each atomic moment's content in the cosmos tells us nothing about what that God does with reference to what occurs in other domains.

Hegel could be understood to have acknowledged a hierarchy of emphatics, ending at their source. The acknowledgment of that source led Bradley to ignore all the subordinate emphatics. Like Hegel, though, he could not account for what he took to be other than the final, fully real Being, except as somehow and to some degree having the status of unrealities or of partial versions of what alone was fully real. Though they provided them with beginnings, Hegel and he were unable to account for what they took to be other than and to exist apart from their final Being.

An account that takes whatever there be—even if it be nothing but a stage in a dialectical process carried out apparently either by humans who are not fully real or by the final reality that had no need to do so—though addressed in apparently objective terms, verges on a mysticism in which everything is more or less absorbed in a final Being. Being must always be understood to be other than and be participated in by everything, with one necessary exception: the ultimate conditions are not inside Being but are produced by it as that which it needs to provide its possibility with what can both sustain and refer Being's possibility to it. That, perhaps, is the reason that their presence and roles was not noticed by these unusually acute thinkers: it awaits the acknowledgment of its source and of the difference this makes to what is being intruded on.

Question: You take time, and apparently space and causation as well, to be the outcome of meetings of two different realities, one a specialization of extensionality and the other due to singular beings. Aren't the outcome's effects achieved over the course of time? Doesn't that mean that the understanding of time requires an understanding of both causality and time?

Answer: No. Acts are continuations of their sources; time, space, and causation are the outcome of the interplay of extensionality and beings.

Q: If the interplays take no time would they not occur instantaneously? Were they not spatially distanced, would they not pile on top of one another? If they had no causal efficacy, could they end in what has a status of its own?

A: Our language is attuned to extensionalized occasions and relations, particularly as occurring in the humanized world. To express what is intensively reached and to express the way in which time, space, and causation are constituted, one must carry out intensive acts. Distances traversed by such acts are not comparable to those traversed over temporal, spatial, or causal distances.

Q: Doesn't it take time to go from depth to surface, or conversely? Isn't the unitary depth of a being at a distance from its public manifestation? Isn't the unitary being the cause of its expressions?

A: Just as it need take no time to be acceptive of an emphatic or to express one, so it need take no time to carry out an intensive act. When and as one is acceptive of something, when and as one expresses oneself, when and as one identifies a conditioning governance, an intensive depth is traversed. Since it takes time to traverse a space or to complete an act of causation, the traversal and the completion of the expression, or of its acceptance, will be different in kind from what occurs when one is engaged in an intensive act, attends to conditions, or refers to Being.

It does not take time for something to be other than something else. Nor is an act of causation or a movement over space required. It may, though, take a while before one is in a position to identify the Rational or the Dunamis. Not distant in space or time, nor causally connected with what occurs, each can be known only by detaching it from the other. Although there are logicians who speak as if references to what is intensive were ridiculous, like the rest of us, they, too, engage in intensive acts to arrive at their forms and laws. The time that they might take in doing this is dismissed as irrelevant. Also, though the acknowledgment of conditions, Being, and beings may take time, the passage to them need take none at all.

Q: Is the just completed determination of a prospect that you take to provide a beginning of a present moment impotent?

A: Yes, the past that provides a beginning for a present is used to provide a beginning for a present that is used by both temporality and a being to make a prospect become more and more determinate, until it is finally completely so and thereupon is able to be a past that will be used to make a prospect be a determinate beginning for the next moment.

Q: Doesn't the idea of emphatics require us to entertain a new idea of causation?

A: I would have been inclined to say "no" were it not for an unknown reader of my book for the press. He said that the idea of emphatics introduced a new idea of cause. I think that it would be less confusing to use "cause" in the usual way and use "emphatic" to refer to what is intruded on what is subject to causation in the accepted sense. That would leave one more ready to focus on the origins and outcomes of the use of emphatics. Once this has been done, it may be desirable to treat expressions of emphatics, and perhaps their use, as beginnings of movements back to their sources and as expressing a kind of cause that, despite its ubiquity, has been overlooked in discussions of causality.

If the expression of emphatics is taken to be causal, one will understand "cause" to cover movements from depths to surface and to allow for its application to the acts of Being, the ultimate conditions, and singulars. This idea, though it surprised me at first, has become more and more appealing.

133

Q: The conditions and the beings that constitute times, spaces, and the commonly accepted causal processes may add emphatics to them, when and as these are constituted?

A: Yes.

Q: Instead of crediting any actuality in space or time with efficacy, you take all power to stem from depths that no one reaches?

A: We encounter the power in its expressions. No one of these is entirely sundered from its sources.

Q: Are space and time necessarily linked?

A: Not in persons, not in the humanized world, not in nature. It is questionable whether or not the Einsteinean linkage of space and time is more than a correlation of the numerals associated with their different measurements.

Q: You say that the past is irrecoverable. Yet at least one moment of it, that which is identifiable with what is an achieved, determinate beginning of a future, has a role in the next moment?

A: Yes. It is given an active role by beings and temporality together. Had no use been made of it by them, a present moment would be just an arbitrary imagined cut in a continuous flow, having neither a beginning nor an end. Instead each present begins with what is determinate and uses this to produce a continuum of determinations of a prospect until this is made completely determinate.

Q: Could there be emphatics that were pertinent only to some subdivision of a moment?

A: I know of none. A "now!" qualifies an undivided present.

Q: Is the time that occurs in the humanized world a limited version of the time that occurs in the cosmos?

A: No. What is in one domain is not a limited version of what is in another.

Q: Do you exist in time?

A: Yes and no. As an individual who has not expressed himself, I am not in time. As one who knows, I use my mind in a personal time. As a member of the humanized world, I live in a humanized time. My organism, as subject to the same conditions as natural bodies, exists in the time of nature, under limitations and subject to qualifications that I impose on it directly or via my person or lived body. That organism contains cosmic units.

Q: Is the prospective end of an ongoing moment a possibility?

A: No. Like a possibility it is indeterminate; unlike a possibility, it is not one of a number. From the beginning of a present moment, until it is finally arrived at, a prospective end is a point at which temporality and a singular converge.

Q: Is the prospective end of a causal act a point at which a causal condition and a singular converge?

A: Not unless the act is governed by a purpose.

Chapter 7

Evocative Emphatics

1. Evocatives

There are no less than four ways in which something may promote actions by something else. Causes may produce effects. Usually when one touches a stranger, or more often when one pushes the stranger, he or she will move away or respond in speech or act. A second way prompts others to act in some desirable way; a cry of pain may elicit some relevant act. A third way prompts a response, but this may be of various kinds; the death of a leader may be met with cheers, jeers, and sneers. All three ways could be included among the familiar emphatics noted in the first chapter. A fourth way of emphatic, intended to evoke others, deserves separate examination.

Evoked emphatics fall into two major groups: those that are used along the lines that evocative emphatics use and those that refer back to the sources of emphatics. All are expressed in that which carries out acts of its own. The first are dealt with in the present chapter. The second are examined in the next. The first group encompasses two different kinds of emphatics: those that act as evocative agents and those that act as principals.

2. Art

A museum, a stage, a picture frame, an audience, and even tickets to and advertisements of performances are emphatics that may alert one to the fact that there are other emphatics to which one may wish to attend.

An artist is a skilled master of ways to make distinctive use of written or spoken words, sounds, silences, movements, rests, canvases, paints, stones, stages, or props, among other things, act as carriers of emphatics that intrude on those who confront the outcome in an active, receptive mood. As great playwrights make evident, a portrayed tragedy may not only show some emphatics operating in a play but produce emphatics that affect those who are alert to those that are stressed there.

A declaration of war, a marriage ceremony, or a divorce decree not only have effects; they add new meanings to a host of occurrences, changing the outlook and the emphases of those involved and sometimes of others as well. There are times when they may be of little or no interest. Sometimes, though, we see someone suddenly startled or awakened by what he or she confronts, thereupon becoming aware of the fact that an emphatic has been evoked, perhaps by some other expressed emphatic.

An artist produces emphatics that intrude on those who confront the work in a receptive mood. His or her work may not differ significantly in theme or craftsmanship from those produced in other ways. Sometimes the work makes a difference to those who approach it with indifference or who are critical or perplexed. Evocative emphatics do not dictate the kind of response they elicit.

It is sometimes said that an artist is successful if and only if he or she produces what is beautiful. Apart from the fact that "beautiful" does not seem to be appropriate to ascribe to the works of Aristophanes, Molière, Gaudi, or Dostoyevsky, it is not evident just what is meant. Apparently a reference is being made to a work as having an experienceable unity in which disparate parts are so joined that they enhance one another, contrasting with "pretty" in its singularity and tensions, as well as in the difficulties that its production has overcome. One is then confronted with the fact that there are monuments, paintings, sculptures, poems, plays, and stories that are quite simple in design. What perhaps is intended is the fact that the emphatic produced by a work of art should elicit satisfying, deeply grounded feelings.

The distinguishing character of a work of art is not that it is produced by a disciplined human—winners of athletic contests are usually well disciplined—but that it elicits emphatics in those who attend to it in an appreciative spirit. They are more than the outcome of a technology perfected and more than what awakens appreciations.

A work of art not only evokes responses, but evokes emphatics in those who are appreciative. The fact is usually expressed by referring to an appreciative encounter with it as manifested in distinctive ways—applause, smiles, an alertness, expressions of satisfaction, and insights into the nature of humans and what concerns them.

Where a psychoanalyst may try to introduce emphatics that will enable one to act in more desirable or acceptable ways, an artist produces some that arouse others to produce emphatics of their own. An artist is hurt more by indifference than by rejection. He wants others to become aware of things in a more nuanced, penetrative way, if only for a short time. If so, art has an effectiveness that a consideration of it, as though it were no more than a work of a skilled technician—who even might have an insight into what things are in depth—could not satisfy.

Understandably artists take their own kind of art, and sometimes a few others, to be superior to the rest in the kinds of emphatics they produce, as well as for the emphatics they elicit from those who attend to the works appreciatively. There is no evidence, though, that any one kind of art provides more effective or more desirable emphatics than others do. Sometimes, though, a work may produce emphatics that prompt others to produce emphatics of their own, emphatics that they might not have been able to produce otherwise. Beethoven's Ninth Symphony begins by expressing a distinctive emphatic that evokes the expression of a number of quite different ones in those who hear it. The diversity of the evoked emphatics is largely hidden by references to their surprise, pleasure, and the like. Correggio's *Jupiter and Io,* though it skips the details focused on in pornographic works, exhibits a satisfying sexual experience that the others do not and evokes emphatics that they could not. What is portrayed makes one alert to what had just preceded and what will succeed it, in ways that few if any other works do so well, in part because what had gone before and what is yet to come are already compressed within the portrayal of one moment of a deep, tensed, satisfying sexual experience undergone by Io due to a formless, unexposed insistence by Jupiter.

There are works, other than those produced by artists, that are sources of emphatics, prompting their recipients to express emphatics of their own. Differing radically from one another, such evoked emphatics are to be distinguished not only from the familiar emphatics that intrude on the routine and the commonplace, but from the ontological emphatics that enable one to move back into their sources in individuals, conditions, and Being.

One who appreciates a work of art is subject to emphatics that evoke others by him. These may be quite different and could be expressed at a different time and in different ways from the ones the art work presented. At the end of a great theatrical, choreographical, or musical experience, one sometimes faces the familiar in a new spirit and may be ready to produce emphatics expressing an altered attitude. The language of criticism and appreciation falls far short of conveying the nature of the emphatics that great art expresses. It surely does not do justice to the qualitative tonality, the multiple nuances, and the various emphatics that it evokes many to express.

Although performers produce works whose merits are at least in part determined by taking account of emphatics elicited by the intrusion of other ones and conveyed by applause and sometimes by expressions of dismay or disgust, most artists do not usually wait for the responses of others before they decide whether or not a work has been done well. What may prove to be most evocative of expressions of appreciation may even be thought by their creators to be inferior to those that the creators favor. It is usually not wise for an artist to keep in mind the kind of emphatic that the work might evoke since this will, more likely than not, turn the artist's attention from the production of an excellent work to the production of what might satisfy a patron, a dealer, or some group.

A creator usually produces works that elicit emphatics from him- or herself that may not coincide with those elicited from others. The creator's approvals, and sometimes even disapprovals, may be rejected even by great critics. The effect that the work may have on the creator, the critics, and others may sometimes be unexpected. Some of the French painters who were refused a showing in an exhibition at the beginning of the nineteenth century are now heralded, and those who had been endorsed by authoritative figures, forgotten. Van Gogh sold only one painting in his lifetime; today his paintings command the highest prices; yet it would be difficult to find anyone who thought they should be placed at the head of the available works of all other painters.

It is rarely easy to determine whether or not there is any work of art that is evocative of the same emphatics in all who attended to it, or even if it has the same effect on everyone in a particular culture, of a certain age, or with a particular background. Until that issue is satisfactorily resolved, we must be content to note that different emphatics may be evoked by a work and that we can learn what these are by seeing how they affect what is then done.

Art historians and technicians, like those artists who are concerned with the kind of acclaim their work will arouse, tend to overlook the essential role that evocative emphatics play, because they view the works as being no more than the outcomes of creative acts, as related to the works of other artists, or as reflecting or helping alter the course of current practices.

Those who, on acknowledging an emphatic that is taken to be due to God, go on to act in ways that enhance others, do something similar to what is done by one who is acceptive of an emphatic due to a work of art. There is still a great difference between them. Without any prior commitment or supposition, one can be prompted by a work of art to express oneself emphatically in new ways; nor does a work of art usually produce an emphatic that enables one to attend to its source.

Critics and dealers often focus on various parts of a work of art, looking for novelties and repetitions. Sometimes they are interested in knowing how and when the works were produced, looking for what had not been noted before or for tensions and difficulties that had been overcome. Again and again, they are confronted with what is simple in design and apparently had been produced without having to overcome great obstacles. The crucial task faced by an artist is not the overcoming of great obstacles, but the creating of what is evocative of effective, desirable emphatics, both in those who are cultivated and in those who are not.

This view of art is opposed to two others, themselves opposed to one another. One of them takes its stand with the work of art as offering an instance of a final, absolute beauty or harmony. A second takes the work to be a source of pleasure. Both separate parts of a single whole, with the first taking a work of art to be that which is to be appreciated and the other taking it to be an occasion for undergoing a desirable experience. Both slight the fact that a work of art emphatically evokes the expressions of emphatics in those who attend to it.

The acknowledgment of the emphatic nature of art does not make evident just what is being expressed. What this is, is so obvious to artists that they cannot understand why it is not known by everyone.

As has already been noted, each work says something like "This is what it is to be!," "Indeed!," "Attend!," "Yes!" in a distinctive way, whether or not it evokes emphatics in any one. It may evoke any number of other kinds of emphatics, but the one it is intended to evoke is an awareness that something is being shown to be insistent on making evident that it is.

What everyone, with the exception of current epistemologists, apparently adumbrates and occasionally discerns is presented by a work of art. Different arts do this in distinctive ways and evoke emphatic expressions of different kinds in those who accept the works as presenting a depth brought forward, a surface owned, a self-proclaiming reality. To say this to artists, I have discovered, is to say what is obvious to them. Often enough, the artist is perplexed by what almost others say he or she has done.

Apart from a failure to provide a vocabulary that would allow an artist to explicate what he or she believes has already been made obvious, all of us have suffered from a common failure to make evident that a work of art provides an emphatic that evokes desirable emphatics in those who attend to the work. One solution to the difficulty is to promote a readiness to be evoked by the arts. That is one of the results a good education makes possible.

3. Education

More evidently than any other source of emphatics, education is occupied with enabling and perhaps arousing others to achieve positions where they can produce desirable emphatics. The clarity of its function tempts one to take art, as well as discipline and acculturation, to be no more than specialized versions of it.

Institutions where no art is taught sometimes place their offerings under the heading "arts and sciences." The "arts" here may refer only to political or social history, languages, or reading some classical poetic or dramatic writings, with no attempt made to understand how an artwork is produced, what it expresses, or the kind of emphatics it should evoke.

Education, particularly when it focuses on the improvement of desirable habits and the mastery of various skills, is primarily occupied with evoking emphatics that promote others, making possible the achievement of desirable goals. Since even the gifted must learn, it is tempting to suppose that education is the primary and indispens-able discipline and that all other activities, even those where one learns only by experimenting, are specializations of it.

When occupied with the formation and strengthening of desirable habits, education focuses on the production of emphatics that evoked them and that may then provide beginnings and occasions for con-tinued growth and mastery. When directed toward the young, it will often concentrate on the evocation of emphatics that are similar to the emphatics that were previously evoked but that are to be used in new situations with possibly different effects.

Even those who are preparing to become teachers are prompted to produce emphatics of their own. If well taught, they will not try to duplicate the emphatics that their own teachers provided but will instead produce emphatics that enrich and thereupon become sources of others, some of which have little or no educative role. The primary aim of education is not to have teachers produce teachers, but to evoke the production of desirable emphatics by others. Teaching prospective teachers is but one of the many ways in which this can be done.

Good teaching is begun before one is ready for school, and it may be carried out by those who are not explicitly engaged in teaching or interested in evoking others to produce desirable emphatics. When an evocation is an incidental accompaniment of an observation of the attitudes and acts of someone admired or feared, imitation rather than education occurs. Imitation duplicates, at some remove, what evoked it; it falls short of learning in its failure to produce strong, individually tinctured emphatics.

One who has been well taught has been prepared to express emphatics that originate deep within, below where one would other-wise be ready to act. Rage, affection, and concern seem to be even more deeply grounded but are quickly qualified by the individual as affected by the emphatics that learning had evoked.

It is an arresting fact that many, perhaps all, educate themselves to some degree and in some manner. Even those who learn from others do so in their own ways and at their own pace, though few, if any, are pure autodidacts. Some of the emphatics are evidently evoked by those who are admired, thereby making manifest that there are emphatics that are elicited rather than imposed. A child who wants to learn, an apprentice who is eager to serve, or someone who is anxious to advance in the world sometimes prompts others to impose emphatics that will evoke desired acts.

The conventions and complications involved in good living by different people point up the need for teachers who can evoke many different kinds of emphatics in those they instruct. Repetition falls short of learning in its failure to elicit strong, individually tinctured emphatics by those who are taught. That does not mean it should be avoided, since it may prove to be a way of making something more evident than it had been.

Focus here has been mainly on formal education, too often taken to be little more than a process of rearticulating text books and a confounding of it with discipline and training. Too many in our leading colleges and universities today think that they have completely escaped Gibbon's criticisms of the dons of his time. He said that they were full of port and pride; most professors do not drink much port.

A great deal is learned informally, without following a prescribed route, taking prescribed steps, or having distinctive aims. Much is learned through observations and interchanges, as well as from approvals and disapprovals, particularly by those who follow them up by action. Usually we keep in reserve a judgmental attitude about the producers of emphatics who promote the expression of others by those they have influenced. It is not just, of course, to take all the faults and errors committed by the taught to be due to their teachers; the taught have a freedom to accept, advance, or distort what is made available to them.

A teaching that is confined to the rearticulation of texts confounds discipline and training with teaching or, at the very least, obscures meanings behind an array of facts. What is an essential part of education is often bypassed, leaving students with remembered data and references without prompting or enabling them to produce desirable emphatics of their own. Often we keep in reserve a judgmental attitude toward the evokers of emphatics in the young and the pliable. Evidently we expect education to be a means for evoking commendable emphatics in those who are subject to it. The "we" here, unfortunately, does not include many of those who had presumably assumed the role of teacher.

Although a good, strong case can be made on behalf of athletics as providing splendid sources of emphatics that evoke desirable ones by the participants and even by other students and some of the faculty, it is far from evident that the benefits are great or widespread. It may be claimed that a good athletic program offers a fine way to raise funds to support research and to make possible the hiring of distinguished scholars. One may then still fail to use athletic programs in ways that help students to acquire or strengthen such virtues as persistence, determination, and cooperation and to avoid a sense of worthlessness when defeated.

Education, of course, is not confined to schools. Nor is it dependent on the teaching and training provided by knowledgeable and communicative masters of special subjects. It also needs the help of dedicated teachers who promote the achievement and use of good habits of questioning, probing, experimenting, and thinking, an awareness of distinctive objectives, an understanding of and a training in the avoidance of errors, an overcoming of disinclinations to persist, and the carrying out of radical self-criticisms.

Like gardeners and mothers, teachers—at least those who are occupied with teaching the very young—are interested in flourishings and growth. They focus on the evocation of emphatics in those in their charge. These should carry forward not merely what they were taught, but the ways in which this was done. One who does nothing more than teach a subject that has been mastered, evidently does less than what one should be do.

Before and after time has been spent in classes and before and after one attends a school, one is caught up in an educational process. Although there is considerable merit in Dewey's claim that a child learns by doing, the claim falls far short of what is needed, precisely because it emphasizes action and tends to bypass the fact that there are many other ways in which teachers may use different kinds of emphatics to evoke the use of more desirable ones by those in their charge.

If "doing" means no more than that evoked emphatics should not duplicate the teacher's at some remove and if "doing" requires students to produce desirable emphatics of their own, carried out in ways that enhance that on which they impinge, it surely deserves acceptance. To be most helpful, it should also be understood to evoke the production of other desirable emphatics by the student. These emphatics need not be, and rarely will be, much like those that evoked them, failing as they do to have the backing of needed habits and judgment. A student is to be affected in such a way that he or she produces the kinds of emphatics that enhance. To do that, a student must have some awareness of the nature and promise of that with which he or she deals, backed by the likelihood that what is done will be appropriate and commendable.

Adventure, exploration, questioning, and experimenting need the backing of knowledge, part of which may be incorporated in habits. Presumably it is these that recommended "doings" are intended to provide and strengthen. That, though, is but to say that evoked emphatics should both use and strengthen some tendencies rather than others. Doubting and a readiness to accept evidence also should be encouraged, not only in workshops, law schools, and laboratories, but in the course of all instruction.

Since the emphatics to be imposed on students should arouse them to produce desirable emphatics of their own, education should give greater attention to them than the arts do. While the arts not only express emphatics but evoke others that express a heightened sensitivity and insight in those who are appreciative, educators evoke emphatics that more or less continue along the lines that increase knowledge, apply and enhance skills, correct what had been misconstrued, and promote an occupation with desirable but neglected projects.

Evocations may be produced necessarily, deliberately, or adventitiously. They may be wholly or partly successful, and they may sometimes be ignored or rejected. What they evoke may be emphatics that are not only quite different from those that elicited them, but may have their expressions qualified in other ways.

Some recipients of emphatics may respond excellently, others poorly, with most more or less responsive to the evocative emphatics produced in the arts and by education. It would not be helpful, though, to grade the emphatics that are then evoked. They do not fit into a prepared set of boxes. The practical wisdom that might support the attempt should not be allowed to obscure the fact that neither evocative nor evoked emphatics are well-demarcated, simple units.

Emphatics, due to conditions and to what makes use of them, often have a sufficient degree of success to tempt one to suppose that evoked emphatics are unavoidably expressed by those who are subject to them. As a consequence one may be inclined to hold that there are some, perhaps even many, who can have emphatics evoked in them that continue along a path that may have been traversed by emphatics evoked in others. They will likely be characterized as insensitive.

4. Training and Discipline

There are educational institutions where coaches of successful teams receive a higher salary than the most learned and successful of teachers and where outstanding athletes are viewed as having reached the highest of goals, short of that which they might attain were they to become professional athletes. It is not unusual, and for many not surprising, to hear a distinguished coach addressed as "doctor" after he or she has received an honorary degree and other learned colleagues, who earned theirs, addressed as "mister" or "ms."

Twist and turn as we may, there is a great difference between those who coach or train and those who educate—and, of course, between those who are coached, trained, and disciplined and those who are educated. It is, though, possible to be well trained, disciplined, and also educated.

There are few who would seriously question the need to train and discipline the young. These must be helped to build good habits, backed by strong characters. Most obtain that help from early childhood on, to and through adolescence. A few schools focus on doing just that. Others look to their athletic departments to carry out the work, usually without supervision and assessed mainly in terms of victories achieved against defined rivals. Military academies devoted to the task of training officers not only do that, but make those in their charge carry out specific tasks in disciplined ways.

Training focuses on building desirable habits. Discipline is intended to strengthen some habits and improve the character of those who are subject to it. Without the discipline the habits will tend to be elicited by circumstance and will be neither well directed nor well controlled; without the habits discipline will end in submissions and unfocused reactions. Both can and should be parts of an educational program, but they can be and too often are carried out apart from one. It is not enough to learn how to function well in ways that others already well trained and disciplined do; one should also learn how to produce emphatics of one's own that may not have been expressed by others, or perhaps not as well.

Unlike the arts that evoke emphatics expressing an alerted sensitivity to what one may then confront and unlike an education that encourages the expression of emphatics that may be unlike any that evoke them, training and discipline usually evoke a readiness to act along prescribed lines. The former stress the distinctiveness and individuality of those they affect; the latter stress the desirability of acting in established ways. Ideally both should be evoked. This is what military establishments try to do, though it is inevitable that when choices have to be made, the latter will be favored.

Training and discipline do not focus on the establishment of a position midway between undesirable extremes. That is a task reserved for those who want to achieve desirable habits and characters. Training usually evokes a readiness to respond properly; discipline usually evokes a readiness to control. Ideally one should be both trained and disciplined, and thereupon readied to produce emphatics that promote a mastery of what is dealt with.

Evocative emphatics may do no more than produce a tendency or a readiness to express similar or dissimilar emphatics by others. Art and education, for example, sometimes evoke no more than a readiness to produce emphatic expressions by those who are subject to them. Sometimes they evoke no more than a tendency to respond in prescribed ways to what is confronted. Other evocative roles of training and disciplining may then be overlooked. If so, they will become indistinguishable from a molding or a transformation of those who are subjected to them. Where the trained and disciplined tend to reexpress the values of those to whom they have been subject, those who have been affected by art or who have been well taught add evaluations to what they emphatically express.

It would be difficult to draw a line making off where training and disciplining are distinguished from education, particularly since education involves the formation of habits and the building of character, and the others do sometimes affect one's outlook and attitude. Still, where training and discipline lean toward a strengthening of habit and character, education passes imperceptibly into training and disciplining when one is occupied with pointing the unprepared in the right direction. There is no need to concentrate on the production of evocative emphatics of only one kind. One can benefit from an appreciation of art without compromising one's ability to learn history or mathematics or to be trained or disciplined. Some people are educable more easily and successfully than others. No one knows just why. References to dullards, incompetents, and immaturity or to the gifted, the brilliant, and the like hide more than they reveal.

A readiness to be evoked by one kind of emphatic does not preclude evocations by others. One can be appreciative of art, be well educated, trained, and disciplined, and still be subject to emphatics that promote other ways of expressing oneself emphatically. The more evident and important of them, acculturation, as encompassing commitment, cooperation, and reasonableness, deserves attention. One will readily suppose that it does no more than produce refinements or variations of emphatics evoked in other ways, if the distinctive positions where, and the channels through which they are expressed, are ignored.

The knowledge of the primary kinds of emphatics that can be evoked depends in part on what one knows about the major abilities that we have and what could promote their excellent expression. A distinguishing of different kinds of evocative emphatics does not require one to hold that their sources or their outcomes are sealed off from one another. The fact tempts one to take some such source of evocative emphatics as education, training, or disciplining, and sometimes even art, to be primary evocative sources of emphatics and all other sources to be specialized and perhaps distorted instances of them. A knowledge of the major sources and channels that are used by most of the emphatics that we provide offers a good safeguard against the commission of that error.

Some of the familiar and some of the ontological emphatics already noted are occasionally evocative. A physician or some other authoritative figure sometimes expresses emphatics that evoke others in those who are ready to do what they are told to do. The training of nurses and the disciplining of the hospitalized serve to keep evoked emphatics expressed within required limits, presumably promoting desired outcomes.

One who was not affected by art or was not properly educated, trained, and disciplined may still be able to make good use of familiar emphatics and be subject, as others are, to those that are ontologically grounded. They will be inclined, though, to depend on cues to set off required actions, and they usually will do so in unreliable ways.

Training and disciplining at their best are primarily productive of evocative emphatics that promote appropriate and successful ways of functioning in particular areas. It is not unusual to suppose that those emphatics could evoke eminently desirable acts elsewhere as well. Again and again army generals have been thought to be eminently qualified to govern, as if the affairs of a state could be best carried out by commanding acts from those who are forbidden to make any alterations except along prescribed lines. President Truman presciently remarked that General Eisenhower would discover, and be dismayed to learn, that the orders that he gave as president would be carried out in quite altered and unexpected ways.

It is part of the training of army officers and those they lead to carry out the orders they receive; it is part of the task of those in civil government to tailor requests to fit the circumstances. Where the first are trained to obey, the others are expected to modify what they are required to do in order to make them appropriate. Subordinates in the armed forces are, of course, required to use good judgment, and subordinates in a government are expected to carry out orders, but the first are trained and disciplined to do this in a certain way, where the second are expected to make orders fit particular cases. The two ways need not be radically divergent. The first are to be qualified by good judgment about the demands made in special cases; the second should not violate the intent of the initial demand.

5. Acculturation

The emphatics that are produced, as well as those that are evoked by art, education, discipline, and training, though not often focused on, are fairly well known. All of them could be taken to contribute to the production of an evocative emphatic that enables one to share in a common heritage. It is tempting to view all of them as different strands in the production of a single evocative emphatic that enables them to be integral parts of a community in which a common heritage is both continued and modified. Admonitions, example, criticisms, threats, and punishments force most into line. The likelihood that some one emphatic will be widely accepted and supported makes one receptive to those emphatics that are expressed in the community's traditional ways and thereupon enables one to fit into it and be ready to act appropriately.

Communities, through their established languages and practices, their acceptances and rejections, acculturate their members by evoking emphatics that enforce the established ways. Even social upheavals and rebellions, as well as radical changes in direction and values, are often supported and carried forward by those who share in and continue a common heritage. Those who have already been acculturated may then have to undergo radical changes to which emphatics, due to one's education, training, and disciplining, may contribute.

Acculturation provides an habituated way to conform to the dominant practices of a community. This, through multiple channels making use of specific evocative emphatics, promotes attitudes and practices that accord with and promote a common morality. Filtered through those in acknowledged commanding positions and subject to multiple evocative emphatics, the members of a society are prompted to act in concordant ways.

Were a society's ways and outlook stable, acculturation would be indistinguishable from a socially sustained training and disciplining. None, though, can escape the need to modify even well-entrenched and respected practices so that they can be carried out well in new situations. Inexorably a society's heritage is faced with new problems, some due to changed circumstances and some to challenges posed by incursions from other societies.

Acculturation is the outcome of evoked emphatics by a society. It prompts its members to continue along established lines while making adjustments in changing circumstances. In the absence of evocative emphatics, the members of a society will tend to continue established practices that no longer help in the ways that are needed if the continuance and strengthening of the society are to be promoted. When problems arise, as they always do sooner or later, though not often in cataclysmic forms, an achieved acculturation blocks the way, sometimes with good and sometimes with bad effects. Aware of the fact, it is usually desirable to provide education, training, and disciplining that are broad and strong enough to withstand some and to accommodate other radical changes in social functioning.

Some make use of a well-mastered technology to enable them to continue to know and function well, no matter what changes their society undergoes. Others instead take the stand that mathematics, logic, or a presumed precise use of words is able to provide truths that are unaffected by social needs and changes, without affecting the acculturation that is needed if one is to prosper together with other clear-minded people. A good acculturation accommodates both. It may make use of emphatics evoked by masters of other enterprises but will usually need to be supplemented by emphatics that promise socially desirable results.

Acculturation, even in the calmest and most satisfying of times, depends on the evocation of emphatics from depths in individuals that are channeled primarily through their lived bodies and incidentally through their persons and organisms. It enables them to find a maximal accord between what they are at root and what they are as involved with others. Changes in language, laws, morality, and religion, backed by authority, rhetoric, force, rejections, and punishments, compel many not only to change their ways, but to acquire new habits and to produce emphatics that are acceptable to those who govern.

Art, education, training, and disciplining could be taken to be specialized versions of an acculturation, each evoking attitudes and acts that make primary use of one or another subdivision of a human. It would still be difficult to determine the sources of the different evocations or to know exactly what emphatics they evoked, mainly because there are no neat, evident boundaries separating the different divisions from one another. An expression of sensitivity is tinctured by thoughts, expectations, hopes, fears, biases, and circumstance, and these by it. Each movement in a machine, in contrast, is a distinct unit.

A machine might write "*d*," "*o*," and "*g*" when anything resembling a dog appears on a screen, but the machine will neither know nor refer to an actual dog. It may be so made that it will point to an actual dog and be able to frighten it, but it will intend neither—or anything else. It never expresses any emphatics, though it may run off designations of these if it is designed to do so. Indeed anyone, in a mechanical way, can add exclamations and question marks anywhere in a sentence without doing anything more than get in the way of the reading of it.

Carelessly placed at the end of a sentence, a "!" or a "?" will not have the status of an expressed emphatic, though it may evoke acts in those who attend to them. The evoked emphatics will differ from those already examined, in not being due to the expression of some other emphatic. Emphatics evidently may be evoked in many ways and on many occasions. They are properly identified as "evoked emphatics," in the sense here intended, only if they are due to the expression of other emphatics.

When a computer produces what are taken to be alarms, it does no more than what might prompt an appropriate reaction in a living being, but the computer will neither know nor refer to anything. Nor can it be evoked to produce an emphatic. Though a mob's shouts and acts are more than aggregations of those of its members, it is these who produce emphatics and evoke the expression of emphatics in one another. In a more controlled form, somewhat similar evocations are produced by the members of an army. Although acculturation, like the outcomes that depend on the use of evocative emphatics, takes a while to move close to a completion, it is usually carried out independently of its evocative source. Like the effect that an appreciation of a work of art or even that education, training, and disciplining produce, acculturation may be carried out and completed long after the initial evocation was operative. This does not mean that it can be properly understood if no reference is made to that evocation. One may be subject to an evocative emphatic, no matter what one may then do, or when.

The most violent of rebels is an acculturated being. The rebel's oppositions, negations, and invocations may be functions of the same evocations to which others are subject. Unlike them, the rebel will produce negations as well as qualifications that others reject. Some, less conspicuously and effectively, on being subject to the same emphatics that are being evoked in others, will sometimes respond in similar or in quite dissimilar ways.

Evoked emphatics are in part a function of the habits, attitudes, and dispositions of those who are affected and in part a function of the way they are being evoked. An overemphasis on the power to evoke emphatics may outrun but will not necessarily do what does not accord with the demands and needs of its source.

An evocative emphatic stops short of compelling the beings it affects. No training, disciplining, threats, rewards, or control is able to impinge on an individual though he or she may be so constrained or feel threatened as to express independent acts within prescribed limits,

152

close to what is desired or demanded though not necessarily close to what that individual would prefer to do.

The independent beings and aims of individuals set limits to what evoked emphatics may do. Sometimes those individuals are quite successful in minimizing the effect that evocations of emphatics will have on them. None offers a wholly passive place where the evocations operate; everyone of them adds freshly produced qualifications to what intrudes.

There are some, particularly animal trainers and those who have studied some of the higher forms of animals in their customary surroundings, who claim that animals express emphatics that have been evoked in them. There is no reason to doubt them or even the claim that various acts by some subhumans are followed by the acts of others that contribute to the achievement of desirable outcomes or that end in duplications or qualifications of the initial acts. Other subhumans may not only be altered, but may be prompted to act in ways crucial to their continuance or welfare. There would be nothing amiss in holding that they evoke emphatics in others that enable those others to distinguish what is important for the welfare of a group or kind from what is not.

What is evident is that humans can emphatically evoke a wide range of emphatics in one another and that an attribution of similar abilities to subhumans usually reexpresses the human in a modified form. Much that we attribute to animals is a variant of what we know to be true of humans. Evolutionary theories, often enough, read back into the past pallid versions of some of the things known about humans.

Great changes in the ways that both commerce and leisure can be carried out are not entirely separable from those that highways, bridges, trains, automobiles, airplanes, telephones, and computers produce and the differences they make to commerce and leisure. Viewed from the standpoint of the past, they could be taken to evoke at least some of the emphatics that we introduce into what we then confront. What is done by machines does not, though, impose emphatics that evoke others.

6. Governing Evocatives

The evocative emphatics that have so far been noted are carried out by others that exist together with them. Emphatics of quite a different kind are evoked by controlling conditions. These may have the form of alterable laws, natural or human, or of laws that hold always. Each elicits acceptances and submissions by the others, but only the eternal laws always evoke a conformity to their demands. Although surmises are unavoidable from the standpoint of that with which they interplay, a law is an evoked emphatic.

It is one thing to be so acted on that one carries out an act, and it is quite another to be evoked to carry out some emphatic. The latter, but not the former, has an emphatic expression elicited by what acts on it. It would therefore be reasonable to suppose that when a singular and a condition produce particulars, each of them evokes the other to make a contribution. That claim moves beyond the point reached earlier when nothing more was affirmed than that a moment of time is constituted by a union of temporality and a singular. If this is done, it would then be reasonable to say that particulars, for example, are not only constituted by a meeting of universals and singulars, but that each of these evokes the contribution of the other. Time, space, causality, too, would then be understood to be the outcome of meetings of evocative emphatics that singulars and extensionality elicit from one another.

Laws evoke sustainings of themselves and thereupon govern what does this at the same time that beings insist on themselves and specialize the laws. What is not evident is whether or not all laws and all singulars separately or jointly evoke emphatics in what they intrude on to make this insistent on accepting them.

Following the lead of either Plato and Aristotle, many have been content to assume that there is a kind of receptacle, or matter, that is somehow powerful enough to provide a lodging for intrusive forms. Later thinkers, Kant in particular, refer to "experience" without making evident whether or not this added anything and without showing if or how it could provide the needed lodging. The receptacle, matter, or experience to which reference was made would have had to be evoked to resist, for otherwise it would be crushed, overwhelmed, or swept away, leaving the supposed intruders unable to find a lodging.

Question: This chapter is totally unexpected. It makes evident that what seems to be surmised by many—that you write down what pops into your head, and that, despite your persistent use of such terms as emphatics, Being, conditions, and the Dunamic-Rational, you do little more than present a number of essays that are yoked together by means of a loosely applied set of terms.

Answer: I have heard that charge many times over the years, even when I presented charts and made evident the natures and roles of pivotal realities—singulars, ultimate conditions, and Being—the inescapable ways that they were related to one another and their roles in constituting the members of the different domains. Some were understood by me quite early; others much later. Instead of treating any of them as cartons or translating everything else that was known into versions of them, I used what I understood of them as guides and warnings.

Different investigations were begun from different positions but were constantly checked against the fact that there are singular beings, of which I am one, that these have persons, lived bodies, and organisms and that there are a number of domains, governed in different ways. It took me a while to learn that there is a final reality presupposed by everything else and even longer to realize that every being participates in its excellence to some degree. I have tried to keep in mind what commonsense and logic insist on, the claims made by great minds over the centuries, and the fact that humans express themselves in and through their characters, habits, persons, lived bodies, and organisms. I never lost sight of the fact that we make adumbrative moves into individuals, but I did not see until later that we also make discerning moves as well that reach in one move what adumbrations attain in several or that the latter are often carried out over routes that had been traversed, in the opposite direction, by emphatics.

After a position had been explored, I raised difficulties, some of which are reflected at the end of each chapter in the present work—a practice begun in *Being and Other Realities.* Each work was rewritten many times, usually after I reflected on the criticisms that late drafts elicited from acute critics. Then, once more, I rewrote the whole from beginning to end.

Q: You attend to art, but pay no attention to natural beauties. Don't the Rockies and the Grand Canyon intrude on the routine with an incredible force? Doesn't the sun sometimes go down in the evening in a breathtaking way? Don't they evoke expressions of delighted amazement? Why not include natural wonders or even a poet's flower in a crannied wall, among evocative emphatics?

A: We would, and we should, if we understood them to be singular expressions of nature, but we would be hard pressed to find anything there that was not beautiful. We would find a dying blade of grass, a decaying carcass, a number of wolves tearing a lamb apart to be beautiful. We would not, though, take what we saw to be evocative of the kind of desirable emphatics that works of art produce. What is not evident is whether or not, in the absence of humans and a possibly unnoticed translation of nature into what occurs in the humanized world, any natural occurrences are evocative of the kinds of emphatics that humans can evoke.

The question of the kind of acquaintance humans have with what is in nature is one that has not been adequately treated by me or, to my knowledge, by anyone else.

Q: Heidegger saw the old shoes painted by van Gogh as revelatory of the hard life of a weather-beaten peasant.

A: A painter is neither a sociologist nor a historian. No one now knows whether or not the shoes were owned by van Gogh, scuffed up a bit by him, or made to look shabbier than they in fact were. I confess that I do not trust anything that Heidegger said; he was a Nazi, and that means that truth was not cherished if it seemed to get in the way of the promotion of a great outcome. For Nazis paintings were conveyors of information; it is not odd to find one of them taking a painting of old shoes to be a way of telling us about a peasant's life. It should, though, alert one to the fact that he perhaps knew that what he was supposedly reporting was no more than an instance of the kind of service all art is supposed to provide.

Q: You have tried your hand at painting, drawing, sculpting. You have written a play, taken dancing lessons, attended classes for actors, watched films being made in Hollywood, discussed poetry with poets, painting with painters, sculpture with sculptors, architecture with architects, written two books on art, and—

A:—still remain baffled, not confident that I have gone as far as I should go if I am to say what it is that the arts achieve, and what they do to us.

Q: Has it been your theories rather than your experience that has so far guided you?

A: I have never tried to separate or to connect them. I must confess that I have never learned much even from conversations I have had with artists as intelligent and as articulate as Auden, Stevens, Cage, Welliver, Slavitt, and Thom, among others. I cannot talk about my ventures into art as coming anywhere near what they have done.

I prefer works that make me smile, pleased, alerted, for reasons I rarely seek—in good part because I am not an artist but have somehow touched on the edges of what they intend.

It disturbs me some that I have learned so little either from talking to artists or from reflecting on what I have done. My awareness of the fact that successful works of art emphatically call attention to the intensive unity of what is expressed is more the result of a reflection on the nature of evocative emphatics than it is on my experiences, though once the idea of evocative emphatics became evident, I have begun to appreciate various works of art in a way I had not before. I have also been encouraged to hear artists to whom I have tried to present this view of art say that this is what they have been trying for a long time to get me to see and to say.

Q: It is not often that anyone, other than a child, says, "I am!"

A: We express it is in everything we do and say. Descartes's concluding that he was, because he was thinking, stated the fact in a limited way. He could have come to the same conclusion had he begun with the fact that he was eating or sneezing or standing up, though that would not have allowed him to conclude that he was just a thinking being.

Q: An artist enables what he presents to evoke emphatics directed at his work, or elsewhere?

A: Sometimes at the one, and sometimes at the other, but ideally at both. In the next chapter, recursive emphatics, which refer one back to their sources, will be examined. The emphatic that a work of art evokes does not necessarily do that; it may do no more than prompt someone to produce an emphatic of his or her own that may have no evident connection with the emphatic that evoked it.

Q: Are an unappreciated or an unopened book of poems, an unread story, a painting in an abandoned house, and the like works of art? Must they wait for someone to be affected by them before they have that status?

A: They are works of art even when not known. They do not, at that point, of course, evoke emphatics in anyone.

Q: It is startling to see you to take pragmatism to have a singular reference to art, particularly in the light of your dissatisfaction with Dewey's account of art and the fact that most pragmatists pay little or no attention to it.

A: What I intended was to point up the fact that pragmatism should have been alert to the role that emphatics have in art. I found fault with Dewey's understanding of art, particularly in the main body of his work devoted to the subject, and with his focusing on paintings dealt with under the guidance of an idiosyncratic, disgruntled collector. Toward the end of his book, Dewey exhibited a better understanding of the subject, but he never took account of the evocative emphatics that the arts provide. Other leading pragmatists have paid little or no attention to the subject. Here they are one with analysts, positivists, and empiricists, conceivably because their commitments to some ideas and methods preclude them from investigating it. The best book on art written by a philosopher, of which I have any knowledge, is Gilson's Mellon Lectures. His daughter was a painter.

Q: You often make distinctions where others do not. When you deal with education, you seem to do the opposite. On your view, would not almost any transmission of information and any cause of changes in practice be identified as educative?

A: "Education" not only has a very wide application, but also a more limited one, keeping it tied to schooling. I have tried to allow for this while remaining alert to some of its other major applications.

Q: Some emphatics are caught up in the routine and commonplace?

A: This was made evident a number of times in the first chapter, and it is touched on again and again in subsequent ones. The fact that one may be subject to an emphatic for quite a while and be occupied with expressing an emphatic that this evokes does not mean that those emphatics are not intrusive. Many emphatics in common use continue to play important roles. A punctuation mark is an emphatic whenever it is properly used. It also can evoke the expression of other emphatics of the most diverse kinds.

Q: An unintended emphatic may evoke other unintended emphatics?

A: Yes. I may betray myself with a frown, and this may prompt someone else to frown as well.

Q: Apparently what you take to be commonplace is identified as a background, and emphatics, both those that are evocative and those that are not, are identified as intrusive on this. What might be an evocative emphatic in one situation might not be one in another?

A: Yes. An evocation elicits an expression; it does not compel.

Q: Implicit in your view, apparently, is the supposition that there is a fairly stable set of occurrences, and that these are intruded on, in some cases in such a way that other emphatics are elicited. Those emphatics may or may not be carried out along lines that continue the influence of the initial emphatics. Even if there were an unavoidable course set by what previously occurred, there may be emphatics, some of which evoke others. Would they necessarily do this?

A: Not all emphatics, nor any at all times, evoke emphatic expressions by others.

Q: One who is self-taught evokes emphatics in him- or herself that may then be expressed?

A: Yes. And I may express emphatics that go beyond the "me" and then curl back to it. It may thereupon evoke other emphatics from that "I."

Q: It sounds as if you thought that you had discovered a perpetual motion machine.

A: No. The expression of an evoked emphatic is different from it. Evoking an emphatic still leaves indeterminate if, how, or when this may be expressed unless the evoked emphatic is recursive, necessary referring back to its emphatic source, a type discussed in the next chapter. When an "I" refers back to itself via its "me," what it receives will be accepted in any one of many ways. It may thereupon evoke other emphatics.

Q: You seem to deplore the sports programs in colleges. Might they not be sources of desirable emphatics otherwise not obtainable?

A: Yes. What I deplore is the tendency in some to make the programs central and pivotal. They could be vital parts of a well-articulated education, but it surely would be an error to suppose that every other interest, procedure, need, and expense must be for the incidental, and perhaps for the expendable.

Q: Do you agree with Dewey about the way students, particularly in the early grades, should be taught?

A: I think he was right to deplore a tendency in many educators of his time to be content with rote learning and the mindless repetitions by the young of formulae expounded by their elders.

Q: Are training and disciplining to be sealed off from education?

A: No. They are usually needed if students are to master techniques and special skills. Some of the emphatics that are expressed in the course of that mastery, though, may not have an educative role. Also, while education focuses mainly on the person and training attends mainly to the organism, disciplining is occupied with a strengthening of the character and its expressions through the person, lived body, and organism. None keeps within fixed borders; each spills over into areas where the others are effective.

Q: To be trained or disciplined is to be evoked to do something?

A: No. It is to be evoked to deal with some things in a more controlled way.

Q: Why not take the different kinds of emphatics to provide different parts of a single process of acculturation?

A: That would foreclose the idea that they need not contribute to this. Some emphatics may be evoked whose expressions do not accord well with a community's outlook or values, then or later. Acculturation gives a greater role than other sources of emphatics do to those emphatics that express a dominant social condition. It may also prevent or limit the effectiveness of other sources of evocative emphatics.

Q: You grant that a machine might produce what might have the effect of eliciting an emphatic from someone?

A: Yes.

Q: Since a child can be sensitized, trained, disciplined, educated, and acculturated without this being an intended result, how will its evoked emphatics differ from what a machine might produce?

A: Although emphatics may be elicited without this being intended, evocations of them begin at deeper levels than their expressions. A machine, though well-ordered and able to function smoothly, exerts no governing control. It is a well-joined assembly of units. Singulars and conditions, in contrast, can govern, prescribe, and express themselves emphatically.

160

Q: A computer may set off an alarm, print exclamation marks, use italics, produce understandable sounds, place things in an order, and enable some others to function in their own distinctive ways. Again and again a machine may intrude some things into what is routine; again and again what it produces is followed by emphatics expressed by humans. Don't advertisements produce emphatics that evoke others in those who attend to them?

A: When an alarm clock arouses one, it does not express or evoke an emphatic, though one may of course then produce an emphatic on one's own. More complicated devices are not able to do better, no matter how complex their movements and how remarkable their outcomes. Just as neither our tongues nor our hands produce emphatics, but at best help convey them, so other agents convey but do not produce any. The movements of a machine or the reading of an advertisement, of course, may prompt one to express an emphatic. Prompting falls short of an evoking; where the latter ends in something producing an emphatic of its own, the former merely encourages one to do so.

Q: There is a great difference between prompting and evoking?

A: Yes. Only evoked emphatics need to be expressed.

Q: Governing evocatives differ from other kinds of emphatics in having their sources in ultimate conditions?

A: Yes.

Q: Platonists take those sources to be always self-same, never affected by what they govern. If they act emphatically, they do this in the same way always, denying "emphatic" any other meaning than that of instantiating eternal conditions. Do you agree with them?

A: No. An emphatic is expressed; an instantiation is a specialization.

Q: Are formal and natural laws evocative of submissions to them?

A: Yes. Otherwise, when they are instantiated, they could sweep away or absorb whatever might provide them with a sustaining locus.

In the chapter after the next, the roles of Being, ultimate conditions, and beings, will be examined in ways that take us beyond the point reached in *Being and Other Realities*. It will then become evident that the kinds of emphatics that finite beings produce are different from those that Being and the ultimate conditions do. Finite beings express different emphatics on different occasions. Being necessarily always expresses the same emphatics. The ultimate conditions

161

necessarily refer Being's possibility to it and may independently express emphatics of their own, when and as those conditions act as Being's agents.

Q: Do formal and natural laws evoke submissions to them?

A: Yes. Otherwise, when they are instantiated, they would sweep away whatever might offer them a place, or they would be altered by that on which they were imposed. The submissions are never complete. They are always qualified by an insistence, by what is distinct from what is being submitted.

Q: There is no passive "matter" that laws organize?

A: What is available for organization has a being of its own. It is never completely passive; it always interplays with the laws that effectively control it.

Q: There is and there could then be no perfect conformity to the laws of logic, the truths of mathematics, or cosmic laws?

A: Not unless that which conforms had no nature of its own.

Q: Somehow, for you, there is nothing but Being that one can surely know to be eternal and perfect. Yet there could be, in fact there are, finite beings that are not only other than Being, but exist contingently and do unpredictable things. Is what the finite beings do known by Being?

A: No. Being does not know anything.

Q: Knowledge is a great good, yet Being cannot possess it?

A: Knowledge is a great good for finite beings. Being, as presupposed as excellent and as what is other than all else, does not need to know anything. What knowledge would arrive at has to be sustained by what is different from this. Being does not provide anything that is sustained by anything other than itself or by itself in a delimited form.

Q: Does Being express itself emphatically?

A: Yes. The ultimate conditions are *its* conditions.

Q: What receives those emphatics?

A: Being enables the conditions that it emphatically produces also to receive its emphatically expressed possibility.

Q: Do animals use emphatics?

A: We know that many can be trained and that some can be disciplined. In different ways they alert some others to the presence of danger, the availability of food and water, etc. There would be nothing amiss in crediting all of them with the ability to produce emphatics that evoke emphatics in some others.

Q: Some emphatics are evoked by other emphatics, and some are not?

A: Yes. There are, moreover, many ways in which an emphatic may be evoked.

Q: Does anyone know how any being, as apart from all else, is affected, and what ought to be done by each?

A: No one knows any being exhaustively or has a knowledge of it that is complete and perfect, that is beyond the reach of error or misconstrual, but many know large, constant truths about them, for example, that they are finite, exist contingently, express themselves in limited domains, are interrelated with others, are confined by and own instantiated ultimate conditions, and participate in, presuppose, and are other than Being.

Q: Your idea about distinct domains seems to resurrect Aristotle's and the medieval idea of fixed species.

A: Not only do I not preclude the existence of domains following after one another, but I also acknowledge a Dunamic-Rational that made it possible for one domain, the cosmic, to be a source of nature, this to be a source of the humanized world, and this to be a source of a domain of persons. The Dunamic-Rational makes it possible for what is in one domain to be related to what is in others. As has already been made evident, it is this that enables one to know what exists outside one's mind.

Q: You still sound antiquated. Why not join Whitehead and, in some accord with leading scientists, content yourself with a cosmology that has room for the acknowledgment of a God?

A: A cosmology has no place for responsibility if it has no place for any being to exist for more than a passing atomic moment. A philosophical cosmology differs from a scientific one in allowing for no changes in its primary parameters. It is justifiably criticized for its inability to account for perception, for the persistence of any finite being for more than a moment, for an inexplicable existence of contingencies, and for its inability to account for the ways in which beings interplay or express themselves in limited domains. It must be passed beyond if justice is to be done to what occurs in nature, the humanized world, and a domain of persons.

Q: You say that there are persons and that these are owned and used by individuals. Yet some find no reason to take humans to be more than complex organisms, composed of determinate parts, moving and interacting in mechanical ways. Has anyone ever seen a mind, or any of the other supposed subdivisions of a person? Indeed, has anyone ever seen a person?

A: These are not to be seen, but to be adumbrated or discerned and understood. Seeing, experimenting with, or in some other way obtaining information about an organism or some part of it, such as a brain, is carried out by what is not just an organism.

What observes a brain? Who or what knows that there are brains? Who or what reports the ways brains act? To whom? Can a brain know, perceive, intend, fear, hope, or plan? Is it responsible?

No one, to be sure, has ever seen a mind. It is not visible. A specialized subdivision of a person, it may make a difference to the ways in which other subdivisions function, and conversely. Even one who takes a stand with physiological processes not only knows something about what is not in his or her mind, but can come to know that there are minds by taking account of such emphatics as "true!" and "false!"

Q: We know that some computers can play masterly chess games, can detect flaws and errors, correct spellings, carry out complex mathematical computations, and send and receive messages, all at great speed. Every word can be designated by a number, every number can be expressed in a series of ones and zeroes, and every member of that series can be reexpressed by opening and closing an electric circuit. Why may computers not do all the things that minds are supposed to do?

A: Computers go through a multiplicity of prescribed moves very rapidly. Chess masters carry out a strategy, punctuated by emphatics. Those who design computers to play games of chess try to find and install the best replies to every move. Those replies may require not only a great number of alternative replies to them, but to replies that might be made to those replies, and so on. A chess master may be defeated by a computer because he or she is unable to envisage the totality of replies that could be made to any move made. Although his or her moves may not assure a victory, they express decisions then and there made to the predesignated moves made by a computer. The designers of the computer have it run through a multitude of alternative answers to any given move, to pick the best of these, and then repeat the process after each move that is made by its opponent.

Computers play no games. They are not conscious. If designed to engage in games of chess, their moves will be preset, with the best ones elicited by the moves made by their opponents. None expresses an emphatic, but every move made by a chess player is an emphatic. To end with a victory over a computer that has been programmed to designate moves that will end in victories in games of chess, it is necessary to make moves that a program carried out by a computer is not be able to counter.

Q: You say that there are persons and that these are used by individuals. Yet there are some careful thinkers who find no reason to take humans to be more than organisms, composed of detectable parts, carrying out mechanical moves.

A: Imagining, inferring, anticipating, believing, hoping, fearing, dreaming, and knowing are acts carried out by persons making use of their minds. Great changes in the ways both commerce and leisure are carried out are not completely different from those that computers and other complex machines produce. They could be imagined to evoke some of the emphatics that humans introduce into what they confront. They do not, though, themselves impose emphatics that evoke others.

Q: Biologists and physicians are still faced with unsolved problems about the nature of the human organism; sociologists and anthropologists confess to being perplexed about humans' social lives. Do you have the answers?

A: No. I have been dealing with these issues within a larger context, from a different angle, and with a different objective in view. Among other things, I am trying to understand how to pass from surfaces to depths, multiplicities to singularities, the dependent to the independent, the owned to owners, and conversely.

Q: If individuals exist beyond the point where any intrusion can reach, how could one know any individual and therefore that any emphatics had been evoked by or in them? I have asked this question in other forms before, but I do not think that you have provided a clear, satisfactory answer anywhere.

A: A clear, satisfactory answer is not necessarily provided in a single statement. The complexity of the subject requires that one deal with it from many different angles and that these inescapably require that one encompass them within a single, integrated whole. We must try to improve our understanding of how it is possible to pass from surfaces to depths, particulars to singulars and conditions, the dependent to the independent, the owned to the owner, and conversely.

Individuals are not sundered from what they own and use. When references are made to them, one may make contact with them as involved with what our references terminate at. We move toward them as singulars, without ever arriving at them as just singulars. What we provide becomes more and more subject to their unifying control. The issue is not one of knowing or not knowing, but of knowing superficially and knowing penetratively.

Q: When one adumbrates or discerns, speaks to and not just at another, does one make use of an emphatic?

A: Yes.

Q: Will that emphatic evoke the expression of an emphatic in some other being?

A: It may, but it need not. An emphatic can play an evocative role only if it is imposed on what is in a position to be prompted by that emphatic in order to produce another. Again and again, we are aware that other realities are accepting our intrusions on them in their own ways, sometimes expressing the fact by producing emphatics of their own. We are not always sure whether the emphatics were evoked or were instead produced for some other reason.

Q: I think you should add, "We are not always sure that what is being expressed is or is not an emphatic." Sometimes you speak as if any expression were an emphatic and sometimes as if only those expressions that in fact intrude on something are emphatics.

A: It is not always evident whether or not something is an emphatic or just a contributor to the constitution of something that could sustain or be evoked to express an emphatic. Misconceptions about the status of this or that item, though, must not be allowed to jeopardize the claim that there are emphatics and that some of them evoke the expression of others on whom they impinge.

Q: Where many take a human to be a soul that is joined for a while to an organism, you take a human to be a singular who expresses him- or herself in and through an owned person, a humanized body, and an organism. Doesn't that mark a regression, not an advance, since we are then left with the question of how each of these is related to the others?

A: The three provide diverse, primary avenues through which an individual expresses him- or herself and thereupon makes him- or herself be a member of some domain. As we have already seen, emphatics enable us to understand how we can personally attend to our organisms, how injuries to our organisms end in personally felt pains, and how we can be members of a humanized world.

Q: Does that not still allow one to affirm that there is a soul in each, individualizing it?

A: Yes, but I see no reason why one should make that claim. The supposed soul is so different in origin, nature, and career from a lived body and organism that one is forced to suppose that it is always alien to them and is somehow forced for a while to be yoked to them. One could with as much or as little justification identify a lived body or an organism with an individual or as an individual's initial possession, then take the other or his or her person to be forcefully united with it.

Q: Since "other than" is a symmetrical relation, will not each being emphatically characterize Being as other than it?

A: Yes.

Q: Will Being not then be changed?

A: No. The emphatic that terminates in Being identifies Being as that which is other than that emphatic and its sources.

Q: This not very clear. More important is the fact that you are now saying what was never before said by you or apparently by anyone else.

A: There are new truths to be discovered in every discipline. None has come to an absolute end.

Q: Is needed advice that is not heeded or an exclamation that is not noticed an emphatic?

A: Yes, but they are not evocative.

Q: Why should one take advice or an exclamation that is heeded to be evocative, when the evocation depends on the emphatic's reception?

A: They are evocative of emphatics in those who are in a certain state. They would not be evocative at all, did they not promote the expression of emphatics in those who are receptive to them and thereupon ready to produce emphatics.

Q: Could an evoked emphatic take one toward the emphatic source that evoked it?

A: Yes. It would then act as one of three kinds of recursive emphatics—discussed in the next chapter.

Chapter 8

Recursive Emphatics

1. Three Kinds of Recursive Emphatics

A recursive emphatic makes an unavoidable reference to its source. One kind emphatically refers to a more recessive source of it— a "me," e.g., recursively refers to an "I." A second kind terminates in what is similar to that from which the emphatic originates—to attend to a person, e.g., one must be a person. A third kind inescapably terminates in what differs in nature to what refers to it; every being, e.g., recursively refers to Being. I will here deal mainly with the second kind and incidentally with the first. The third kind is relevant to what is dealt with in the next chapter.

2. Mind

To know what a mind is and does, one must use one's mind. The mind that is known may be one's own or another's. In either case a recursive emphatic will be used in the act of knowing a mind. A denial that there are any minds, just as surely as the affirmation that there is one, recursively and emphatically terminates in a mind as its source. The fact stands obstinately in the way of attempts to identify a mind with a brain, since no one could make the attempt if he or she did not use his mind. What is recursively terminated at may not then be known; a recursive act is not necessarily cognitive. A recursive emphatic that is expressed when the mind is used well or badly ends at the mind as that which could be used in other ways as well.

The recognition that both affirmations and denials of the existence of a mind recursively and insistently terminate in one defeats all attempts to deny that there are minds. Other emphatics originate or terminate elsewhere, but none gets in the way of the recursive emphatic that every use of the mind inescapably provides.

169

Being does what no mind can. Not only does Being make itself possible when and as it is, converting the possibility of itself into the possibility for itself by producing the ultimate conditions that sustain and refer the possibility to it, but it is presupposed and participated in by every being.

What provides recursive emphatics, ending in a mind, could exist outside a mind and be related to this by a mediator that brought what was made available by an object to one's mind—or, conversely, brought what was in one's mind to intrude on what is outside it. Our knowing of what exists apart from what is present in the mind depends on the mediative help of the Dunamic-Rational, bridging the gap between what is in one domain and what is in another. In its absence there would be no perceiving or any other way of knowing anything outside one's mind. Its neglect leaves epistemologists trapped inside their minds, unable even to know that there is anyone to whom they are able to address or to know if anything that they acknowledge has a lodgement elsewhere as well.

One recursively refers to a mind when one denies that there is a mind and also when one maintains anything. Even a strong skeptic is forced to make a recursive reference to his or her mind when and as he or she denies having one or knowing that he or she has one. To know what is recursively reached, one must engage in a specific act of knowing it.

A recursive emphatic, ending in a presupposed mind, need not be carried out by a mind. Nor need it end in the acquisition of any knowledge. The move instantiates the Dunamic-Rational, and it could be carried out by making use of any one of a number of sub-divisions of a person. Its use does not necessarily hinder the use of other recursive emphatics, ending in the same or other places.

3. Persons

A mind is a subdivision of a person. So is a will, desire, sensibility, and sensitivity. Each has its own distinctive way of acting. The use of any one of these ends in what recursively and emphatically terminates in the mind or in the person who owns and expresses him- or herself by using this mind.

It takes a person to deny or to doubt that there are any persons. It is a person who knows, expects, sympathizes, loves, or fears a person.

When it is said that a dog, a cat, or some other animal loves or fears a person, what is meant is that it acts in ways that are like those that persons sometimes carry out and that it can perhaps feel somewhat the way a person does when fearful, pleased, or in doubt. Whether it does or not, no one knows. Though a human may act in ways that seem to satisfy an animal and though some animals seem to express pleasure on seeing some humans and seem to act dejectedly when separated from them, it is doubtful that any animal is able to carry out an act of adumbration or discernment. Nor is anyone able to carry out such an act in dealing with a human embryo. Both supporters and foes of abortionists pit ignorance against ignorance, leaving it to the courts to settle on an answer that satisfies neither.

It takes a person to deny, or even to doubt, that there are any persons. It is a person who knows, respects, sympathizes with, loves or hates other persons. Although subhumans seem to express fears and expectations, these are not identifiable with the fears and expectations expressed by persons. Persons are owned and used by human beings; these also relate persons to the humanized bodies and organisms that are also owned and used. To acknowledge a human, one must not only be one and be interinvolved with another human as a person, but recursively, though not necessarily, deliberately, or as self-aware, refer to oneself as a person.

When "that is not a person" is used denigratively, what is referred to is identified as a person who has expressed him- or herself in a repugnant way. Whether it is affirmed or denied that there are persons, a recursive emphatic is produced. Attempts to ignore or deny that there are persons emphatically and recursively refer to one.

4. Associated Beings

No one exists completely cut off from all other humans. A lonely wanderer, a hermit, or one who avoids all human contacts lives in a domain together with other humans, with what has a bearing on its continuance, prosperity, and peace or on the attention of others. If this hermit holds him- or herself apart from the rest by refusing to be with or to communicate with them, he or she will still be related to them through an inheritance that cannot be eradicated. It will always play some role in what the hermit does. He is also one among many, even when alone, ignored and ignoring all others, rejecting every means by which he or she can be more closely together with them. These rejections are socially qualified and continue to connect the hermit with other members of the humanized world.

The members of the humanized world are associated as coordinate units. Nevertheless those who provide guidance, governance, or leadership do not stand above the rest. Even those who refer to a leader emphatically end with that leader as one of them. They may speak of the leader as a god, treat him or her as a usurper, or suppose that he or she is so wise and powerful that obedience is intolerable. Their acknowledgment of a ruler, nevertheless, indicates acceptance of this as one who is together with them. The reference is recursive but avoidable and therefore quite unlike those involved in the recursive emphatics that inescapably take us to minds, persons, beings, the ultimate conditions, and Being. The ruled both recursively and emphatically identify those who rule as being their rulers. In the absence of such an identification, they could be controlled and ordered but not ruled. Usurpers are subjugators before they become rulers.

Question: Is that all you have to say about recursive emphatics?

Answer: No. The next chapter is devoted to an examination of Being. This is recursively and emphatically referred to by whatever else there is. It also deals with the ultimate conditions as conveying, confining, and governing every finite being, as well as dealing with finite beings as other than Being. There are other recursive emphatics in addition to these. Instantiated logical and mathematical laws recursively and emphatically refer to those laws as conditions that might not have been instantiated.

One who was interested in presenting a metaphysics that embraced a set of irreducible, inescapable truths could take as his or her task the study of evocative emphatics that take one from beings to conditions and from either to Being. It would not be amiss to say that this is what in fact is done when any efforts are made to discover what the primary kinds of realities are. One would, though, not yet have learned much more than that Being and the ultimate conditions had to be. It would not yet be evident why there were finite beings and that these expressed themselves emphatically in a number of ways, most of which need not have been expressed but some of which inescapably refer recursively to their sources in the ultimate conditions or Being.

It took me a long time before I identified some of the more familiar emphatics, noted in chapter 1. It took even a longer time to identify some of the major ontological emphatics, which are dealt with in the rest of this work. Only then did it become evident that there are recursive emphatics that take one to what is necessarily presupposed—Being, the ultimate conditions, and singulars—by whatever else there is. What would not yet be known is why there was, or how there could be, anything else. To follow the lead of a recursive emphatic is not yet to know all that is to be known about what is terminated at. It must be examined to see what it is, and then one must try to see what it must do and where it does end.

Q: You have done that?

A: Knowing that I am fallible and that the method employed is better and better known and strengthened as I proceed, I still must say "Yes!" That does not mean that I have not found it necessary to rethink and rewrite this work—as I have others—again and again. Nor does it mean that what I finally take to be a work ready for publication is perfect. I am not offering an excuse for whatever failures the work now exhibits but am noting a fact about this and every other philosophic work. At its best, philosophic thought is acutely attuned to the fact that it is engaged in frontier thinking and so far can never do much more than open up avenues to be traversed more carefully by those who follow.

I think of Peirce as America's greatest philosopher, but there is not much in his major writings that does not need refinement, expansion, and defense. A good criticism of what he has done will honor him. It will also make possible the mastery of fields that have so far been neglected. The study of emphatics is one of them. His recommended replacement of entertained ideas by ideas of practical consequences should, among other things, alert one to the fact that ideas of practical consequences could be emphatic versions of entertained ideas. As will become evident at the end of this work, this is just one of the ideas that his original thought elicits. His failure to attend to recursive emphatics is one reason why he did not realize that signs cannot be understood if no references are made to their users.

Q: This sounds as if you had found a good escape hatch. If a philosophical account is so unreliable, why not begin by accepting what leading figures endorse and patch it up where necessary?

A: There are areas they have neglected or dealt with in inadequate ways. Nothing seems to have been agreed on by all. Few pay attention to criticisms that question their primary but often unexpressed assumptions.

Q: You remark that each religion rejects the other religions and that you so far agree with the rejection of each by all the rest. Don't all other philosophical accounts, at least implicitly, reject yours, and conversely?

A: The theologics are dogmatic; they do not invite criticism. None has ever provided a tenable proof of the existence of the reality that they say all should revere. Each insists on acknowledging only a limited number of emphatics that they alone can make available as ways to reach the divine.

A work worthy of the name "philosophy" raises difficulties that challenge its most basic claims. It is ready to acknowledge that what was achieved at one time may need to be qualified and perhaps may deserve subordination to a more comprehensive and better warranted view reached later. Wittgenstein knew that, but he thought that that meant one should begin with the simplest of assertions and see how one could build on them. We know far more than we have been able to say and surely far more than what we can learn from analyzing our claims.

I do not hold that what is now maintained is without a flaw. I have, though, subjected every thesis to criticisms that are as severe as I could manage. The claim and the outcome, I know, are often dismissed as idle, unchecked ruminations of an undisciplined mind. Rarely do I find the charges backed by evidence.

Q: There is, to put it gently, a touch of arrogance and conceit in your reply. Few, if any, in the history of systematic thought match it.

A: I don't agree. There is little doubt in the minds of Plato, Aristotle, Descartes, Leibniz, Spinoza, Kant, and Hegel that they have reached some final answers. Granted the assumptions they made and the methods they followed, they were right to be confident that they had done so.

Q: But you don't think they did?

A: Yes and no. Granted their beginnings and their methods, they came to conclusions that did enable one to see what had not been seen before. I find too much was left unexamined—as the study of emphatics alone makes evident.

Q: You have avoided their errors and have left nothing out?

A: I hope I have done the first; I do not know if I have done the second or even that what I have stoutly maintained will withstand severe criticism. I have tried to subject what I have claimed to examinations from many different positions. I now am not aware of any serious omissions or faults. It would be easy to speak in more tentative ways, but I would then not be honest about what I think has been accomplished. I have been helped in part by my poor memory, which often allows me to return to what I had written as if it were new.

Q: Why not build on the best view that we now have?

A: Granted that this is known, one would be able to build on it in two ways. One could try to patch up and supplement what had been maintained by some great figure or backed by some school, or one could instead, with some awareness of what had been accomplished, try to carry out the work afresh, alert to what is being presupposed as well as to issues not usually noticed. There are many other, different ways in which one could advance; a number of them may help clarify what had previously been misconstrued or alert one to what had been overlooked.

The same primary and pivotal realities can often be arrived at in many ways, each contributing to a result neither could produce alone. One learns about the nature of singulars, e.g., by approaching them from the position of the ultimate conditions that confine them, from the eternally fixed position of Being, or from the positions of other beings.

Q: Is there a necessary end to such efforts?

A: Yes and no. The pivotal realities—Being, the ultimate conditions, and singulars severally, and their essential relations to one another, can be understood, leaving over a multitude of questions, not the least of which is the kind of difference they make to one another through interplays, intelligible vital connections, and emphatic intrusions.

Q: Perhaps advances in the sciences, mathematics, logic, or analysis could help?

A: They might—and they might not. The matter cannot be settled a priori.

Q: Do you agree with your former student, Richard Rorty, that the dominant Anglo-Saxon epistemologically oriented philosophy is bankrupt?

A: Yes. But I do not think that his pragmatism provided him with all his warrants. He did not, and I think he could not, show that there was a "language of mankind," which one should then use. He seems to be unaware that there are emphatics and that some of them are recursive, taking one toward what is presupposed.

A philosopher should free him- or herself from untenable positions. Rorty should have been acclaimed by those he criticized, since he made evident where they went astray, but the praise is muted since he provided nothing to set in place of what he exposed as unwarranted and untenable. His entire critique could have been compressed in single crushing sentence: If all you can know or say is in your mind or language, there is nothing else that you can know, and no one to whom one could report the supposed findings.

The boldness, humility, resoluteness, self-criticism, and range of a systematic study is different from what is characteristic of other enterprises. It could not even be confined to epistemological questions without one knowing something about the nature of knowers and their relations to what is and could be known. Despite himself and despite the anger he aroused, Rorty and those he criticized stopped short of what they had to acknowledge in order to have a view to present to someone.

Although something can be learned from an existentialist's nuanced self-examination, perhaps by overhearing what he or she says to him- or herself, that existentialist is self-confessedly trapped inside a self. Given the created works by some leading existentialists, one would reasonably expect them to show how the works could exist apart from their creators and even to recognize that some of those works both provide loci for emphatics and express others, some of which recursively end at what was pre-supposed.

Q: I must confess that much of what you say is darker than the middle of the night, though perhaps no more so than what Parmenides, Plotinus, or Hegel said.

A: I like being associated with them. I do not find them to be as opaque as some say they are. They address primary issues that others bypass and do so in ways that make it possible to understand both necessary and contingent realities in a way one could not before.

Q: Where should one begin?

A: Where one is.

Q: Where is that?

A: In the daily, humanized world.

Q: Isn't that what Dewey did?

A: Yes, but he was unable to deal with what was not in that domain. He had no way of making contact with anything in the cosmos or even in nature as a distinct domain. What he said about persons is often quite commonplace. What he said about religion, to put it gently, is not very illuminating. He focused on blockages and on overcoming them, but he failed to see that this required him to attend to emphatics, some of which were introduced by humans, as they tried to bring encountered objects within the orbit of human interest and control.

Q: Being can be completely understood?

A: There is no point where one's understanding of it is brought to a halt.

Q: Should we not expect to find unbridgeable differences in other areas, where some may acknowledge emphatics that others do not or cannot?

A: Yes—and we do. The rules of etiquette that prevail in one society are not respected by those in others. Doctors disagree on diagnoses.

Q: What should be done?

A: First, the differences should be made evident. Then the assumptions that lead one to go beyond the point others reach should be exposed. If all differ in their understanding of facts available to them, a reexamination of what is claimed will be needed. Most important, the point where one goes beyond where the other comes to a rest must be made evident, and warrants for the move must be provided.

Q: Evidently there is at least one basic question that you cannot answer. You do not know whether or not there is a God. Does that fact not compromise your attempt to provide a comprehensive account of reality?

A: No. I find nothing more than Being needs to be acknowledged in order to understand why, how, or what anything else is. Different religions acknowledge different gods. Some suppose that there is only one but do not agree on how this is to be characterized. A number justify their views by referring to miracles, prophetic utterances, visitations, and the like. Each finds the miracles defended by others to be implausible or matches these with others no less astonishing. All could and in fact tacitly do agree that Being expresses itself emphatically in everything and evokes emphatics that allow one to terminate in it as both eternal and excellent, but they then unwarrantedly suppose that it is something like a perfect, everlasting, and powerful person or an unfathomable combination of persons that, despite its perfection, does different things at different times. What should be shown is that an account of Being and its relation to all else is necessarily incomplete.

Q: It surely does not meet the demands of the pious.

A: True—if the pious do in fact encounter divinely produced emphatics. The theologians' neglect of these makes one suspect that the pious are occupied with imaginaries, unless one wishes to say that the pious do acknowledge and use emphatics that have a divine origin and that the theologians do not know that or do not know how to deal with the fact.

Q: The pious may be right? There could be a God beyond Being who expresses himself emphatically in some or perhaps everything.

A: Yes. I do not, though, know of any warrant for the claim.

Q: You would apparently maintain that emphatics having a divine source are recursive?

A: I am not sure. If they are recursive, they not only enable one to begin a move toward their divine source, but necessarily refer to it, when and as they become available for others to accept.

Established religious institutions prescribe necessary preparations and identify various objects and acts as the only, the best, or the most appropriate loci of emphatics that have their source in an identified God. If it is maintained that God created everything else, it is hard to avoid the claim that everything whatsoever is a locus of a divinely produced emphatic. One religion would then differ from another primarily in its choice of objects and acts that enable one to make contact, or the best contact, with the divine and perhaps also provide the best answer to the question of whether or not an emphatic, having a divine origin, was recursive. Despite their disdain for one another or a gentle shoving of them aside as respected ancestors, as earnest, or as worthy of respect, each religion ends with the claim that it alone has found the occasions and the methods for knowing where best to make use of divinely produced emphatics.

Q: There seems to be something absurd—since you are not pious and accept no theologian as a reliable guide—in your telling theologians what the pious do and what it is that a theology should explicate.

A: It is no more absurd than the claim made by one from a democracy to know what a tyrant is, does, or might do. Sometimes the pious refer to miracles or to proofs, but the first are ignored or rejected by those who adhere to other religions, and the second have not survived critical scrutiny. Thomas Aquinas, whose brilliance is evident in other works, offered five proofs of God in his *Summa*. One proof would have sufficed, were it impeccable. None, nor all of them together, is tenable.

Q: Are the pious, the unconvinced, and the irreligious irreconcilably opposed to one another?

A: Not on every issue. They may agree on what the virtues are, on the best ways to avoid or overcome vice, and even on what exists in contradistinction to a God.

Q: Don't some of the religious account for the existence of contingent realities that would otherwise be inexplicable?

A: Some don't even try—process theologians are content to stop with the acknowledgment that there is a God and contingent realities as well. Many instead refer to an act of creation but do not explain why or how what is perfect and eternal would or could suddenly produce contingent occurrences. The fact that there are contingently existing realities has never been explained. An attempt to do that is one of the tasks faced in the next chapter.

Q: In this century prominent thinkers have urged us to give up the attempt to provide a systematic account of the nature and interinvolvements of realities and to try to focus instead on what humans say or undergo, as alone providing sure grounds for anything that could be reasonably claimed to be sound and even irreducible.

A: As has already been noted, they have been unable to show that they could know that there was anything outside their minds and therefore have been unable to maintain that there is anyone whom they know whom they are able to address.

Q: You don't seem to notice claims made on behalf of skepticisms, the need to speak with precision, or the recommended ways to escape from holding unexamined, prejudicial, and perhaps untenable views. You spend little time trying to show that their views are weak or indefensible, though some are defended by using the techniques and checks that logic, mathematics, and the sciences provide.

A: I have dealt with these in passing. Since I think that the criticisms I have made—that the views do not allow for the knowledge of anything outside their minds—are devastating, I see little point in making a careful study of what else they say when they try to operate within their self-imposed limits.

Chapter 9

Necessary and Contingent Realities

1. Finite Beings

No finite being need have been. None must continue to be. When any one is, it is, of course, a reality with its own nature, powers, and involvements. Unable to account for them, some suppose there was once a "big bang" when a multiplicity of cosmic entities came into existence. Nothing is said about why the "bang" should have occurred or how. Others, who take refuge in the idea of creation, do better than that, since they acknowledge a something that necessarily exists and that has the power to make something be in place of nothing. Unfortunately they assume that what necessarily is and always is self-same nevertheless carries out acts that could have been better than the one that a supposed infinitely wise power supposedly produced.

Following Whitehead at some distance, process philosophers have been content to hold that there are many finite unit beings, each lasting a moment, that somehow are taken account of by those who succeed them and by a God who makes use of them to provide opportunities for those successors to be better than their predecessors. Nothing but some mysterious "eternal objects," on this view, does or could assume responsibility or be accountable. Nothing but that God outlasts a moment. Even if it be supposed that there is a changing side of God that takes account of the world's activities and another side that is forever fixed, nothing is said and apparently known about the relation of the two. Since what contingently exists need not have been, some account of why it occurs is needed.

To suppose that there is a side to God, whose existence has not been demonstrated, that acts in contingent ways, does not cancel but rather adds to the difficulty. Why does He act in contingent ways? How are His contingently functioning and His necessitated sides related? How does one show that what is claimed of Him and of the world that apparently coexists with Him and goes its own way is true? Could anything on such a view be planned, prepared for, or predicted either by humans or even by that God? Is it not misleading to call that supposed reality a God, if He does not express himself emphatically, and perhaps recursively, and is not the object of worship?

No finite being need ever have been. How could the existence of anyone be reconciled with the reality of what is eternal and presumably never changes? Does there have to be a God who was not only eternally self-same but is constantly changing, so as to accommodate what occurs apart from him, and who somewhat futilely offers each newly, inexplicably produced temporal atom a better prospect than that which its predecessor had realized in its atomic moment? Is it true that nothing is accountable, nothing is responsible, nothing is done? Is a supposed universe of momentarily existing beings, even if credited with the ability to adopt what had just passed away and open to lures presented by an otherwise indifferent God, to be accepted for no other reason than that it enables one to provide an explanation for the occurrence of a sequence of temporal atoms?

There are beings that last for short periods whose presence and natures cannot be understood without references being made to what preceded them and to prospects that are to be realized. This does not mean that no explanation needs to be given for their occurrence. Even the possibility that something exists since it is distinct from this must be accounted for. An account of reality that provides no explanation for the existence of contingently realities is incomplete. If it cannot provide one, it is inadequate.

Anything that did not have to be, even if accounted for by reference to some sufficient cause, is a contingent reality. So is its cause and the entire chain of causes of which this is a part. What occurs may conform to a law, but the conformity is not necessarily complete or steady, and the law itself could have been different and have a different degree of control from what it now exercises.

Finite beings could be caught in a chain of necessities, but that chain might not have been. We will never escape a blunt acceptance of contingently existing beings unless we can show that some of them, at least, are necessitated by that which necessarily exists. They could not, though, be derived from logical, mathematical, or natural laws. Those laws, in order to be able to govern, await their presence.

Anything that is, unless it is necessary in and of itself, is a contingent reality. So is its antecedent cause and the entire chain of causes of which this is a part. Even mathematical necessities and logical laws, governing whatever there may be, would not be, were there nothing that was both necessary in itself, and presupposed by whatever else there was.

2. Ultimate Conditions

Each finite being has its own center. Each also shares features with others. Some of those features are constant; some are adventitious. Owned and used by finite beings that need not have been, those features instantiate common conditions in distinctive ways. They are, as was seen earlier, particulars, i.e., distinct unities of contributions from common conditions and singulars.

Features shared by a number of particulars may be adventitious. They need not have occurred. Some of them may be widely but not universally shared, enabling one, for example, to distinguish some black Africans from Asiatics and Europeans, and all of them from apes. All humans are subject to the same common conditions, but sometimes in different degrees. Some will live together in peace; some will remain apart from others who live across the road.

Common laws and governances are specialized versions of the ultimate conditions. These are constants, instantiated everywhere. None is necessary in and of itself; all could have been otherwise. They govern and relate whatever else there be.

The ultimate conditions—the Assessor, the Affiliator, Extensionality, the Coordinator, and the Dunamic-Rational (as I have found it convenient to name them in light of their primary roles in governing the domains of persons, the humanized world, nature, the cosmos, and the connections they have to one another)—are necessitated contingencies. They necessarily exist, made to be when and as Being is, in order to sustain and refer Being's possibility to it. They could have been different in kind and number from what they are and could do other things besides sustaining Being's possibility and referring this to Being. All that Being does is to enable them to be its perfect agents, never doing what it does not endorse.

Finite beings differ from the ultimate conditions in status and power. The latter are necessarily produced; they could have been different in number and kind, but whatever they are, they exist when and as Being does. They could, but need not, act in other ways than they do. They must sustain and refer Being's possibility to it, but just how they do this depends on them. They exist in contradistinction to Being, and they could therefore act on their own. They are Being's agents, doing what Being requires them to do; but, having realities of their own, they are able to do things that Being does not require them to do but never what it does not endorse. They meet that requirement if and when they jointly confine finite beings, for these are Being itself as recapturing the hold that Being had on the ultimate conditions before these acted on their own.

The ultimate conditions need not have done anything more than sustain and refer Being's possibility to it. So far as they do only that, they act on their own. Necessitated and required to function on Being's behalf, they could do what they must in number of ways, subdividing, e.g., into any number of interlocked units. What they do is a necessitated contingent act, one that had to be performed but could have been carried out in any number of ways. They are then able to but need not act in other ways as well. If they do, the result will be contingently produced contingencies, what might not have been produced but have in fact been produced by the ultimate conditions acting on their own. All that Being does is enable them to be its perfect agent, never doing what it does not endorse. If and when the ultimate conditions jointly act, they meet that demand by enabling Being to recover the hold it had on them. What the ultimate conditions confine is Being itself in miniaturized forms, owning the ultimate conditions to the degree that these had acted independently of Being.

Finite beings need never have been; when they are, they differ from the ultimate conditions in nature and role. Where the ultimate conditions had to be and had to act in certain ways—but could also act in other ways as well—thereupon conveying Being as owners of them to the degree that the conditions act independently of Being, finite beings must own those conditions to the very degree that those conditions acted independently of Being. Each finite

184

being is Being miniaturized, owning the conditions that confine them.

3. Being and Its Productions

The ultimate conditions are always owned by Being. When they act independently of Being, they convey it beyond themselves, in the guise of owners and users, to the very degree that they acted independently of Being. The ultimate conditions are always owned by Being and whatever beings there are, revealing the beings to be Being made finite.

Each finite being is contingently produced; there need not be any. The ultimate conditions are necessarily produced but can act on their own. Only if they do, will they sustain and refer Being's possibility to it. That leaves them able to act in other ways as well. If they do so act, there will not be more reality than Being has—that is impossible—or they will reinstate Being to the extent that they had acted independently of it.

Finite beings are Being itself, recovering the hold on the ultimate conditions that confine those beings. It is one and the same thing to say that the conditions confine the beings that own them and that they convey Being beyond themselves in delimited forms that recover the hold that Being had of them before they acted independently of it. "To confine a being" is an alternative way of stating "to convey Being within limits where it acts to own the ultimates to the degree that these had acted independently of it."

There is no temporal lapse between the owning of the ultimate conditions by Being and the owning of them by beings, though the first is inescapable while the second never occurs unless the conditions in fact are jointly instantiated and confine what owns them. If and when the ultimate conditions act on their own, they carry Being forward in the guise of their possessor. It is one and the same thing to say that finite beings own and use the ultimate conditions that confine them and that those conditions are always owned and used by Being.

Whatever there is, is necessarily produced by Being or is Being in a miniaturized form, owning the very conditions that Being produced so far as those conditions act independently of Being. There is no mysterious Platonic "receptacle" or an Aristotelian "matter" waiting to be infused with Being. There are only a necessary Being and necessitated agents that sustain and refer Being's possibility to it and that convey Being in a limited form as the owner and user of them to the degree that they act independently of Being.

Being is not only necessary in itself and necessarily does what it does. It is presupposed by all the ultimate conditions and by everything else. Not often acknowledged, it is nevertheless always terminated at and participated in by every being. All recursively and emphatically refer to it. Nothing is so independent and so accessible as Being. It necessarily exists, necessarily does what it does, and is always related to whatever else there is, both as presupposed and as an excellence in which every being shares to some degree.

As Anselm saw, a final perfect Being must be possible. That possibility could not be—as he apparently thought it was—something that someone entertains. It does not await anyone's acknowledgment or use. Being encompasses its own possibility, as a possibility *of* it, and has that possibility sustained by and referred to it, made into a possibility *for* it, whether or not there are any humans. A human who has the idea of a perfect Being cannot prove there is a possibility for it unless and so far as he or she already knows that it is a possibility that Being provided.

I have now summarized an account of the origin and nature of the possibility of an eternal reality originally presented in *Being and Other Realities,* but I have also taken account, as it did not, of the fact that Being not only is presupposed by all else, but has two facets. One, as Hegel saw, embraces everything that could be referred to it. The other, as Plato saw, is presupposed by whatever exists apart from it. The possibility that Being makes available for the ultimate conditions to sustain and refer to it is a possibility that is also resident in it.

There never could be less than Being, its possibility, and the perfect agents that do what Being demands be done. As able to sustain and refer, the ultimate conditions are distinct from Being and act on their own. As so able to act, they could do more than sustain and refer Being's possibility to it. When they do, they could not produce anything that could add to the reality that Being has. What they confine is Being, conveyed within the limits they provide when they jointly act in ways additional to those that they must when sustaining and referring Being's possibility to it. Each finite being is distinct from Being and exists within limited confines. Since there is no more reality than that which Being possesses, each finite being can be nothing more or less than Being itself, recapturing the hold on the ultimate conditions that Being lost when and as they jointly confine those beings.

Being always is. Needing an agent to sustain and refer its possibility to it, it provides this. That agent does what Being requires it to do. To do that, the agent must act on its own. It may then do nothing more than sustain and refer Being's possibility to it, thereby doing nothing more than reinstate Being's ownership of them.

The confinement of finite beings by the ultimate conditions is one with the conveyance of Being beyond those conditions, to the extent that these act independently of Being. There never is more reality than that which Being has, but some of this is necessarily expressed as its possibility, some necessarily sustain and refer that possibility to it, and some must be conveyed by the ultimate conditions if, when, and to the degree that these jointly confine the singulars that own and express themselves through them. It is, I think necessary to restate this truth, again and again, in somewhat different ways, for the paradoxical reason that it is so obvious.

Being, the ultimate conditions, and beings have their own centers; neither the conditions nor the beings add to the reality that Being has, but they exist apart from and act in ways that Being does not. When the conditions act on their own, they reinstate Being to the extent that they do so. There is nothing but Being holding on to the ultimate conditions to the very extent that these necessarily act independently of it, both on its behalf and if and when they contingently act to confine singular beings. These might not have been. All beings might cease to be; if and when they do, the ultimate conditions will do no more than sustain and refer Being's possibility to it.

Being and the ultimate conditions necessarily exist; finite beings are the outcomes of acts by the conditions that might never have occurred. Theologians, and some philosophers, following the lead of Aristotle, Descartes, Leibniz, Spinoza, Hegel, and Whitehead, among others, will be inclined to substitute "God" for "Being," bypassing the question of whether this was or was not to be worshiped.

If a theologian substitutes "God" for "Being," he or she will take a stand between a theism and an atheism, holding both that the God is an eternal, self-contained reality deserving worship and that every finite being is that God miniaturized, without denying that each finite being has its own center, carries out its own acts, and expresses itself in and through instantiated ultimate conditions.

3. The Dynamic-Rational

Beginning with Descartes and reflected today in the views of distinguished logicians is the view that the formal, the intelligible, i.e., the Rational alone, has the range and ability to relate any being anywhere to anything anywhere else. The Rational, though, cannot account for actions, changes, passages, and inferences and therefore cannot account even for the acceptance of any proof of it or of anything else. A proof requires a passage from what is begun with to what is terminated at. A rigid deductive system, with one truth rigorously connected to others, allows for no move from any truth to another.

A formal system has no place for any passage. At best, it exhibits the frozen outcome of what had in fact been arrived at by carrying out some act. That act may be well controlled and move in a straight line from beginning to end, but whether it does this or not, it is not reducible to a set of rigid connections.

To think, to infer, to prove, one must begin at one position and move to another. The act may be kept within rigid confines, but whether it is or not, it will begin at some position, then move to and end at another. A proof that there is no passage, change, or movement gets in its own way, for it itself begins at some position and arrives at another, its conclusion.

Proofs, like other acts, involve passages. Even a simple negation involves one. No one saw this as clearly as Hegel did, though there is no need to suppose with him that what it ends at will be joined to is negative on a higher level where a new positive thesis will be matched by its negative until one ends at a final, and presumably the only, reality that there is.

As Kant saw earlier, recourse must be made to something other than the Rational in order to account for any passage, in or outside the mind, from an acceptable beginning to a certifiable end. A purely formal account has beginning and end together. We can start at a beginning only if we start outside where it is formally joined to a necessitated end. We can arrive at a justified conclusion only if we move to it as that which is endorsed by the necessitated end.

A sound inference starts with an endorsed beginning and ends with an endorsed outcome, but it may move from the one to the other in any one of an endless number of ways. Correct reasoning requires nothing more than that one begin with what is endorsed by what is formally accepted as a beginning and that one terminates with what is formally necessitated as the end. It does not prescribe how one must in fact move from the endorsed beginning to the approved end. One thinker may do this with great rapidity; another may do so only after wandering about for a while. Both will reason soundly if they begin and end at the same place. The move is dynamic, instancing the Dunamis, accepting and ending with what is Rationally certified.

The Rational is not a fixed condition that an alien Dunamis encroaches on. The two are always intertwined, but not always to the same degree. It is also possible to ignore one of them for a while in order to maximize one's understanding of the other. The Rational will still be qualified by the Dunamis, and conversely.

Those who acknowledge only the Rational allow no place for their acknowledgment or use of it. They cannot account for adventures, discoveries, inferences, or errors. Those who instead acknowledge only the Dunamis, such as Bergson, can never take a stand where they could refer to it, compare different parts of it, or show that any of their inferences are sound. In order for what is in one domain to be connected with what is in some other, a domain's characteristic set of conditions must be dunamically and rationally connected with those characteristic of the others.

The Dunamis is related to the Rational somewhat as individuals are to the conditions that confine them. It owns and expresses itself through the Rational. This, with the help of the Dunamis, makes its termini relevant to one another. The purest of transition begins and ends with what remains apart. Unless one could avoid all universals and therefore all laws, one must acknowledge the Rational. Unless one could avoid all passage, one must acknowledge the Dunamis.

A participation in and a presupposition of Being are not neatly separated from one another. Not only are they joined in Being as it is in itself, but even when they function independently, each is qualified by the other. Neither evokes emphatics in the other; indeed, each so imposes itself on the other that their differences in nature and functioning is emphasized. The two together are under the governance of dominant conditions in each domain and alone enable one to pass in thought or fact from one domain to another.

Question: This is incredibly obscure, or to speak kindly, it is very difficult to understand. Hartshorne, who has known you for about sixty years, has in effect stated that you are a twentieth-century obscurantist matching Hegel's opacities with your own.

Answer: Although I think Hegel's book on art orders the arts in a foolish way, supposing that architecture is the lowest form because it imposes ideas on brute matter, and although I cannot always see the reason why his dialectic takes the steps it does, I find his work filled with daring insights on crucial issues. I am not sure to what Hartshorne was referring since he gave no instances.

Q: What is clear, though, is that there were positions that you had once stoutly maintained and which you have now abandoned. Not only have you rejected what you once maintained about God in *Modes of Being,* but you have modified what you had previously affirmed about the Dunamis and have stopped making references to the Habitat, though this played an important role in your recent book. In this work, for the first time, you affirm that finite beings both presuppose and participate in Being.

A: I think these changes mark desirable advances and do not jeopardize the rest. It is absurd to think that one should not make advances on what one had once achieved, pulling back, canceling, and, where necessary, adding. I think it is still right to hold, as I have over the years, that there are a number of domains, that these are governed by ultimate conditions ordered in distinctive ways, and that there is an eternal Being. Each has its own distinctive ways of functioning; the full understanding of each requires that account be taken of the others. If I am wrong, I hope that what I have maintained will provide an occasion and a goad, making possible a better view. I do not see why, with everyone else, I should not both critically assess and correct what I have maintained.

Q: I think you have missed the point: I am not saying that you are wrong but that, at times, it is hard to understand what you are affirming.

A: I have not rewritten anything the hundred times that Plato supposedly did with the *Republic*. I now view what I have written as undoubtedly needing to be modified in many places, without jeopardizing its main thrust and its major claims. Try as I may, some issues remain more recalcitrant to clarification than others do. I nevertheless record them in the belief that what I now see obscurely others will see clearly, just as I now see clearly what others have seen obscurely. Along with everyone else, I want to assess critically, correct, and clarify what is being claimed.

It would take a lifetime to get anything about reality perfectly clear; those who have tried have ended with very little. I do not think we have learned much when we are told that the meaning of "life" is life, i.e., "life" without the quotation marks, or that "y says 'y'" is more precise than "I say 'y.'"

Q: No one should accept what you here claim?

A: Acceptance should come after a critical reading. I do that: each work has been subject to many rewritings, with some issues in better focus than others, without ceasing to be known as focal, and some of their major features and roles made evident. Clarification should follow discovery. There is not much to be gained by restricting oneself to the clarification of some terms. At the very least their sources and referents should be acknowledged before these are dealt with from some selected perspective. Analysis should be preceded by the acknowledgment of what is real and important; it cannot tell us what this is.

All that I claim is that pivotal realities have been noted, major connections identified, and explorations carried out without prejudgment, with some persistence, and with an alertness to crucial issues. It is, I think, all that any one could maintain about what could be achieved in a philosophic account. No one could do less without assuming much that needs to be examined, modified, and perhaps discarded. Advances will undoubtedly be made by those who subject a philosophic study to a careful reading that initially begins from other positions and proceeds along different lines. All the while, much may be found to withstand severe, critical study. Philosophers, like mountain climbers, can take advantage of one another's achievements, while remaining alert to their own limitations and the limitations of the others.

All that anyone could justifiably maintain is that an advance has been made on what had been previously done and ground prepared for further advances to be made. One thing seems certain: a refusal to deal with the whole of reality, the permanent and the transitory, Being and beings—and what connects the two—tacitly accepts what has not been examined but whose understanding may jeopardize what is claimed. At the very least pivotal realities must be acknowledged and their connections understood. When one attempts to do this, sooner or later, neglected truths (e.g., that Being is always presupposed and participated in, that ultimate conditions necessarily exist, that beings are Being miniaturized, and that there are emphatics that make a difference to that on which they impinge) will become evi- dent.

Q: It is still true that what you are maintaining is difficult to grasp or to warrant. You maintain, for example, that finite beings are miniaturized versions of Being, even though Being is eternal, self-sufficient and is both presupposed by and participated in by every singular.

A: If you approach something from different angles, you will find that you must characterize them in different ways. That will still allow for the acknowledgment that persons are different from but related to lived bodies and organisms, that they cannot be understood in the same way that humanized beings, natural beings, and cosmic units are, and that one can deal with all of these only if one acknowledges a Being beyond all of them that is both presupposed and participated in to some degree by every being.

Q: It is still true that what you are maintaining is difficult to grasp or to warrant. One reason is that you characterize them in a number of different ways. You hold, for example, that finite beings are miniaturized versions of Being, that they are other than Being, and those that are humans express themselves in and through such different channels as persons, lived bodies, and organisms.

A: A being, in relation to Being, has to be characterized in a different way from what it would have to be, as expressing itself in and through its different subdivisions, as related to different orders of conditions, or as related to other beings.

Q: Are you now maintaining, in some disaccord with what you once thought, that were a God to exist there would necessarily be a number of eternal realities that He produced that both sustain and refer His possibility to Him, as well as distinguish themselves from Him?

A: Yes. Some religions in fact refer to eternal angels or to lesser gods as utilizing what a supreme God produced. They hold views that are not in much disaccord with what is here maintained, but they also go beyond the point where understanding stops. One needs a faith to be able to identify the emphatics that enable one to move to a God as existing beyond Being and therefore beyond the point where understanding stops.

The references that Aristotle, Descartes, Leibniz, Spinoza, Hegel, and Whitehead, among others, made to what they called "God" were references to Being credited with powers that they had no way of knowing that it had. No one worships the God of any of them. Those who worship use emphatics that apparently are not available to any who are not pious, sustained by a faith, and thereupon able to move beyond the point that knowledge can reach. I am sorry that I have not always been clear about what now seems to me both obvious and undeniable.

Q: Critics of metaphysics maintain that Being is beyond the reach of knowledge.

A: What they mean is that it is beyond the kind of knowledge that is occupied with beings and their interplays. Once they ask themselves whether or not there is something presupposed by those beings and their interplays—or even, as we saw earlier, if they ask themselves about the nature of particulars or truth, they will find themselves occupied with issues that force them to attend to ultimate conditions, Being, and singulars, and they will become alert to the presence of emphatics, whose nature and roles deserve to be understood.

Until one can identify a divinely produced emphatic, there is no way of moving toward its source. What would then be learned, no one who has not done this could know. Some of those who refer to angels or lesser Gods hold views that are not much in disaccord with what is here being maintained about the ultimate conditions that exist when and as Being does and that always act as this requires.

I go much further than most who are religious in not only granting that there could be a God, but in maintaining that if there were one, He would be emphatically available everywhere, with different religions favoring some entries, under conditions that they define or control.

Q: In effect, you are offering a secularized and partially altered version of what others grasp in other and more arresting ways?

A: No. Although there are striking similarities between dominant religious as well as theological accounts and what is here maintained about what is eternal and presupposed, there also are great differences. Not only do the theologians rest their case on dubious historical reports, but they assume that what they claim is true. As a consequence they fall short of showing why or how there ever could be anything more than a necessarily existing Being. Everyone uses emphatics that make possible a move toward Being as presupposed; everyone, too, uses emphatics to begin or to increase a participation in Being's excellence.

Q: Why has this part of the subject not been examined?

A: In part, I think, because it is not common for theorists, though common for most others, to take account of what is reachable through adumbrations and discernments and of what may provide emphatics that may be imposed on others and enable one to move back to their sources.

Q: Presumably those who worship identify emphatics that enable them to move toward their divine source?

A: Yes. To say this is to place all religions on a footing.

Q: Why not do so?

A: Everyone of them objects. Each takes itself to provide the only, or at least the best way, for making emphatics supposedly due to God available for use.

Q: Why not ignore their special pleadings? Why not, with Lessing, take them all to be good paths leading to the same goal? Their different prayers and ways of worshiping could be accepted as equally valid. Just as different cultures use different languages, cuisines,

194

forms of address, and the like to carry out similar functions, so one could take different religions to be so many different ways of making divinely produced emphatics available. Formalists have long recognized that the Rational has a range that is not limited to any one domain. Do you differ from them on this issue?

A: No—so far as they have gone. Yes—if they suppose that no one could, should, or does go further. Usually, though, they fail to take account of the fact that there are a number of distinct domains in which the dominant condition is not the Rational, and that the Rational is never instantiated without being involved with the Dunamis. What is not evident is whether or not the two ever exist or function apart from one another. I have wobbled on the issue. The Rational has the kind of absolutivity that rationalists have taken it to have, but I am not confident that it is even then not provided with a vitality that enables it to stretch between alien terms. "*A*" entails "*A* or non-*A*" holds everywhere and always, but it could not do that unless the "or" began with at either the *A* or the non-*A* and ended at the other. The connecting of the two does not take time; it occurs when and as there is an *A* and a non-*A*. There is a power to a negative, as Hegel saw; there is also a power expressed in an entailment, demanding a required end.

Q: Your account of ultimate conditions as coexistent with though dependent for their presence on Being is suspiciously close to the views that some have expressed about subgods, or angels, and others about lesser gods.

A: There is a great difference between the two views. The ultimate conditions have neither wills nor desires. They carry no messages, and are instantiated only as conveyors and confiners of limited versions of Being.

Q: You speak with great confidence about a Being that at once is participated in, is presupposed, and is other than everything else and of finite realities as participants in Being, as presupposing and as other than it while able to be related to one another. You have not said this before.

A: I did not attend to Being in *Modes of Being*. I began to focus on it decades later, in *Being and Other Realities,* and then only as that which is presupposed and is the source of the ultimate conditions that are instantiated as confining the beings that own them. Only here have I acknowledged the fact that Being is both presupposed by and participated in by every other being. Only here have I stated that each being is both other than Being and related to other finite beings.

It is somewhat strange that it is usually expected that philosophers should present just one view and even carry it out in new areas but that they are not supposed, as are artists and scientists, to subtletize, to enlarge, and sometimes to abandon what they had once attempted when they used too small a canvas or when this was marred with holes and wrinkles.

A philosopher who identified him- or herself as one who has taken a position at some place and will not allow any issues to make him or her change what had previously been maintained in effect holds that fresh thoughts and radical discoveries are not to be expected from him or her and that at best one may expect suggestions on how some limited inquiry might be subtletized, expanded, or modified. No artist, scientist, or mathematician accepts that proscription. A systematic, speculative thinker is like them and therefore quite different from a defender of a view maintained against all challengers; criticisms are welcomed and critics applauded when they help free the thinker from limitations and help take care of gaps previously undetected.

Q: Many would accept some of the things you say, but they want to explore them in ways you do not.

A: I see nothing objectionable in doing that, though I think that if no attempt is made to provide a comprehensive, self-critical account, much will be ignored, and many limited truths misconstrued.

Q: You agree with existentialists in holding that there are persons?

A: Yes. To be a person, though, is not to be precluded from being an individual who owns and uses it, has a lived body and an organism, and knows truths about what is real apart from all of them.

Q: Pragmatists maintain that they are members of a humanized world.

A: They are right to do so, but they ought not stop short of asking what they presuppose, what everything participates in, and what exists outside the humanized domain. This does not mean that there may not be a distinctive way of matching the ways in which one might view them as personalized, as parts of nature, or as cosmic. One thing is becoming more and more evident: pragmatism, as now practiced, falls far short of doing justice to what is not in the humanized world.

Q: Didn't Dewey try to take account of every kind of reality and every basic kind of interinvolvement?

A: He did, and he did not. He tried to provide accounts of the nature of logic, mathematics, science, politics, education, religion, psychology, and art, little of which was found acceptable to those who had occupied themselves with these subjects. Still, I think he was right to do this; a philosophy should be interested in every major kind of occurrence and adventure.

One can, and sometimes should, replace what is entertained, not only with action, but with appropriate hopes and fears relevant to the needs of others and even with appreciations and insights into what things in fact are. One should stop not only to overcome what is in one's way, but to enjoy what is confronted, and to appreciate what realities are in depth. That should, as I make evident at the end of this work, lead one, among other things, to envisage a multifaceted pragmatism that has a number of specialized forms.

Q: Would it not be better to postpone such a venture until we had more knowledge, better groundings, and clear indications of what it ought to achieve? At the very least, would it not be better to wait until the subject of emphatics has been well mastered?

A: Not necessarily. Sometimes new advances will clarify what had remained obstinately obscure.

Q: Your account of the nature and finality of Being leads one to suppose that you are a Platonist. Are you?

A: Yes and no. With Plato, I hold that one can arrive at what is presupposed by whatever there be. I do not think, though, that Plato correctly stated or even intimated what this was. Also his "Receptacle," as I have already noted, in which eternal ideas could be received and sustained, is so weak that it would not be able to do more than retreat before the presence of his Ideas and could perhaps even be destroyed by them. I find difficulties too with what Plato says about poets and about politics, while learning much about other matters and about the need to push philosophic inquiry to its limits. While agreeing more or less with him about the reality of universals, I think they are different in number and nature from what he took them to be.

Q: Are you an Aristotelian?

A: Yes and no. I think Aristotle was right to identify a number of distinct domains but that he did not identify them correctly or understand the ways in which they were related. He did not see that the domains had come to be sequentially and that the reaching of one from another requires the use of the Dunamic-Rational. He supposed that we know other realities by adopting their forms, as freed from an apparently unknowable matter. He did not take account of adumbrative and discerning moves that can be made toward singular realities, and he did not see that a person, a lived body, and an organism are interrelated and also owned by an individual that is both the other of Being and participates in its excellence. We now know that he had too limited a view of logic, had misconstrued the relation of species to one another, and did not have a good grasp of the nature and presence of what he called "final causes." These are, of course, easy criticisms to make after some thousands of years of progress made in logic, biology, and other inquiries. Plato and he both have much to teach one today, even about subjects that are today pursued in different ways and with outcomes that were beyond their power to envisage. Many of our advances would not have been made were it not that they had offered accounts that were worth examining with care, even if only to be refuted and replaced.

Q: Are you a Thomist?

A: Yes and no. I think he was right to recognize that an understanding of finite beings requires one to recognize that nothing is just a union of matter and form, but that there is a possessor and user of them. He did not acknowledge that emphatics have a divine origin, did denigrate women, did not object to slavery, and never clarified what he meant by "transcendentals" or showed why these had to be. His God was perfect but still could be persuaded to change his course. Insufficient attention was paid to the need for and the natures of "angels," and he gave no adequate account of the claims of those medieval thinkers who were primarily occupied with understanding how one could participate in a primal excellence.

Q: Are you a Cartesian?

A: Yes and no. I agree with Descartes in thinking that every crucial idea deserves critical examination. He did not adhere to his program when he envisaged a deceiving devil or when he maintained that there is a God who honors as true only ideas that are clear and distinct. He had no clear and distinct idea of the devil or God or of the ways they act, though he made use of them to build his case.

Q: Are you a Spinozist?

A: Yes and no. I agree with him in holding that there is a reality that necessarily exists and necessarily does what it does. I do not see how he could know that this had an infinite number of attributes, how these were related to one another, or why we know only two of them. The Dunamis has no place in his account, precluding him from accounting for any inferences or from arriving at his God through something like an act of love, which he endorsed.

Q: Are you a Kantian?

A: Yes and no. I agree with him in holding that there is a depth in beings, but not that there is nothing to be found at the end. I think he was right to maintain that the ontological argument is faulty and that a study of Being is carried out in a different way from that which is needed to understand finite beings. I think he erred in using distinctions endorsed by logicians of his time, along with some embellishments that he did not fully justify, in order to define a set of categories encompassing all that could be known, and in his supposing that there was no way in which one could know an individual being. His criticism of the ontological argument supposedly shows that a necessarily existent God could not be derived from the possibility that there is a God. What he did not see was that there was a possibility that was needed by Being to sustain and refer Being's possibility to it. He could not account for the existence of his categories except by having recourse to a set of logical distinctions that could have been reduced or increased. They look as if they had been invented after he had decided that he needed twelve categories in order to encompass whatever was experienced.

Q: Are you a Hegelian?

A: Yes and no. I think Hegel was right to hold that if we acknowledge finite occurrences, we are able to begin moves that end in what necessarily exist. He was right, I think, to hold that a final reality is participated in by all other realities, but I do not think that they exist only within it. He began his *Phenomenology of Spirit* confessedly unable to acknowledge any "this" and therefore anything other than what was inside his supposed final reality. He did not show how any of the items caught up in his dialectic could ever have avoided being swallowed, without a trace left, by his final reality.

These comments are too brief and rough to do justice to the subtleties and insights of these great classical thinkers and the fact that I am greatly indebted to all of them and to others as well.

Q: There are many other thinkers I would like you to comment on, but I suppose it would help most if I asked about the one philosopher whom you have read extensively and with care. Are you a Peircean?

A: Yes and no. I agree with Peirce in holding that there are no issues that should not be critically examined. I think he unnecessarily confined himself by trying to deal with many basic issues by using just three categories, and he did not have a good understanding of humans as individuals or as members of a humanized domain. He did not provide a systematic, comprehensive view and did not subject his studies to radical criticism. He also skipped over many issues that deserved careful attention—emphatics among them. He is, I think, America's greatest logician and greatest original thinker. Royce deserves to be remembered because he was perhaps the first and surely the most appreciative of Peirce's contemporaries of the originality and greatness of Peirce as a philosopher. James was a lifelong and generous friend, but he was apparently unaware of Peirce's unusual range of gifts and of the magnitude of his contributions.

Q: Hartshorne has recently republished a number of his articles. They were preceded by an interrogation of him by a disciple who asked him questions about some of the historic figures now being mentioned. Did either of you know of the interrogations of and replies of the other?

A: The present set of question and answers comes after his was published, but his was preceded by those in *Being and Other Realities*. His and mine were carried out independently. Although the matter is of little importance, a comparison of the two sets of questions might have some interest for those who would like to see how friends—who have followed different courses over the years, who had some of the same teachers but have not been in close contact for decades, were familiar with a good deal of the same literature and worked together to publish the six volumes of the Peirce papers selected from the voluminous published and unpublished writing that the Harvard philosophy department bought from his widow some years ago.

It bothers me that Hartshorne refuses to answer crucial questions that his writings raise: Is no one ever responsible for any act or its consequences? Does nothing finite ever exist for more than atomic moment? Why are there any contingent occurrences? What kind of reality do laws have? When his defense of the ontological argument for the existence of God was shown to be untenable, he said that he had other proofs, but he has not told us what these are. Nor does he provide instances for his claims that almost every other thinker, including his accepted leader, Whitehead, engages in an apparently disreputable rhetoric.

Q: You may differ from one another on many issues, but you are one in ignoring what is at the forefront of current discussions. Neither of you pays much attention to the epistemological struggles and the answers proposed by contemporaries to epistemological questions.

A: Whitehead, in a little book, offered a minor variant of the current epistemological view and never showed how anything in the external world could be known. I do not know any place where Hartshorne has addressed the issue. I have done so in this work and elsewhere.

Q: You, more stridently than either, dismiss current epistemologists as narrow, perhaps otiose and evasive, assuming much that is not examined. Hartshorne scolds where you dismiss, but you are one in not dealing with their views in detail, hardly noticing their claims that they are being careful and precise and that they are appreciative of mathematical and scientific achievements and their claims of results achieved by carrying out careful examinations of the way language should be used.

A: I have tried to concentrate on crucial issues and have pointed up what I think are crucial, irremediable faults and failures in current epistemology. My objections are often in considerable accord with those made by Dewey and his disciples, while finding their alternative to have too narrow a range. It is possible that I have misconstrued some of those I have criticized, though I did try to examine them carefully and appreciate their strengths even when I concentrated on making evident their serious faults and limitations.

Philosophy is an adventure, alert to neglected issues and open to unexpected answers. At its best it carries out daring ventures and subjects its premises, procedures, and outcomes to radical criticism. It does not defend some dogma, no matter how defective it is found to be; instead it holds onto and benefits from the use of whatever is discovered. If one has a program or view that does not demand or permit a careful examination of what is presupposed or participated in, much that is questionable will be accepted, and much that deserves study will be neglected. That does not mean that the issues are unimportant or that they have vanished.

Q: Would it not be better first to master a good method, get firm groundings, and clear indications of what can next be learned? We have been beset by a number of supposed systems that have questionable beginnings, proceed in questionable ways, and end with what has not been shown to be.

A: These are serious faults. They are not to be attributed to the enterprise, but to their practitioners. If what is done is faulty in method and ends with what is unwarranted, it should be corrected if possible or else dismissed.

Q: Analysts, following Wittgenstein, want to begin with what they surely know, and then they want to proceed carefully, step by step, as far as they can go. They are dismayed by the irresolvable disagreements other philosophers have with one another, their grandiose and uncheckable claims, and their failure to proceed with meticulous care from one firm position to another.

A: When I began my graduate work, I was one of them, trying to use techniques and achievements as impeccable and irreplaceable. I began to move away from them in the attempt to answer questions that were ignored—even such an obvious one, as that which asked about the nature and role of the relation between $\emptyset$ and x in $\emptyset x$—while avoiding the faults of those who, like Hocking, leapt from one Himalayan peak to another in mysterious ways.

Avoiding both extremes, I have tried to begin with the acknowledgment of the fact that I am an individual being who exists for more than a moment, who owns and expresses himself through his person, lived body, and organism, who is responsible, who is taken to be accountable, and who is other than everything else. That has led me to attend to laws and other conditions and to that which enabled these to be, as well as to the emphatics that they produce and those that terminate at or in them.

I have now arrived at the stage where I can take a fresh look at the question of evil and wrong and be ready to see if there are other ignored but illuminating ways of looking at what is real.

Chapter 10

Evils and Wrongs

1. Evil and Wrong

E very reduction in value, intended or not, is wrong. Evils are intentional acts that reduce the value of those who produce them as well as what they affect. Every evil act is a wrong act, but many, perhaps most wrong acts are not evil. Both wrongs and evils have many degrees. Both can be subdivided into many kinds. Both presuppose a prospective, ideal good that could have been realized to a greater degree than they had enabled it to be realized. A refusal to try to realize what is good is at the root of evil. The finitude of the individual inevitably makes him or her do what is wrong.

No one can do all that ought to be done. Each must be content to promote and to approve acts that are less wrong than others would have been in the circumstances. If to do wrong is to be guilty, everyone is inescapably guilty for failing to do some of the things that he or she ought to have done. An individual may be occupied with producing a great good, perhaps one greater than anyone else would or could produce; he or she may promote happiness and health in many to an incomparable degree; or the individual may receive and may well deserve great rewards. Inevitably, though, he or she will neglect to attend to some things that are outside the scope of his or her attention and acts; inevitably each will fail to do all that needs to be done.

Some time ago, in the course of an examination of the biblical story of Job, I distinguished ten different kinds of evil—among them bad intention, wickedness, and vice. The ten were particularly relevant to that story. A different list is needed if evils are to be distinguished on the basis of their relevance to the existence and prosperity of persons, lived bodies, and organisms, or to societies, civilizations, the environment, humankind, and other important areas in which our obligations and failures are signally relevant and in which they could be illuminatingly classified and related. One way to provide it is to envisage any and all prospects as more or less, or as positively or negatively, instantiating a constant, possible Good constituted by the convergence of the ultimate conditions at a single end even when not engaged in confining actual beings. The outcome of every act would then be seen to promote, or even to preclude, the realization of that Good to some degree on that or other occasions.

The Good itself is too feeble to prevent the realization of any prospect, even one envisaged as radically destructive of what is of value. It is strong enough, though, to make the realization of any prospect that is other than it be deficient to some degree. Understood to be the point at which all the ultimate conditions converge when they exist apart from Being, the Good will always remain unrealized, no matter what is done by those conditions or to the singulars that these confine.

Evil is an emphatic that is expressed by one who seeks to destroy what should be preserved or enhanced. Not only is it what ought not to be, but it stands in the way of the realization of what is good. What is done may be needed as a preliminary or might even be necessary in order that a greater good be achieved but, if it is evil, it will still be evil.

To do good is to enhance or, at the very least, to preserve what is good. Those who torture others, blow up hospitals and schools, destroy what others rightly cherish, or abuse the defenseless sometimes think of themselves as freeing the world from what they take to be sources of evil, perhaps made evident by distinctive appearances, religious practices, institutions, and beliefs; by poverty; or for any number of other reasons that mark off some from most of the others. Whatever the reasons, the acts are evil.

Both the Communists and the Nazis were convinced that the Good could not be realized unless what they took to be evil was extinguished, despite their confidence in the inevitable realization of what they took to be good in the form of a perfect state, governing dedicated Communists or pure Aryans. It is not clear, though, whether or not they identified any of their own destructive acts as evil. Apparently they thought that what they did was needed and, so far, was at least instrumentally good.

If a wrong neglected or prevented the realization of good and enhanced whatever else there was, the existence of evil would raise an unsolvable problem. In the biblical story of Job, terrible acts are carried out by Satan, who is not only permitted but challenged by God to make Job's life as miserable as he could, for no other reason than to show Satan that Job's faith could not be shaken, no matter how great his sufferings. It is a terrible, shocking story, one in which a supposedly perfect being allows his adversary to kill Job's family and his slave/servants as well, to see if that would make Job lose or qualify his conviction that God is good and does only what is good.

Asked by Job to account for his miseries (but not for the annihilation of his family and for those who worked for him), God does no more than to say that His majesty and the reasons for what He does are beyond Job's ability to understand.

Job is not an attractive human being. His friends are conceited boors. The acknowledged God shows no sympathy, love for, or any interest in those who suffer and are wantonly destroyed. It is savage to suppose that new children and new helpers will somehow compensate for the willful slaughter of their predecessors. No concern is shown by Job or by God—or, indeed by any of the commentators I have read—about those whom Satan is permitted to destroy. In the end all questions of this kind are ignored, and Job's request for a reason is answered by God's reference to His incredible power and wisdom. No evidence is offered to show that He is just, rational, or good or has any interest in humans and their welfare. Instead He is portrayed as boastful, cruel, and inconsiderate, seeking to make a point that need not and should never have been made. Why should Job's faith be subject to terrible challenges underwritten by God? Why should God care what Satan believes? Why should innocent people who are associated with Job be destroyed? Is it right to allow them to be killed as a way to test the strength of Job's faith?

Twist and turn as we like, we are faced with the fact that Job is made to suffer and innocents destroyed for no other reason than that God wants to show Satan that Job has an unbreakable faith. In what? Surely not in God's wisdom, justice, goodness, compassion, or love. God's claim that He has His own reasons does not tell us anything more than that it is not for us to know why anyone, even a purported man of faith, should suffer, or why innocents should be destroyed.

Not all injuries, pains, or losses are unnecessary or inexplicable. Some are unavoidable. Like slight burns, some may provide needed warnings of great dangers. Some injuries are unavoidable outcomes in the circumstances; some sufferings may be desirable parts of a process of learning what is to be avoided on other occasions. The fact that discipline may be promoted by restraints, restrictions, denials, and defeats or that these may in fact help or prevent greater, undesirable occurrences in the future does not compromise the truth that some loss occurred. One who produced it, though not necessarily evil, did what was wrong, even if he or she also produced a great good.

Even when a small loss reduces the likelihood of a greater loss later and even when this is an inevitable part of a great good, it will still be regrettable. Both a poor and a fine landscaper will kill some plants and trees. Neither may do what is evil, but both will do some wrong. The latter, though, will use the wrong as an occasion for producing something as good or better.

Too ready a forgiveness may get in the way of someone becoming the person he or she ought to be—one who avoids doing evil things and also tries to make good whatever losses in value are the unavoidable accompaniments of his good acts. Overindulgence, a refusal to criticize, admonish, correct, help, or restrain, may not only fail to preclude undesirable acts and bad attitudes but may also encourage others to produce what may be worse in nature and outcome than they might have been.

"Sin" is primarily a religiously sanctioned term, referring to what opposes or ignores what some religion defines as good or what it takes to be a precondition for the attainment of that good as this is understood by religious authorities. It could have been avoided. Sometimes it is identified as a precondition for the attainment of what is good. There are theologians who speak of "Adam's fortunate fall," since it made Christ's incarnation a needed corrective. Some have supposed that it suffices, in order to live a perfect life, to do what some religion or religiously sanctioned work claims one should say or do. None can claim that all wrongs will be avoided, since some of these—neglect and insufficient control, particularly—end in unavoidable failures to say or do what should have been said or done.

Different religions have different lists of sins, and defenders of those religions sanction different acts that will erase or compensate for them. Each ignores some things that other religions take to be essential—often a distinctive profession of faith and the accompaniment of it with some distinctive gesture or act. Sometimes what one religion endorses another abhors. Christian men take off their hats when they pray; Orthodox Jews would never do that.

Emphatics identified by the adherents of one religion are rejected by the adherents of others, and a concern for and use of the objects in which those emphatics are taken to be available are dismissed as idolatrous. No matter how civil the defenders of one religion are to those who favor some other and no matter how much they coincide, each remains irreconcilably opposed to all the others, differing not only on what is to be included in a list of evils, but how these are to be avoided and what punishments they entrain.

It is not reasonable to think that there will be no more wars. They occur in every century. No matter what the day, there is perhaps no one who has lived when some war or preparation for war was not being carried out somewhere, often enough with the contestants claiming the sanction of some dominant religion or somehow to be defending it. It is also true that there have been terrible wars fought by those who accepted the same religion, as well as others fought by those who were indifferent to religious claims and actions. The ecumenical councils that have now superseded the violent and disparaging confrontations of religions in the past are unfortunately governed by an anemic politeness in which discussions of basic issues and differences are avoided or glided over to leave the contenders with little more than a presumed respect for the sincerity of those whom they think are profoundly mistaken.

Sometimes the sins that some religion identifies are indistinguishable from what a society or state condemns. "Wrong" covers a greater range than any of these acknowledge. It characterizes every neglect or minimization of what ought to be done, even if it is unavoidable and whether or not it interests a religion, a society, or a state.

There are some, among them the great Jesuit theologian Rahner and Pope John Paul II, who believe that their God's mercy is so great that it is possible, likely, or certain—just which is not made evident—that He punishes no one. There is a hell, they say, but they think that there may be no one in it. To keep in consonance with good sense and a healthy understanding of what is evil, they should have at least added that those infants and children whom the Nazis placed in gas ovens because of their ancestry are granted special privileges. The idea of Hitler and his followers eternally enjoying the presence of God alongside the innocents they slaughtered trivializes the evils Nazis intended and produced. A God who supposedly forgives everyone, no matter what is done, has too cavalier a view of evil to make Him recognizable by anyone who has a robust sense of what ought and ought not to be.

2. Disloyalty

A secular version of sin is exhibited by traitors, those who take bribes, or in other ways more or less act as some religions decree that they should not. An economically tempered version of this evil is supposed by Marxists to be characteristic of the capitalists they oppose. Sometimes it is said that the lives of those others are empty of meaning or that they express perverse, selfish, detestable habits or intentions. These criticisms are met by countercharges that the criticisms are the expressions of envy, timidity, befuddlement, or viciousness.

It is doubtful that there ever were many who never thought of doing or who never intended to do what loyalty requires. If there were, they would have to take themselves to be indebted to no one, no matter how much they had been helped. There are some, though, who are ungrateful, self-centered, and/or indifferent to others, but it is doubtful that they keep a constant course or that they are never responsive to any kindness or help. It is also doubtful that there ever were any who chose to act so that a lesser good was promoted when they saw that a greater, with no more effort, could be realized or its realization greatly advanced.

Some, perhaps most of those we take to be depraved human monsters trying to do great harm, think that they are doing what it is right for them to do at that time, for themselves, for others then or later, and/or some imagined worthy end. What they do is wrong, but they are not necessarily evil, unless they wanted to do what they knew ought not be done. Still, not even wars that are fought in defense of a homeland, culture, morality, tradition, or state or uprisings against dictators, tyrants, enslavers, the mad, the dishonest, and the corrupt could ever be freed from the taint of destroying some things that deserve to be preserved.

From the position of a final good that ought to be realized and whose realization everyone should promote, there is no one who is not a kind of secular sinner. Those who maintain that there will be a time when there will be no more religiously defined sinners are matched by those who claim that there will be a time when we will live as we ought, in perfect societies and states.

Given the finitude of humans, our limited knowledge, and our incomplete control of our persons, lived bodies, and organisms, it is not unreasonable to expect that there will never be a time when we will not fall short of doing what we ought to do for our families, friends, society, state, humanity, or even ourselves. The few who are said to have devoted themselves to promoting the realization of superlative goods that benefit others and who always act in the most desirable ways have to be credited with remarkable knowledge, splendid characters, fine habits, unusual insight, and great control. Supposedly they would be without self-centered thoughts and would never favor themselves over all others at any time—in short, not be like any known living human being.

3. Pain and Other Emphatics

One can read Dostoyevsky's story about the "underground man" as maintaining that some do what is evil because it gives them pleasure to show that they are individuals in command and that the claim can be well expressed in a rejection or a destruction of what others might cherish. I think that the "underground man" is instead emphatically pointing up the fact that each individual has a desirable value and may rightly insist on this over against the more familiar, socially approved goods that most of us seem to prefer to all others. From that standpoint, which the story seems to assume is well known and usually found to be acceptable, the underground man is an oddity who perhaps cherishes evil and pursues it for its own sake. From his position, he is insisting on the importance of a good that others minimize or neglect. He would usually be said to be envious and jealous or to like disturbing those who are harmlessly enjoying being together. In fact, he is emphatically making evident the nature of a human as a singular whose presence and rights are greater than any that could be achieved in the most convivial of situations.

The pleasure that some seem to find in torturing others, the determination to dominate by humiliating or by destroying what others cherish does not necessarily show that some seek and enjoy inflicting pain or by getting in the way of others' pleasure. They may take this to be an incidental part of the act of achieving a great good for many. To do evil one must unnecessarily preclude or destroy what is good.

No one does all the good he or she ought to do and presumably could do. All fail to recognize goods that are theirs for the taking—pleasure in nature's glories, the joy of learning, good conversation, friendship, admiration of great achievements and their sources, success achieved by oneself or others in difficult ventures. Each knows that he or she is unique, a being who is never reducible to any or all of his or her expressions. Few, though, are willing to accept the fact, in thought or in act, over against other claims made by state, society, family, or friends.

Even if, as some ancient rabbis claimed, it is better not to have been born and even if those who are responsible for the birth were held to have done what they ought not to have done, each of us is indebted to many others for many goods that they have made available and that have been accepted by us. Alone, unaided, none of us could have survived infancy. Whether one is advantaged or disadvantaged, there are goods that one ought to realize and payments that ought to be made. Not deliberately, often hardly noticed, all of us act in regrettable ways. We may or may not be aware of our indebtedness to others or that we could have acted in other and better ways. We may be responsible for no evil and may have done all that we could do to preclude it. Yet no matter how good we are in intent and in act, we neglect doing some things that ought to be done, and we often do some things we should not have done. We will, so far, allow for and be responsible for doing what is wrong.

Given any prospective good, we may know no way to obtain it, except by ignoring some warranted demands and by using means that we do not altogether control or always know how to use in the best possible way. No one knows exactly what will and what will not benefit others. The outward signs of suffering often fall quite short of conveying the anguish that is being lived through. We may sympathize, console, relieve, help, and even try to compensate for debilitating experiences, as well as for losses undergone by others, but no matter how acute and penetrating our discernments, we never experience what another is undergoing.

It has been said that if a woman could recall the pain that she had suffered during childbirth, she would never, despite the incomparable joy of seeing an infant that had just emerged from her body, want to have another child. The forgetting is a blessing, but it does not eradicate the fact that the pain occurred. There is an undeniability to pain, a forced focusing by one's person on what one's organism or lived body, and sometimes on what subdivision of these, undergoes. If some animals feel pain, as they sometimes seem to indicate that they do, they must own and be affected by a simulacrum of the kind of person that humans have. This does not mean that they will have wills or the ability to speculate or that they could vary the degree to which they participate in Being's excellence.

A pain is an emphatic that one's organism imposes on one's person. A wrong is an emphatic reflecting someone's failure to attend to rights and needs. Evils are emphatics that unnecessarily reduce the value of that on which they intrude. Their production is not usually accompanied by any pain and may express a strong and warming desire. When a responsibility for an act is accepted, the perpetrator acknowledges that he or she did what ought not to have done.

If the fact that a person, lived body, and organism are owned and used by an individual is ignored, we would be faced with no less than three unsolvable problems: a person–lived body problem, a lived body–organism problem, and a person-organism problem. The notorious "mind-body" problem usually focuses on a subdivision of the last. All are solved, or rather dissolved, once it is remembered that an individual is a being who not only owns and expresses him- or herself through all three but who can also use the lived body as a sign of the person for the organism or conversely use the organism as a sign for the person. Unavoidable wrongs originate and are suffered in any one of the three.

Neither a lived body nor an organism does what is evil, though either may so act that values are unnecessarily reduced. Evils are intended. They depend on acts of will and may or may not be backed by bad habits and misconceptions of what is at stake.

It is questionable whether or not anyone does or could concern him- or herself with doing what is evil, if he or she did not anticipate its being accompanied or followed by a possible enhancement of what is cherished. One might imagine that there is a devil who enjoys doing evil for no other reason than that it is evil. Sometimes it is said that there are humans who are no more than miniaturized versions of such a being, but they would then have to be less complex, with different impulses and desires than humans in fact have.

If what humans ought to do could provide them with no satisfactions, one would have to take them to be no more than machines that indifferently destroyed what was valuable. To intend, to desire, to want, no matter how this is misconstrued, is to seek what presumably will satisfy and, so far, is good.

4. Suffering

When one's acts are primarily affected by one's character, what is done is qualified by a virtue or a vice. No positivistic, analytic, or linguistic study of what is said or done could therefore do justice to the presence of either. Having no place for emphatics, they could not know that what was said or done could be overlaid by what has its major source in one's character.

Not only ethics, but morality with its permissible and forbidden acts as well, plays a role in the humanized world. Both use and produce emphatics. Societies and states, though, are mainly concerned with morality, tinctured here and there by an awareness of ethical issues. Taking the sources of undesirable and desirable acts to be lived bodies, they identify virtues and vices as habits that are expressed in and through public acts, while using a language that will usually have seeped in and carries forward long-entrenched traditions and beliefs. Whether one is virtuous or not, some suffering is unavoidable. Understood as that which is consciously undergone, it unavoidably involves a person, usually as interinvolved with a lived body or organism. There are some sufferings that are traceable to one's awareness of a supposed or actual status or role in one's group, society, or state, but one could also suffer from anything that slighted one's imagined, assumed, or actual position relative to others.

Suffering may be personal, lived through, organic, emotional, short-term, or long-term. At all times it exhibits an unwanted subjection to what precludes pleasure and serenity. It is sometimes said that there are those who enjoy their suffering or at least enjoy telling others about it, but that enjoyment or communication leaves it untouched though sometimes momentarily or partly overlaid by what is less disagreeable.

Sometimes an effort is made to show that suffering is beneficial, making one aware of one's finitude and faults and perhaps of hardships undergone by others that otherwise would not have been noticed. Whether or not it is a prelude to great goods otherwise not obtainable, it is not itself desirable. Not often considered in discussions of evil and wrong, except where it is inflicted without warrant—perhaps in an effort to express control, elicit submission or to test fidelity, perseverance, determination, and the like—it precludes good acts that could have been carried out.

There are a number of basic types of suffering—personal, physical, lived, or social. There are those who suffer some of these because they have been denied opportunities or alleviations. Fear sears the expectations of many, often making them suffer in anticipation, and when the anticipated arrives, sometimes for periods after that. In different ways all subject us to experiences that are more or less indifferent to what we want, should have, or could have.

Great or minor sufferings may accompany the realization of what is good, somewhat as strain and pain sometimes do when one carries out a difficult act. When great goods are obtained at little or no price, they are not usually appreciated to the degree that they otherwise might. This is but to say that suffering may have an instrumental value; it does not compromise the truth that, as undergone, it is not desirable.

Those who are aware of the value and promise of some things sometimes suppose that they are justified in ignoring and sometimes in opposing other insistent demands. Some so cherish themselves that they resent any claim that is made on behalf of a family, group, society, or state. Others devote themselves to one of these at the expense of the rest and sometimes of themselves. No one but a perfect being would be able to give each claimant its full due at all times and places. No actual person has sufficient knowledge or control to do that. There are some, though, who are so concentrated on a part of an important whole that they effectively force other rightful claimants into the background. The extreme cases are due to a vice. Others are wrongs, reducing values, perhaps as a consequence of an unavoidable neglect, carelessness, or ignorance. The status of neither is necessarily reduced when regretted or even when efforts are made to recompense for them.

Wrongs are sometimes emphatically identified. When they are, the expressions of the emphatics may shock and unsettle those who take no notice of the motivations and partial justifications that may have prompted the acts. In some accord with Dostoyevsky's "underground man," one may make one's feelings, emotions, passions, singularity, and self-awareness so evident that it becomes patent that almost everything else has little comparable value. What seems minor or shameful when one is enjoying comradeship, and common, harmless pleasures is brought forward as more vital and thus of greater importance. The "underground man" gave expression to this; the rest of us do not, or at least not so violently.

Sometimes in self-defense, one who destroys eminently desirable goods or who precludes their achievement will claim that a greater good will thereupon be achieved or promoted. The claim is sometimes made on behalf of really great prospective goods whose realization may more than compensate for the losses involved, somewhat as a painting may be justified for its using up paints and canvas, and its minimization of some parts so that the whole is enhanced. A similar claim is sometimes made by tyrants, haters of foreigners, racists, and bigots of other sorts, and so on down a long, depressing list. Sometimes it is held that this is the most efficacious, the most expeditious, or even the only way to achieve a great good. There is little evidence that it is.

There are some who speak of "just wars." It is hard to find any. Even the Nazis were initially fought not because of the evils they produced and those that they were prepared to add, but because they violated a treaty. It is indeed fortunate that the two world wars ended as they did, but it would be naive to suppose that they were wars between those who were bent on doing evil and those who were determined to stop them for that reason. Neither side aimed at the achievement of a good for all. The Emancipation Proclamation did not free the slaves in those states that remained on the side of the Union during the Civil War. It was a needed, great first step, deserving praise, but it was not without its note of punishment for seceding states.

On behalf of a society, state, ideal, tradition, morality, or religion, one might try to justify an opposition to a destruction of goods that had already been or that might yet be achieved. Those who are threatened or attacked may have been dedicated to producing a greater good than what could have been achieved by those who opposed them. That, of course, does not assure their victory.

There are those who speak of benefiting all, or at least those who are identified as worthy of receiving benefits if only because they have a favored ancestry, citizenship, color, wealth, power, education, and/or religion. It is hard to know whether or not they are deluded, actually believe what they say, and know what their acts are intended to support. More likely than not, they do not understand the import of what they decided to do, or allowed to be done.

One does what one ought to be done if one realizes a good that is greater than that which could otherwise have been achieved and possessed. The realization of claims of other components is also needed, if the best outcome is to be obtained. What is overlooked or precluded may be the result of a concentration on otherwise neglected or unduly minimized factors. This does not mean that it may not involve a neglect or a minimization of others. To be successful here and now, we must neglect some demands, and therefore must fail to do some things that should be done. Only an omniscient, omnipotent being could always act as it ought.

Without concentration, with its inevitable slighting or neglect of what is not focal or essential, it is not likely that anything great could be achieved. Everyone minimizes or overlooks what promotes or preserves what ought to be. A needed concentration on this or that does not mean that one is not wrong if one ignores the merits, prospects, and claims of anything else. The fact that it is impossible to do all that ought to be done does not absolve anyone from the charge of having neglected what should have been done.

5. Heedlessness

Heedlessness is both unavoidable and regrettable. Not intended, perhaps deplored, it is chargeable to everyone, no matter how noble the aim, how great the success, and how inescapable the neglect. Wrongdoing, in the form of an unavoidable heedlessness of the needs, rights, and demands that cannot then be attended to even by the most adroit, governed, and powerful, entails a tacit acceptance of an obligation to do what still needs to be done. This is but to say that one is obligated not only to make good the losses that one had caused, but also those that result from the neglect and use of some things when one is occupied with doing something else that ought to be done. It does not justify a Rousseau's sending his children off to an orphan asylum, expecting a society or state to do what he should and could do. There is a great difference between an unavoidable heedlessness due to one's inability to deal with a situation as well as it deserves and a heedlessness that is due to an indifference, though both fail to promote goods that ought to be realized.

One has a right to insist on oneself as an individual whose person is precious, deserving to be cherished and expressed. Whether this is focused on or not, some just claims will be neglected. The fact that one is engaged in promoting goods, perhaps even some that are more important than those which interest others, does not cancel the fact that one is neglecting the rightful claims that could have been promoted or should have been satisfied.

Although it is not intended, a heedless act emphatically intrudes on a number of otherwise neglected objects. Like the emphatics that are due to Being, the ultimate conditions, and singulars, the neglect that heedlessness expresses requires no intent and may also be regretted.

It is not possible to avoid doing wrong, if only in the form of an unavoidable neglect of what deserved attention, preservation, or promotion. The issue would be faced more directly were advantage taken of the way Aristotle dealt with the virtues. Tendencies in one direction are to be promoted by undergoing a training that ends in the acquisition of habits in which opposing tendencies limit one another. That view, if modified so that it is relevant not just to habit or to the training of the young and well born—and if account is taken of a considerable number of other habits—promotes the avoidance or the reduction of some wrongs. Failures to attend to some justified demands can also be reduced by cultivating the practice of finding a position where appropriate weight is given to more relevant and important items.

Instead of trying to avoid extremes by incorporating aspects from contenders in a single habit or in a fine way of functioning, one should try to achieve a position that allows for the realization of maximum good. The wrongs that cannot then be avoided are to be compensated for by providing the neglected existences and functionings.

Each individual, even while concentrating on what should be produced, or on what is, is obligated both to do what he or she can and to make good his or her neglect of what should have been dealt with appropriately. At the very least, the individual should identify others as his or surrogates, emphatically crediting them with the obligation to do what he or she had failed to do.

What is to be realized is not just what is focused on and that one might be able to realize in a more successful way than others could, but what also promotes the realization of other goods that one could not then achieve and that may not even have been envisaged. Everyone has an obligation to try to make what is being neglected be dealt with later by him- or herself or by others. To the extent that this is not possible, each has an obligation to support those who are able to do what he or she did not do and perhaps could not have done. All moralities, and an ethics as well, build on the fact that an obligation is an emphatic that is imposed on each individual by others and on others by each of them. Even the most splendid of acts demands compensatory moves, expressed initially in the form of commitments to promote the goods that are being neglected or to enable or support those who will most likely then will deal with them in the ways they deserve.

One reduces the charge of doing what is wrong by accepting oneself as a sustaining member of a group in which some of one's failures are matched by successes achieved by others. One can also reduce it by promoting the realization of goods that one could not then realize and that he or she may not even have envisaged. Each, therefore, should recognize the obligation to try to have what is neglected be subsequently dealt with. If this cannot be done, each should recognize that he or she has an obligation to support those who are able to do it. Vice is a persistent source of emphatics that reduces the value of that on which it intrudes.

In addition to other reasons for being a contributing member of one's society, such as safety, care, training, fellowship, and support, there is the need to have others do some of the things that one could not do at that time or place and perhaps could not do at all. We are obligated to do all the good we can and to promote the goods that were neglected or were improperly dealt with by others. In addition we should support those who will more likely deal with those goods in better ways than we have dealt with them and perhaps than we ever could. The fact that a neglect is unavoidable does not mean that it is not wrong or that a wrong is thereupon reduced. One is obligated to sustain and to help others promote what good they can and is obligated to sustain and to help those who could realize what one had to neglect.

The best of acts is set in a context of omissions and neglects. We rightly praise any who promise to support those who will at least try to do all they can to realize the greatest good then realizable. What is too often overlooked is the fact that the promise is implicitly made by everyone. Each of us is dependent on others to do what we neglect or deal with inadequately.

Obligation defines what otherwise would be accompanying or merely future as subject to demands made on us but which we did not and perhaps could not satisfy. It is therefore not altogether correct to hold that all wrongs, or even all evils, are due to failures to exercise sufficient self-control. One may misunderstand much, but even what one does understand involves some neglect; the best of acts is set in a context in which only part of what should be done is or could be done.

When expressed as an obligation to provide or to compensate for what ought to have been done, the wrong of heedlessness is turned into an obligation which requires that all condemnation be held in abeyance. Although the charge of guilt for failing to do what ought to be done or could have been done is thereupon deferred, one would still be guilty. Whatever wrong was done, in any case, has its condemnation canceled when the obligation is satisfied by others, provided that these are accepted as one's agents or surrogates.

As long as there is a future and humans are interinvolved with one another, able to make up for the slack that is inseparable from a concentration on the production and preservation of what is good, an unavoidable heedlessness will make evident some of the things that others ought to do. Since they, too, will be heedless of some things, heedlessness will never be eradicated.

The wrongs that could not be avoided are to be compensated for by providing the needed factors and functionings. Each person is a member of a single humankind in which the good that he or she should have but could not have done is to be produced. If we have no successors, there will, of course, not be anyone to do what we could not. Nevertheless it will deserve to be done.

Unable to do all that we ought and required to do some of the things that others failed to do, we continue to benefit from what others achieved. The good that anyone does is so little, though, compared either to what was received or to what one ought to do, that it would not be amiss to call a human "the irremediably guilty being," hopelessly mired in debt even when contributing to the good of a group and, incidentally, to the good of its members and perhaps others as well. What he or she does may not be appreciated, but as long as he or she is one among others, sustaining and perhaps adding to commonly available accumulations and opportunities, some recompense for unavoidable heedlessness is possible.

A despot might take observations like these not only to justify the demands that are made on others to sacrifice themselves for the glories that will supposedly ensue, but to justify any number of onerous demands made on the young to be ready to sacrifice themselves for the good of the country or for the glorious world that supposedly will ensue and to justify any number of onerous demands made on all. The world the despot envisages, though, will be occupied by other heedless individuals. No societal good ever could fully compensate for what had to be neglected. Each has him- or herself to perfect. In addition each is indebted to those who made it possible for him or her to be part of a world from which much can be obtained that is needed in order for each to become the person he or she ought to be and to do the things that ought to be done.

A commendable response to the wrongs each does because of involvements in the production of some other good would be forgiveness. One would then underscore the fact that some failure was unavoidable. That, of course, will not wipe out the fault, nor will it compensate for it. It is also questionable whether or not anyone has or could have the right to forgive the acts without overstepping one's limits as an individual within a group. Each is a moral and an ethical failure in a world one did not make.

A wrong might be produced by someone who was no more than a vehicle for carrying it out. Though not responsible for it, that person would still be condemnable and might even be held to be accountable for it because he or she was found to be where the deplorable act or an unavoidable omission occurred. Education, punishment, and protest might lead to an improvement in behaviors; they will not preclude or eradicate all such wrongs.

Splendid humans, well-ordered societies, and well-governed states may help all to become better. Some have made some progress in helping the guilty. They have, to date, not achieved much. Prisons are a governing body's confession that it does not know how to prevent the need for them.

Suffering is personally undergone. Depth searching and intentional moves into a perpetrator show a greater respect than a light, careless punishment or an indifferent forgiveness could. They are also more sensitive than a detached act of mercy or kindness is, since they respect the singularity of the perpetrator, even honoring him or her as one who was a primal source of what was done. No forgiveness, of course, could ever distinguish the evils that one had produced or the wrongs that one's acts inescapably entrain. This does not mean that there is no difference between heinous and indifferent acts. There is no known way to compensate for a murder; wrongful imprisonments, exile, torture, or deaths. Compensations might express emphatics, but they cannot, givin the nature of the case, do more than provide convenient ways for expressing the judged, public value of a loss.

We may be forced to choose between undesirable alternatives, and we may look to others to do that which we ought to have done but which we could not do because we were occupied with doing something else that was right for us then to do. We can do no better than to try to make up for what we had reduced in value or for neglecting rightful demands, having been forced to do so in order to realize some other, perhaps eminently desirable good. This does not mean that we must ignore or resist our predilections or that we should alter what we are doing.

It is perplexing to an outsider to hear some stoutly maintain that there is a full human at the moment of conception and then refuse to baptize it. Even Thomists do that today, quietly abandoning Thomas's claim that male embryos are divinely endowed with immortal souls only later, and female embryos some weeks after that. Thomas, of course, did not know that God placed a soul inside each embryo and surely did not know that He took account of the gender of the embryo before He acted or that He ignored the likelihood or, from His perspective, the certainty that a terribly distorted child would be born that would die at the moment of birth.

We know embarrassingly little about some very important things—when a fertilized human egg becomes one of us, what the extent of its initial obligations are, or when it is that it has, and expresses itself as, a person. In the end it will be tradition, common practices, convenience, the prevailing morality, and the state that will make practical, enforceable decisions about these and related issues. They will also determine what must be done to avoid, at least in part, some outcomes of some wrongs and evils. Whatever position is adopted by the courts, the people, or a religion on the practice of abortion, we can now justifiably do little more than grant that a fetus is an incipient human that may, in less than nine months, express itself through three channels, one of which, the lived body, may be used as a sign linking the other two and be interinvolved with other members of the humanized world.

For some it suffices to do what is supposedly commanded by an accepted God or, more precisely, by what is said by those who claim to speak on His behalf. Yet there is no one, pious or learned, who, purportedly chosen by this God, does all that is required or who never does anything that this God is said to forbid. Even the demand that we do nothing but attend to some commands of some religion's acknowledged God or that we obey the laws supposed to have been promulgated by Him falls short of what is required if maximum good is to be achieved.

A demand that one give oneself to the service of a God always contains a hidden note to the effect that one must try to keep oneself strong and well enough focused to be able to do so. A religion that demands that we do nothing but attend to some supposed divine command or that we obey the laws supposedly laid down by Him may offer a good, general guide for the ways we are to conduct ourselves, but it will still fall short of what is required if maximum good is to be achieved. That does not mean that it could not or does not help some to live good lives, or at least better ones than they would have led otherwise.

Those who live in accord with the demands of some religion may not look elsewhere for guidance. Indeed they usually find, to their astonishment and discomfort, that the emphatics that they take their God to have made available are in fact ignored and even denied to be present by many, some of whom are also religious.

Idolatry is the charge leveled against those who take some things, that others do not, to be where an object of worship has made itself emphatically present. If this were the creator of all else or if this were interested in whatever else there was, it would, though, not be unreasonable to suppose that it expresses itself emphatically in and through everything else.

Humans could be viewed as emphatics only if and so far as they were identifiable as intruding on what already exists and were making possible a movement to the source of these emphatics. Were they no more than the products of an evolution, they, and preceding kinds of beings as well, would not have the status of emphatics unless and so far as they were intruded on something that sustained them. In any case they now can emphatically intrude on what they had themselves had helped constitute.

Both what is stressed from the "underground" and from the positions that find ready accommodation in the humanized world deserve expression, with the one purged of most of its violence and disdain and the other of its smugness and trivialities. The anger of the one and the indifference of the other makes evident that they had failed to attend to what they could and should have considered.

The outcomes of both an avoidable and an unavoidable heedlessness define others as required to do what had not been done. Everyone of us, even the most saintly and generous falls far short of doing all that should be done. Neither the "underground man" nor those whom he despised took adequate account of the complex nature of humans. The shock that the former's expressions initially produces is only partly due to the fact that the emphatics and their sources are usually neglected, sometimes disowned.

Thomas Aquinas knew that there was an "existence" beyond the accepted form and matter that was commonplace for the Aristotelians of his day. He never sufficiently explored this insight, leaving it to modern existentialists to identify it with a radical subjectivity from which no one can escape. With the "underground man" they fail to do justice to those against whom they revolt, and they fail to attend to the emphatics that individuals express again and again in many different objects as well as in many different places and at many different times.

All of us have obligations that far outrun our abilities to satisfy. All of us are necessarily heedless, failing to do what deserves to be done. Necessarily failing to do what we ought, we are at fault, if only because our task is greater than any that we could carry out. Each must look to others to do what he or she ought to have done but could not. Necessarily and emphatically each accepts them as surrogates who are to do what he or she could not do, although obligated to do so.

It is not easy to determine if what one does is primarily due to the use of one's character or to one's habits, particularly since the former makes use of the latter. A character is singular and steady, though not beyond modification; habits are many and may be qualified, supplemented, strengthened, or overridden by the expression of a strong character. Where habits are primarily geared to acts, a character is primarily directed toward goals. Neither precludes some wrongdoing since at the very least its use involves a neglect of other acts needed to achieve desirable outcomes.

One's character is modified over the course of a life, with some tendencies strengthened and others weakened or curtailed, usually without one being aware of what is occurring. Habits, in contrast, may be useful or useless or may promote good or bad acts. Despite a common practice the habits should not be characterized as good or bad. They are means making it likely that a certain outcome that accords with what the character demands be promoted or precluded.

When we concentrate on meeting a demand in some place or at some time, we will necessarily neglect our obligation to preserve or enhance what there is elsewhere. Each of us has obligations that far outrun our ability to satisfy them. Each of us necessarily fails to do what deserves to be dealt with.

No one can attend to everything. No one has the ability or even interest or inclination to do so. Every one of us is inescapably heedless. In addition we are heedless because we are not properly prepared to act in such a way that others are benefited, to the degree that they would have been had they been focused on. A solitary, alone in a wilderness, living on what nature might happen to have made available, will not last long or be able to carry out a difficult mission if he or she does not help provide at least what is needed by that on which he or she depends. More still has to be done, but no matter what is done, that solitary will still be unavoidably heedless and will neglect doing what could be done to enhance others.

The "underground man" did not think of the fact that he depended on, and should have in some way taken heed of the needs of others who made it possible for him to eat, drink, grow, rest, be protected against the elements, and so on. Heedless of the merits and desserts of those who cherish other goods, he was also heedless of those who, unknowingly, made it possible for him to concentrate on his own sensibility and its expressions. He did what was wrong, all the while that he rightly insisted on expressions by a person, character, and/or being that others find it improper to express.

A society is an interinvolved multiplicity of humans who are obligated to do what others both necessarily and unnecessarily neglect. Each member satisfies obligations in part by recompensing for what others are forced to bypass in order to meet their own obligations.

There is no one realizable good that justifies the neglect of others. When we concentrate on any, we must make possible a compensation for what we had been forced to neglect. Although we do not demand that an animal do what it cannot do, we do, and we should demand that a human do what ought to be done, even though he or she may not then be able to do it.

A needed concentration on the preservation and satisfaction of one's person, lived body, and organism is inseparable from the obligation to make good whatever losses in value are traceable to an unavoidable neglect, even if this is regretted. It makes little or no difference that some of our regrettable acts are not intended. We are obligated to so what is rights. Unavoidable ignorance, miscalculations, bad judgments, lack of control, the limits of our powers, and the brute fact that we cannot be in many places at the same time do not affect our obligations. These are not measured by what we can do.

There is no one particular good that justifies the neglect of all others. When we concentrate on any, we must make possible a compensation for the achievement of what we had been forced to slight or ignore. It makes no difference to our obligation that the neglect is the result of an unavoidable ignorance, miscalculation, bad judgment, lack of control, or even the brute fact that we cannot be in a multitude of places at the same time. That does not mean, of course, that there is no difference between one who fails to do all he or she ought, simply because he or she is finite, and one who does not do all that could be done in a particular situation.

Even those who had in fact achieved or were dedicated to the production of a greater good than that sought by those whom they oppose could be bent on doing not what benefits others but what benefits themselves alone or a chosen few. Criticisms of them are often ignored or dismissed. It is hard to know if some believe what they say or are just confident that whatever they maintain is true and that what they seek is well worth the price that must be paid to obtain it.

One does what ought to be done if mutually enhancing factors are jointly realized in a good that is greater than any other that is then realizable. What will be overlooked or precluded may be the result of a needed concentration on an otherwise neglected factor or the result of one's not being in a position to do what ought to be done. That leaves the obligations still in place. Since there may never again be an opportunity to do exactly what is required, the obligations must have a form that allows for satisfaction in other ways as well. To be obligated is to be required to allow for, invite, or produce that which is to receive it.

Doing what ought to be done ends in an emphatic addition to what is achieved. No emphatic need be expressed in the form, way, or place one may request or want it to be. Even emphatics elicited from humans may not be expressed in the way one may have requested or wanted. Again and again one regrets having asked someone to offer a toast, tell a joke, repeat a story, or to convey one's sympathies.

Sometimes, in self-defense, someone who destroys an eminently desirable, commonly recognized great good or who prevents its realization will claim that a greater good will thereupon be realized. On behalf of a society, state, tradition, morality, or religion, one might try to justify a destruction of what already had been achieved as providing the most efficacious, the most expeditious, or the only way to achieve a great good. Too often there is little evidence that the results are worth the sacrifice. Whether they are or are not, the outcome will result from a meeting of an emphatic with what provides this with a lodging that may distort, reduce, or reject it. Emphatics that destroy that on which they intrude are like forest fires. They cannot be sustained.

It is not altogether correct to hold that all wrongs, or even all evils, are due to an individual's insistence on his or her uniqueness or freedom. If they were, the insistence would be due to an error in self-understanding. Much, of course, may be misunderstood, but it may still be wrong, just so far as it invites a neglect of what is needed if what ought to be is to be realized. When we focus on an expression of ourselves, some provision should therefore always be made for taking care of what then had to be neglected.

Neglect is turned into a deferment if it is expressed in an obligation to provide or to compensate for what was not then done. A charge of guilty would still be justified. "Guilty" would then be an emphatic, requiring the expression of another emphatic that ends with the preservation or enhancement of what compensates for what had been reduced in value.

Kant's categorical imperative is an emphatic that is imposed on a person, presumably by him- or herself and thereupon affects what he or she might decide to do. Its acknowledgment depends on the supposition that each human knows what he or she would have others do for that person. It would have been more useful were it stated negatively: do not do what you would not want anyone to do. That, of course, would still require one to have self-knowledge. Apparently Kant expected that individuals would open themselves up to such demands as "know thyself" and "cherish and express what you are in depth, as one among others."

It is tacitly assumed that the Kantian imperative is self-imposed. Could an unethical being want to do that? Could it be done if one were not an ethical being? Is it anything more than a way of alerting one to the fact that an ethical being is one who determines what is to be done by understanding what he or she would like to receive? Evidently Kant thought that each human knows what he or she would like to have done to or for him or her and that this is what others would like to have done to and for themselves.

No one can attend to everything that ought to be attended or do so with the degree of attention that a successful outcome requires. We are obligated to enhance or, at the very least, to preserve whatever good there be, but when we concentrate on meeting that demand in some particular place or time, we will necessarily neglect obligations to preserve or enhance what is elsewhere.

Each human has obligations that far outrun the ability to satisfy them. Each is necessarily heedless, failing to do what deserves to be done. A society is an interinvolved multiplicity of humans who are required to do what others there both necessarily and unnecessarily fail to do.

We are obligated to preserve or enhance whatever there is, but when we concentrate on meeting that demand in some place or at some time, we will necessarily neglect our obligations to preserve or to enhance what else there is. It would therefore not be amiss to refer to heedlessness as never separable from what ethically or morally fails to provide or to compensate for what has been neglected. The ascription of guilt can be justified and punishment prescribed only in cases where neglect could have been reduced.

Insensitivity points up a failure to attend to crucial differences, but, despite its common recognition in daily life, it is rarely focused on. One does all that one ought to do, if one reduces the range and injury that an unavoidable heedlessness entrains. Heedlessness should be turned into a deferment of acts that ought to have been carried out.

Both avoidable and unavoidable acts of heedlessness entail a tacit acknowledgment of others who are to do what one does not, and perhaps could not, do. We provide some evidence of that acknowledgment in acts of acceptance of what is worthy of consideration, preservation, attention, or enhancement. This is but to say that what we had to neglect is the object of an obligation not yet satisfied. All of us have obligations that far outrun our ability to meet them.

We hold ourselves and others to be responsible, not just accountable, for some acts and omissions. We may be taken to be accountable for acts and outcomes for which no one holds us responsible and to be responsible for acts and outcomes for which no one holds us accostable. Responsibility is assumed by persons; accountability is determined by authorities. Temporal atomisms have no place for either. Heedlessness, though unintended, always adds to one's responsibilities but may not add to one's accountabilities. Insensitivity points up a failure to attend to crucial differences, but despite its common recognition in daily life, it is rarely noticed that it reflects an unavoidable failure to do what ought to be done.

What is overlooked or excluded may be the unavoidable result of a needed concentration on what would otherwise have been unduly neglected or minimized, but some wrong will still have been done. Heedlessness is turned into a deferment of acts that should have been carried out if it is replaced by an obligation.

A human is more than a highly complex machine or organism. He or she is an individual who owns and uses an organism as well as a person and a lived body. Sympathy, compassion, insight, and support, and an alertness to the needs and hopes of others are possible for almost everyone most of the time. Still, even if some act promotes a good greater than what it slights or neglects, it involves some losses.

We may not be responsible for lies and injurious acts attributed to us, and we may be rewarded for what we did not do. Generals and admirals are commended for victories achieved when they are asleep or were at some distance from a successful completion of a crucial engagement. The awards may nevertheless be deserved, since what those generals and admirals prescribe is what is done.

Were a human no more than a highly complex machine, he or she would not be an individual and would not be able to provide a terminus for discerning acts by others. Sympathy, compassion, insight, consideration, and an alertness to the existence, needs, and hopes of others are possible for almost everyone most of the time. Still, even if some act promotes a good greater than all those it slights or neglects, it involves losses. We might take the promised good to provide an ample repayment, but any loss is regrettable. The choice of some course or object is inescapably accompanied by an at least tacit acceptance of others as surrogates who will compensate as much as possible for wrongs produced.

Granted that some act promotes a better outcome than all those that it precludes or slights, it would still be true that it was deficient. Even if we take a promised, desirable outcome to provide ample repayments, its achievement would be bought at the price of neglects and would involve some irrecoverable loss.

Although love is not always and could not always be expressed at high pitch, a mild, diluted, and variable form of it can and ought to be manifested in every act. Good will, respect, and even decency express it in minor ways. Unlike the categorical imperative, it requires one to attend to the needs and hopes of others before or, at the very least, when one attends to one's own. At the risk of losing its spontaneity, overriding its nuances, ignoring its degrees, and misconstruing how it is to be expressed, it could be encapsulated in the imperative "Be worthy of a love that some deserve!" or, in a more readily acceptable form, "Be worthy of the respect that you know that some deserve!" In either way one invites the presence of an emphatic that underscores one's status as a good human being.

We cannot always avoid failing to be sufficiently sensitive. Our insensitivity may be manifest in different ways on different occasions. Used to refer to one who is subject to but who is insufficiently aware of ethical considerations, it points up a failure to make good evaluations and decisions. No one is sure just what age must be reached before one can be rightly credited with or be denied having exhibited a needed sensibility in this or that situation. On life and death matters, it is quite early.

Flagrant acts of wrongdoing or endorsements of them, even by those who are quite young or confused, may be deeply regretted. So may severe injuries to others or carefree destructions of what some take to be precious. All may be traced back to bad examples and poor training. That will still leave untouched the fact that one who does wrong is often able to do what it would be right to do in many other situations and could control inclinations that favor the doing of great wrongs.

No one knows exactly what dimensions of the self are to be emphasized on each occasion or to what degree and when. Most understand themselves and others to be responsible and sometimes accountable for failing to act with sufficient sensitivity to the natures, needs, rights, and promise of others. Even those who are confined to prisons or institutions or who have been wantonly subjected to grave injuries are expected to be aware of some things that it is right or wrong to desire, plan for, or do.

There is perhaps no stronger evidence of the fact that we take others to have an intentionalized grasp of a fellow human than our immediate condemnation of those who fail to express an appropriate sensitivity to what another is living through. Still, no one knows on every occasion what dimension of the self is emphasized, to what degree, or with what effect. No one has such a complete understanding or control that one always acts exactly as one should in order to promote, preserve, enhance, or realize what is to be done in every situation.

The Good that ought to be realized in all occurrences is instanced by every other prospect. Of little interest in itself it can be occasionally glimpsed as a constant, lacking details. Those specialized, determinate prospects with their more limited ranges, even those whose realization makes comparatively little difference to what occurs, are focused on by everyone.

6. Vice

Vice is a state in which one tends to do what reduces values in oneself and/or others. It could be identified with any undesirable habits or dispositions. If it is to match its opposite, virtue, it will require a reference to the character and the habits that it utilizes.

Antisocial practices, though undesirable and perhaps traceable to failures in character, absence of needed habits, and poor training, are not vices. Neither these nor virtues are confined to acts that are able to be indurated by repetition. Both are backed by a readiness, the one to do what ought not to be done, the other the opposite. The first allows for a narrow range of actions; the second allows for an endless number that are alike in promoting what ought to be. Both take a while to acquire. Sometimes they make use of the same habits and exhibit a persistence in continuing to work on a difficult project with a needed caution, care, and control. Only the virtues, though, will promote the realization of a prospective good. Antisocial acts ignore or block its realization.

One's character is always being modified, with some tendencies strengthened and others weakened, usually without an awareness of what is occurring. Habits may be useful or useless, strong or weak, but they will not be either good or bad, except so far as they are used by a good or bad character or either help strengthen the one or correct the other.

There are some who fail to do justice to what should be done at particular times. Overroutinized, they carry out general policies without paying sufficient attention to particular circumstances. They could be said to be in the grip of a vice because and so far as they fail to provide a proper expression and satisfaction of a virtue. Over the years "vice" has acquired a singular negative meaning in which a deplorable, habitual practice is viewed not only as becoming steadier, but as crowding out other possible ways of acting until one seems to be its captive rather than one who vitalizes and directs it.

It is not necessary that one first know the nature of a virtue before one is in a position to identify or understand the nature of vice. It suffices if it is known to be a character-sustained, habituated way of so acting that a reduction in value is promoted. One could have that knowledge without knowing how to preserve or increase the value. It is also possible, of course, for one with a particular vice to do good occasionally, just as it is possible for one who is virtuous occasionally to do what ought not to be done.

Virtues and vices are dominant tendencies. Neither precludes all the acts that accord with what the other promotes. Usually they get in one another's way. They may also qualify one another. One can be both brave and conceited, forgiving and judgmental, kind and proud.

Like virtue, vice does not have to be exhibited constantly or steadily. It suffices if there is an established tendency to act destructively. A character-sustained practice of reducing values of a particular kind may vary in degree of intensity or efficacy over its course, at different times and on different occasions. No single act, no matter how noble, destroys whatever vice may have been or is ready to be expressed, though it may more than compensate for a harm previously done. Since every kind of evil that is habitually carried out is usually credited to a vice, "vice" is best used as a generic term that applies to all character-sustained habits that reduce values in oneself or in others. That would still leave over a plurality of evils that are not sustained by a character or that are not habit-bound. It is one thing to formulate a law or a rule, endorse an imperative, admonish, advise, or threaten and quite another to utilize what is recommended.

Rules, as well as prescribing and proscribing demands, offer aids to those who attempt to produce maximum good in such and such a situation and on such and such an occasion. Those rules and aids never suffice. All fall short of determining what must be done then and there.

To know what a human is in fact or in promise, what his or her place is among others, how he or she could both benefit them and benefit from them, one must also have some knowledge of what it is best to use at that time and place; what needs to be sacrificed, neglected, and supplemented; and how some redress could be provided for whatever evils or wrongs one had produced or promoted. No one, unfortunately, has a complete, detailed, accurate knowledge of all the relevant factors. Experience and success, along with some knowledge and awareness of the most likely causes of failure and success, make it possible to avoid many of the mistakes made by the innocent, the ignorant, and the careless, the overly bold, and the overly timid. Again and again, though, even apparently unwarranted expectations and acts have ended in the saving and sometimes in the enrichment of what would otherwise have been diminished or destroyed.

There is no set of rules that could be followed, no map, no well-marked road or beckoning by what will be finally realized because one has decided to attend. Teaching, training, discipline, reflection, and practice make for more and more successful achievements, but it is doubtful that anyone has ever benefited maximally from all that he or she could have used. Even one who is well-rounded has no position from which to do justice to all available opportunities or from which all obstacles may be overcome.

Control is eminently desirable, but so are passion and decisiveness. Discipline can get in the way of daring. Dedication to the achievement of one great goal usually precludes the full and proper pursuit of others.

We do not know ourselves or our circumstances well enough to be able to give all our abilities the degree and kind of backing or supplementation that they should have on different occasions. We rarely know exactly what will produce the best results or how they could. Twist and turn as we may, the fact remains that something will have to be sacrificed. A wrong is no less a wrong because it is inescapable or regretted. Compensating, even overcompensating for it, does not erase it. This does not mean that it is impossible to live a rich, good life.

A reference to a good life seems to offer an almost empty objective. It lacks details, nuance, and apparent relevance to what has to be done here and now. Content, distinctions, and qualifications are needed if an ideal is to make a difference to what one is doing. Some account of the rights and abilities of others, as well as the warrant for it and the benefits to be obtained, is needed if one is not to make too many missteps. The achievement of that ideal unavoidably depends on opportunities backed by some control and appropriate action on different occasions.

Instead of holding, as did Freud, that everyone is born polymorphously perverse, it would be more correct to say that everyone initially, perhaps most of the time or even always, has tendencies of which he or she is not aware and which he or she may or may not ever control. Sometimes one may end by acting in ways that are not acceptable to the community and may fail to do justice to what others rightfully claim. Unfortunately no one knows exactly all that he or she or others need or deserve or how to provide it.

7. *The Good*

By making oneself receptive to Being's omnipresence, one becomes enriched in ways other than those achieved when one recognizes that Being is a presupposed source or when one is receptive to whatever enrichment would result from an acceptance of what other beings make available. The Good is not identifiable with any of these. It is a constant, ideal end, specialized in the form of limited prospects that we seek to realize. Impotent and indeterminate, its realization awaits the successful completion of acts that realize limited prospects.

Evil and wrong reduce values in finite realities. Evil does this inexcusably. Wrongs sometimes do it necessarily. Both are suffered in intensive forms that no subsequent achievements could ever annihilate or reduce. Compensations of any kind, even those that are far greater than those expected or warranted, are no more than anodynes, palliatives, never erasing the harm that was done.

A prospect is a possibility that invites efforts to realize it. Even when it is not explicitly noted, it may be effective, eliciting needed acts. Did it not contribute to its own realization, it would at best mark the end of some endeavor, not necessarily the one that was carried out. The Good is a constant that never achieves all the determinations it needs in order to be fully realized. Unlike other prospects it is never realized except as ordering the others as more or less desirable.

Neither purposes nor other kinds of prospects exert control over what promotes their realization, though they may be used as guides and objectives. There are purposes that provide effective prospects for present moments. Those that are due to individuals need help in order to become effective in the moments of passing time that the individuals help constitute and, as we have seen, on which they may intrude emphatics.

It is the claim of historically minded Hegelians, both Marxists and non-Marxists, that there is an inescapable outcome acting on whatever occurs. What will eventually be achieved in fact or thought, it is supposed, is always operative, pulling versions of itself into itself without remainder. Why this has not already occurred is not explained. Presumably anyone who professed to have arrived there would never be able to stand away from it. The more successful a Hegelian dialectic is at arriving at its end, the more surely must what is less than this be a mystery. Success for the Hegelian leaves him or her unable to account for the fact that there are positions where what is not fully real provides steps that inexorably end in what is all-powerful, perfect, and fully real.

Art, education, training, disciplining, medicine, empowerment, politics, religious practices, explorations of the planets, and indeed almost all kinds of activity make suppositions and follow routes that reward examination. To be comprehended, particularly when understood as having realities of their own, they are dealt with as apart from one another but still interrelated and able to insist on themselves as other than whatever else there be.

To know what someone is in fact and in promise, what his or her place is among other realities, and how he or she could benefit from them requires some knowledge of what is best to use; the best ways to use it; what is not to be sacrificed, neglected, or risked; and how redress could be made for whatever evils or wrongs were promoted or produced. A prospect is a possibility. Even when not identified, it may elicit desirable acts. Unfortunately no one has a complete, clear, detailed knowledge of all that is involved.

Perhaps there is no one who does not cherish some things because he or she sees that they are in fact good, though no one knows exactly what place they have in a hierarchy of prospective goods, all ordered under a supreme, final Good. The Good's radical indeterminateness, even its ubiquity, makes it less attractive for most than many more specialized prospects are, even those whose realizations make comparatively little difference to what occurs or to them.

A refusal to attend to the same issues again and again from new positions and with new insights leaves an inquirer tied to what had once occurred. Every work should build on, but should also critically deal with, what seems to have been mastered by oneself or by others. One should go over old territory in new ways, correct errors, look for emphatics that may have been unnoticed and for new ways to see what had been seen from other positions. No one should try to squeeze even the most satisfying of methods or results into dogmas or categories.

A philosophic inquiry that is not both an exploration and an adventure checked by self-criticism has little merit. What is to be sought is not a position that one will cling to, no matter what the problem or the facts, but what will make evident the primary realities, how they are known, what they do, and how they are connected. No one, of course, could master all at the same time..

The great temptation for any systematic thinker is to suppose that what is known to hold in one domain holds in others. It is easy to forget the fact that different domains not only have different members and that the conditions to which they are all subject are in different orders all the while that they are subject to and participate in the same final Being. No account could be more than fragmentary if it failed to show how these are interrelated. No one, of course, could master all at the same time. Each reality pulls its referents toward it. A disjunction of realities has them tamely alongside one another.

Experience and reflection and an awareness of the most likely causes of success and failure make it possible to avoid many of the mistakes and to escape the limits within which the innocent, the ignorant, the careless, and the dogmatic are confined. Specialization is needed. So is use of what had been achieved by others. What had been overlooked will continue to be involved with what is focused on. This might take a lifetime. The outcome of an early venture may not be seriously affected by what is learned later, but it usually can be enriched by fitting it into a larger, justified setting. There is no set of rules that should be followed, no map, no beckoning by what would be finally realized, did one but allow oneself to be well guided.

Teaching, training, discipline, reflection, and practice make for more and more successful achievements. Advances clarify the nature and import of beginnings.

The claim that some enterprise is alone reliable, that it alone deserves study, is a precondition never justified. Philosophic thinking is carried out in a distinctive way, at once occupied with recognizing often overlooked distinctions and connections and with carrying out radical self-criticisms while attending to crucial, pivotal issues.

The one, always indeterminate, always prospective, final outcome is noted by only a few. It interests even fewer. Although no one ever succeeds in making it fully determinate and though all of it is beyond the power of anyone to realize, it is available for use as that which orients and qualifies and more or less orders the limited prospects that are realizable.

There is no set of rules that should be followed, no map, no beckoning by what would be finally realized, did one but allow oneself to be well guided. Teaching, training, discipline, reflection, and practice make for more and more successful achievements, but no one has maximally benefited from all. Opposition is sometimes needed and often desirable. So are persistence and flexibility.

The claim that some enterprise alone is reliable or encompasses and can account for whatever there is, could be, or could be known is a dogma never justified. Still, it may be desirable for some who are engaged in a particular type of inquiry to keep in accord with the practices and to accept the suppositions of others who are also so engaged. Artists and inventors, though, rarely do that. Systematic philosophic thinking too is carried out in a distinctive way, at once occupied with recognizing distinctions and connections often overlooked and with carrying out radical self-criticisms while attending to crucial issues, some of which had been long neglected, perhaps not even envisaged.

The one, always indeterminate, always prospective, final Good is noted by only a few; it interests even fewer. Although no one ever succeeds in making it fully determinate and although all of it is beyond the power of any being to realize, it is available for use as that which orients, qualifies, and orders the limited prospects that one might be able to realize. There is perhaps no one who does not cherish something because it is seen, in fact, to be good though one does not know exactly what place it has in a hierarchy of goods. One may not be responsible for what one then does, but one might be held accountable because he or she was found to be where a deplorable act had been begun or had been carried out and because the prevailing laws or customs define this as punishable.

Forgiven or not forgiven, excused or not excused, neither evils nor wrongs are expunged. We can do little more together than to try to make good what we reduce in value. This does not mean that we must give up our present predilections, but only that, when and as each does what is wrong, it may take many, with oneself perhaps as one of them, to make good whatever losses, deliberate or inadvertent, occurred.

~ ~ ~

Question: This discussion is spoiled in part because you spend so much time trying to say what philosophers should do. If they are philosophers, they know what to do. To whom is this being addressed?

Answer: To those who think of philosophy as an inquiry that has been carried out over the ages by those who want to know what is real but find that there are many today who dismiss all of them and attend only to logic, the use of words, or criticisms of one another. There are thousands of members of philosophical societies in the United States alone who not only refuse to attend to anything but these limited projects dealt with in limited ways, but who pay no attention to any who try to share in the great adventure that has attracted great minds in the past and that deserves, even at some remove, to be continued. As the study of emphatics makes evident, there is much that needs to be explored. Precision, care, and the use of new instruments and ways of proceeding are eminently desirable but should not be taken to preclude adventure, comprehensiveness, and systematization. A teacher of courses in the history of philosophy or in some other specialty, such as logic, history, or epistemology, is not necessarily a philosopher, no matter what his or her title.

Q: You are not objecting to the teaching of such courses?

A: No. What I am trying to make evident is that philosophy has a noble past that should be continued in the form of new adventures, some into unexplored territory. A failure to deal with reality in its primary forms is to leave unexamined much that is being uncritically assumed. Caution is always to be encouraged, provided that it is not understood to preclude adventure.

Q: You deal with a great number of issues in order to make evident the presence and roles of emphatics in limited ways, but, particularly here, you spend much time going over the question of wrongs.

A: That is to be expected. I have been trying to open up the one and to subtletize the other. The first needs to have its nature and scope made evident; the second tries to make what is widely known be better understood.

Q: Nevertheless this account does not seem to be governed by any principle. Why are there just so many kinds of evils and wrongs? Is there no way of knowing just how many basic kinds there are, and how they are interrelated? Granted that you are looking into areas that have not often been dealt with, or not as well as they should have been, it would help to know how you proceeded, if only to see if you had overlooked or slighted some that deserved examination.

A: Your questions and suggestions are in stark contrast to the ones I usually hear. Again and again, I have been admonished for supposedly making use of a somewhat arbitrary set of categories and for using them in mechanical ways.

A set of categories, no matter how useful, leaves one confronted with a need to provide for the degree and manner in which they are to be used. It falls short of providing an accounting. Instead of doing that, I have tried to attend to what I think are crucial questions, examining what is presupposed, seeing what positions could not be avoided, followed by a reversal of all the moves in the attempt to discover what was assumed and to see if there was something overlooked. Once aware that there is a depth to every being that could be moved toward in convergent, intensive moves, it is possible to see how there could be emphatics that are intruded on what those beings had helped constitute—a fact made most evident perhaps when one takes note of the "now!" that is sometimes emphatically added to a moment of time by one of itss constituents.

Each being is obstinate, resistant, acceptive, and insistent, the result of the termination of many different moves, some intrusive but welcomed, others intrusive but resisted, and still others evocative or recursive. It would be easier to produce a systematic, comprehensive account if one decided to make everything fit within some set of predetermined positions, but it is not the object of a philosophic inquiry to find an easy way to learn what the primary kinds of reality are and how they are related to one another. It does not look for an easy way to learn what there is, though it will not object to having one.

A philosopher should be systematic and both a resolute self-critic and a daring adventurer. He or she does not reject but indeed endorses the meticulous analyses of the positivistic minded and the outcomes of the introspections of the existentialists, all the while remaining alert to what they have taken for granted and what they bypass. What is sound in them will find a place within a sound, comprehensive whole, though it may not be as exalted as its defenders would have liked and though it may have to be qualified and reinterpreted in order to make its truths fit together with other truths established in other ways.

Today there are no acknowledged philosophers without academic connections. Descartes, Leibniz, Spinoza, Locke, and Hume, among others, had none. Too many today think that they must imitate the practices, at some remove, of mathematicians or scientists, only to find that what they achieve does not interest their models or apparently anyone else outside a small group that makes the same assumptions, keeps within the same limits, and dismisses all other ventures as worthless or careless.

It is evidently desirable to be precise and to be alert to differences, but that does not provide a warrant for neglecting issues that require one to acknowledge Being, ultimate conditions, and singulars, the ways these are connected, and the emphatics that they produce or to which they are subjected.

Q: I think you have missed the point. Those who concentrate on being most meticulous are in revolt against those who have presented them with large-scale accounts in vague terms, backed by little analysis or justification. They seek to find a solid ground and to use a well-controlled method before they consider such broad issues that you deal with—if you will pardon me—heed-lessly.

A: I, too, want to base what is dealt with on solid ground. "I exist, interplay with others under common conditions, and am able to do many things separately and together" is surely as solid as Wittgenstein's "*x*" says *x,* with the "says" left unexplained. It surely is as primitive as a phenomenological description that is confined with unexplained boundaries by persons who are unknown. It surely is better warranted than a reductionist's claim that there are no minds but only brains, and no one to know them.

Q: You, though, quickly focus on singular beings, the ultimate condi-tions, Being, and emphatics. Must we choose between accepting a few, strongly entrenched though quite-limited truths and an all-comprehensible account that claims to know what individuals are, even Being itself? Isn't the Good positive, what ought to be, and isn't what is wrong or evil negative, what ought not to be?

A: "To be positive" is not to be identified with "being determinative." To lack is not yet to be negative. A law is positive but is expressed in general terms. A hunger expresses a lack but in an insistent, demanding way. The bad occurs with the lack it has. The Good is flawless but indeterminate; there is nothing in which it is imbed-ded.

Q: Might the Good be an emphatic that the ultimate conditions nec-essarily produce, when and as they are, apart from all instantiations as confiners of finite beings?

A: Yes. In the absence of any finite beings, though, it would be an emphatic that they intruded on Being, when and as they referred Being's possibility to Being.

Q: Might the Good not be an ever-present, operative lure, pulling all things toward it? Might not the bad be the results of a maladjust-ment or a willed rejection of the Good?

A: No. The Good does nothing. No one might attend to it. Evils may be deliberately produced though I doubt that anyone seeks to do evil because it is evil. At the very least, the evildoer enjoys exercis-ing power, expressing rage or hatred of what others are or what they cherish. Jealousy, envy, lust, fear, conceit, or a desire to be in control may be dominant, all the while that there is some accep-tance of oneself. They are regrettable, but they may also express an appreciation of what has some merit. The misconception of the value of what has been done or of the role it played need not affect the merit of what is achieved, even when it distorts one's understanding of oneself or one's accomplishments.

Q: You seem to deny that there ever were or will be genuine, saintly humans.

A: If by "saintly" you intend to refer to one who never yielded to temptation, never thought well of him- or herself, never had to recompense for thoughtlessness or self-regard, never did any wrong, or even whose every act was as splendid as it could be, I confess that I do not see how that would be possible, unless this "saint" were as unselfconscious and as self-neglectful as an infant. Hagiographies are not written by careful, well-trained, critical, disinterested observers. This is not to deny that there are outstanding men and women who have reached a stage of self-mastery and who are generous and thoughtful, far beyond what others attain, even for every short periods.

Q: To be or to do good, one must have a good character and good habits?

A: One can do good, even if one has a poor character and bad habits. One cannot, though, live and act as one ought for long, if one does not have a fine character and good habits, backed by an understanding of what others are, need, and deserve.

A child may sometimes make selfless, self-sacrificing moves and be remarkably generous. An adult who imitated such a child would have to overlook the evils and wrongs others do and, in effect, bypass what should have been prevented and should be condemned.

Q: Since we come into a world in which there are many desirable and needed things that are provided by others and made available for our use, ought we not also blame our predecessors for the poverty and other failures that are entrenched when we enter the scene?

A: We should—and we do.

Q: Don't restraining laws and traditions play essential roles?

A: There is a sedimentation of good practices that help one make good choices. Unfortunately they are not well marked off from poorer practices and from the likelihood of making bad choices.

Q: Doesn't the realization of the Good presuppose some lack, perhaps some evil or wrong, in order to show itself as that which is not only opposed by but should overcome them?

A: No. Evil and wrong would then be attached to the Good. Instead they exist apart from it, with the Good awaiting suitable action before it could be realized.

Q: No matter how useful or indispensable something may be, evil is what ought not to be. If it contributes to the production of a great good or prompts one to try to realize this, is it still what ought not be?

A: It ought not be. No achieved good recompenses for what is evil or wrong. Even if either were a prerequisite for what was eminently desirable, it would still be what should not have been.

Q: If the Good is impotent, how could it compensate for anything?

A: As an impotent prospect, it could not. Realized to any degree, it compensates for but never eradicates the lacks and losses that were due to evils or wrongs.

Q: Is the Good an emphatic?

A: Not as a mere prospect; there is nothing that intrudes it on anything else. Brought to bear on what is being realized, it is an emphatic that is used to give an additional import to prospects.

These rather unqualified remarks about the Good go beyond what I firmly know of it. At best they express insights that are not often or readily repeated and should, therefore, be taken to point toward rather than to express what is true of it.

Q: Don't some of those who are occupied with doing evil take an evil to be an inviting prospect?

A: Yes and no. They see evil to be a necessary condition for the realization of the good or to be good in fact, not necessarily because they have a mistaken idea of it, but usually because of its challenges, its enabling one to chasten others for assuming privileges, or for finding pleasures where one does not, does not want to, or cannot. Jealousies, rivalries, and willful opposition point up the injustice of privileges, rights, and opportunities that are available to some and denied to others. I am referring, of course, to those who are are sane, not acting in ways about which they have no knowledge and cannot control.

Q: Some, evidently sane, shout with joy at an execution or find pleasure in the humiliation and abuse of others who are different from them.

A: Yes. The harm that they seek to inflict is part of an expected satisfaction. They could be prompted by almost anything—gender, ancestry, beliefs, skin color, accents, complacency, poverty, wealth, religious practices, and/or convictions.

Q: You take Dostoyevsky's "underground man" as insisting on a good—and so far, to be good—and also as doing what is wrong, because he does not take proper account of other goods?

A: Yes. Everyone, in fact, does that at some time and to some degree. The "underground man" differs from the rest of us in the degree of his insistence on often ignored and neglected dimensions of his person.

Q: Heedlessness is unavoidable?

A: Yes.

Q: Why criticize anyone for being heedless? Would it not be as justifiable to criticize a fish because it cannot run up steps to save a child in a fire? Why not criticize a dog for not answering the telephone? Are the fish and the dog to be judged adversely because they cannot do these things? Are they heedless? If heedlessness is unavoidable, why do you treat it as a wrong?

A: Heedlessness is to be condemned because and so far as it involves a neglect of or a reduction in the values that should be preserved or enhanced. It is a wrong that could be reduced here and there but could never be avoided. If avoided in one place or at one time, there would still be something else that would be neglected.

Q: Are you assuming that all humans tend to what is right to do?

A: No. I am maintaining that they are obligated to do so. So far as they fail to do what they ought, they must take others to act as their surrogates.

Q: Mustn't discipline, training, understanding, and practice be provided? Don't these also require one to neglect a multiplicity of other tasks?

A: Yes. There is no escaping heedlessness, but its scope and the severity of its effects can often be limited and some recompense provided.

Q: Do wrongs and evils add emphatics to what occurs?

A: They must, so far as what occurs has not been subject to ethical or moral determinations.

Q: If the emphatics are not accommodated but are instead rejected, repulsed, or qualified, are they still emphatics?

A: Yes. The fact was made evident at the beginning of this study, particularly when references were made to what violates the demands of an etiquette.

Q: You write as though the study of emphatics had been ignored over the centuries. Has it been?

A: I have not made a search to see if there have not been sustained studies that dealt with the issue. It would be surprising to discover that there had been none, perhaps restricted to accounts of the effects of the arts, education, discipline, etiquette, the actions of the divine, or expressions of the supernatural.

The present examination has been guided by what I had already learned about the inward nature and power of realities and about the effective governance of conditions and laws. It would long ago have been a focal topic, had philosophers, in their reaction to scholasticism, taken art instead of mathematics as a guide, model, or inspiration while remaining alert to its demands and achievements.

The dominance of the medieval philosophic outlook was abruptly brought to an end by two great mathematicians, Descartes and Leibniz. Since that time mathematicians, logicians, and the scientists affirm and presumably have kept themselves in close accord with what these demanded and affirmed. They have dominated a great deal of philosophic thought. Throughout this time attempts have been made to take account of more vitalizing and intensively reached realities. Schopenhauer and Nietzsche alone, though, understood the distinctive nature of the arts and what these made evident. Bergson and the existentialists followed along the routes that these had opened up, but they spoiled their insights by failing to take adequate account of the role of the rational, the formal, the stable, that always plays some role. Sartre, a writer of great ability, like others near the head of the revolt, did not seem to have much interest in or show great perceptiveness about the arts that do not make use of writing.

Q: What would have occurred had the revolt against the dominant medieval attitude, commitments, and procedures been carried out by those who were as much at home with the arts as Descartes and Leibniz were with mathematics?

A: Presumably, then, the role of emphatics would have been recognized, theology would have been dealt with from new angles, and mathematics, logic, and the sciences would not be supposed alone to be able to determine what is real or alone be able to say what occurs.

Despite my many discussions about the nature of art, particularly with Neil Welliver, W. H. Auden, Robert Thom, David Slavitt, my daughter, and my son, as well as others with actors, architects, composers, choreographers, and novelists, I do not think that I have entirely freed myself from the outlook that has dominated the modern era. My opening of the subject of sport to philosophical inquiry, I now see, because it does not take adequate account of the athlete's emphatic insistence on the controlled use of the lived body and organism in challenging situations, falls short of making evident what he or she is trying to do—exhibit a mastery of the organism and lived body at various times and places, some well-defined and others, like mountain climbing, open to unanticipated challenges.

An understanding of sport can benefit from an approach to it that is sensitive to the emphatic nature of art. In different ways and with different stresses, it calls upon individuals, sometimes separately and sometimes as interinvolved, to make themselves emphatically present through their organisms, within a humanized world. My references to sports' appeal to the young paid insufficient attention to the efforts they make to become masters of limited spaces, times, and causal acts.

As is true of earlier studies of other topics, I think that most of what I previously maintained is sound and illuminating or, at the very least, on the right track. The present study of emphatics does, though, make evident that earlier studies were not subtle or supple enough to do justice to their subjects. The study of emphatics should provide much needed rectifications of what has been taken by me and by others to be crucial problems and should alert us to nuances, issues, and answers otherwise overlooked.

Q: Does a philosophic account itself express an emphatic to be imposed and thereby alter the way everything is to be understood?

A: No. A systematic, comprehensive philosophic account notes the major emphatics that make the pivotal realities evident, but it does not affect them. The kinds, sources, and loci of the emphatics that beings intrude on one another are more like identifications and introductions than qualifications or alterations, making evident what is always present. It is to these that one should attend if one is to have a good understanding of the reason why there are contingently existing realities, as well as others that always exist.

One check that I have used again and again is to see how limited topics fit together. Alert to claims made on behalf of logic, mathematics, art, ethics, history, politics, and languages, among other subjects, but without claiming to have mastered any of them, I have tried to attend to issues and problems that promote the understanding of reality in the little and the large, transient and as necessary, commonplace and arresting, functioning as intruders, sustainers, and as members of distinctive domains. I have also tried to place obstacles in the way of every one of my major claims. One consequence that pleases me is that some of those obstacles have proved to be less formidable than they had at first seemed to be. Over the years I have been able to understand what I had before grasped poorly, and I have begun to see what was implied.

Q: You sound as if you were educating yourself in public. Why not wait until you get to a final position and see if it is worth considering or deserves to be studied?

A: There is no final position, fully filled out, that anyone can warrantedly claim to have reached. The great works of philosophy provide fine beginnings, suggestions, recommendations, and openings, just as surely as they make evident what had not been well understood or even surmised before. There is no reason why one should not try to take the same depersonalized attitude toward one's own work as others should, can, and sometimes do.

Too often the latest work of one who is occupied with getting at the root of things, if published posthumously, is assumed to be as dead as its author. Paradoxically, if an author has been ignored by most of his contemporaries as Peirce was, his collected works will be taken to contain pieces of equal merit, especially if there are no good clues about the dates of composition.

Since some or all that had been maintained might be found to be defective, a contribution should not only be rethought; it should be dealt with from many different positions. A philosophical work that is just read, or even studied, has not yet been understood.

Conceivably some or all that has here been maintained is seriously defective, and the entire venture may have to be rethought from top to bottom. Even then, what is presented will be found to have dealt with neglected and important issues in ways that open up new areas and that may also make an advance over what had been dealt with by others in splendid ways.

Q: Twist and turn as you like, you do claim to offer an account that is better than all others and that presumably will hold always. It is hard to free it from the acrid smell of silly boasting.

A: I don't see why. What I have presented is what I think should be examined with care, its errors, oversights, dogmatisms, and claims carefully examined and discarded or else modified where necessary, perhaps followed by inquiries dealing with the same realities in other ways. That does not mean that I think that what is now presented is not right on the whole.

When I am inclined to think that I have at last completed an account of what seems to be without a flaw, I sometimes think about the conversation that a farmer had with his son when he tried to ex-plain why there were no chickens in the chicken house that morning.

Farmer: I heard a noise last night, coming from the chicken house. I called out, "Who's there"? I heard an answer: "There's nobody here but us chickens." So I went to bed. Was I surprised to find all the chickens gone this morning! Son: Dad, chickens can't talk. Farmer: Of course they can. I hear them gabble all the time. Son: They don't speak English, like us. Father: I never thought of that.

Sometimes, what I had not thought about becomes evident suddenly, usually as that which is present, even intrusive, but which I, and apparently many others, had not noticed. Em- phatics, despite their presence in many different forms, could have been and should have been noted and studied by me decades ago. Had I given sufficient thought about the converses of adumbrations and discernments, I undoubtedly would have become aware of emphatics. When I first began to think about them, I did not understand them very well. Even now, my grasp of them is unsure.

Q: Now your work is completed?

A: In fact, new areas are now being opened, I am now planning to institute an inquiry into the nature of surrogates, i.e., the use of entities as replacements for what is accepted.

Q: What has led you to that?

A: It was the outcome of a convergence of three different questions:

1. If emphatics add a meaning to what occurs, is there not something that gives the occurrence that role?
2. What, from the position of a principal, is the status of an agent, and what is the relation that joins them?
3. Are all known and still other not-yet-explored pragmatisms special cases of a primal pragmatism?

A promising answer to all three is that if we begin with the acknowledgment of anything, there may be a good reason for warranting the election of something else as a surrogate for what was initially accepted.

I am now beset with a wide range of questions whose answers will help me examine and perhaps determine if there are conceivable purposes which justify the replacement of anything accepted in some way with something else. A number of things become immediately evident: there are replacements that could be offered for an entertained idea; there are many reasons one might offer for accepting these as surrogates for what is not in the mind, but in some other part of a person, in some part of the lived body, or the organism—and conversely.

I have now set before me a wide range of questions that I will try to keep in mind when I try to deal with these issues:

1. Is there anything that could not be a surrogate?
2. Is there always some purpose that warrants the acceptance of a surrogate in place of what is initially accepted?
3. Is the sustainer of an expressed emphatic a surrogate for the source of that emphatic?

4. Is the acknowledgment of a surrogate an emphatic act?

5. If y is a surrogate for x, can x be a surrogate for y?

6. Could the time, space, or causality characteristic of one domain affect what occurs in some other domain?

7. Is the object of sign a surrogate for the user of the sign?

8. Are works of art surrogates for realities as expressing themselves from their unitary depths?

9. Is a surrogate the justified terminus of a purpose?

10. Is there a primary purpose justifying the use of anything as a surrogate for something else?

11. Do governances have surrogates?

12. Are used emphatics surrogates for their sources?

13. Does Being have any surrogates? Would an affirmative answer not require that Being be related to those surrogates by a purpose? Would that purpose not overarch and thus escape control or governance by Being?

14. Is there a hierarchy of purposes, or are some coordinate with others or have no relation to any others?

15. Is every reality that is other than Being a surrogate for it?

16. Are "agent" and "surrogate" interchangeable terms?

17. Are instances of a condition surrogates for it?

18. Are a person, a lived body, and an organism surrogates for their singular owner and user?

19. What is the major reason for using surrogates—to increase control, range, or satisfy a purpose?

20. Could time, space, and causality have surrogates?

21. Could they be used as surrogates?

22. Is space-time a surrogate for space and for time?

23. Could space be a surrogate for time?

24. Could time be a surrogate for space?

25. Could space-time be a surrogate for causality?

26. Could causality be a surrogate for space-time?

27. Is it possible for anything to be precluded from being a surrogate?

28. Are the major warrants for surrogates different in different domains?

29. Could one type of inquiry be a surrogate for another?

30. Are dreams surrogates for what had been or might be?

31. Could memories be surrogates for what had been?

32. Could the expected be a surrogate for what occurs?

33. Is the acknowledgment or use of a surrogate an emphatic act?

Q: Some of these questions are arresting. Others seem strange, apparently evidencing poorly understood ideas, perhaps by me or you and surely by others. It would be helpful if you dealt with some familiar view and indicated how a study of surrogates would enable one to understand it in a way one would not likely have understood it, apart from such a study.

A: As I have already noted, one of the reasons I have come to the point where I find the study of surrogates to be needed is an awareness that there is a primal pragmatism that different pragmatists have specialized in different ways. Peirce, James, Schiller, Mead, Dewey, and Lewis—to focus on major, better-known ones—recommended the use of different surrogates, all having some bearing on practice, as replacements for what one entertained. Peirce was primarily interested in providing ideas about practical consequences for ideas entertained; Dewey instead was concerned with providing not ideas about but action and control of what was in the humanized world. Neither asked if there might be other things that their surrogates could replace, such as memories, hopes, sympathy, love, mathematical truths, or Being—though Dewey seemed always to be on the verge of doing this.

Surrogates need not provide only conceived or actual practical outcomes for what was entertained. One could, and sometimes does, replace practical involvements with ideas, thereupon reversing the pragmatic emphasis. We do and should do this again and again, particularly when we want to understand just how to function as persons and organisms, as well as members of the humanized world.

The surrogates that the pragmatists recommend are not only some of those that could be chosen for any number of reasons; they can be matched by others in our wills, imagination, aspirations, or sympathies or could allow us to understand what is in domains other than the humanized. Clear and distinct ideas, as Descartes saw, are desirable surrogates for those we usually entertain; they need not have any practical import. It is often desirable to replace one's conceptual or actual involvement in practical affairs with the enjoyment of nature, idle ruminations, fantasies, or memories. Outside the interests of all pragmatists, apparently, are surrogates for what occurs apart from all persons. A multiplicity of different kinds of entities—ideas of what is presupposed, emphatics, what is adumbrated or discerned, hopes, the imagined, the absurd, play, and sport—may not only be recommended and used as surrogates but may themselves make use of them. Anything, in fact, could be used as a surrogate for anything else for some reason. A psychoanalyst promotes the replacement of a distressing personal experience by a memory of it and new acts. The story of Job points up how a God could use a surrogate in the form of Satan to test Job's faith. Reciprocally, Satan can be understood to use that God as a surrogate who provides him with victims.

Q: A wide-ranging study of surrogates will be the last of your studies?

A: I doubt it. What will next require study will undoubtedly become evident toward the end of an examination of the major types of surrogates, just as these became an evident, important topic as the study of emphatics came to a close. Once it is noted that emphatics make a difference to the values of things and that surrogates provide new roles, it becomes evident that the question of how realities and subdivisions of them may be relevant to one another has to be faced, to be followed by another about the ways in which units might function together.

I have now leapt too far ahead of what is evident. What can now be warrantedly maintained is that the study of emphatics prompts an awareness of the need to deal with many kinds of surrogates, for many kinds of acknowledged entities, and for many different reasons. There is no more satisfying a closure than one that makes one aware of what is next to be done.

INDEX OF NAMES

INDEX OF SUBJECTS